# ORGANIZATIONAL BEHAVIOUR

# ORGANIZATIONAL BEHAVIOUR

**Jyotsana Singh**

CENTRUM PRESS
NEW DELHI-110002 (INDIA)

**CENTRUM PRESS**
**H.O.:** 4360/4, Ansari Road, Daryaganj,
New Delhi-110002 (India)
Tel: 23278000, 23261597, 23255577, 23286875

**B.O.:** No. 1015, Ist Main Road, BSK IIIrd Stage,
IIIrd Phase, IIIrd Block, Bangalore-560085 (INDIA)
Tel: 080-41723429

*Email:* centrumpress@gmail.com
*Visit us at:* www.centrumpress.com

*Organizational Behaviour*



First Edition, 2011

ISBN 978-93-80921-06-8

PRINTED IN INDIA

*Printed at* Balaji Offset, Delhi.

# Contents

# Preface

Organizational Behavior is the study and application of knowledge about how people, individuals, and groups act in organizations. It interprets people-organization relationships in terms of the whole person, whole group, whole organization, and whole social system. Its purpose is to build better relationships by achieving human objectives, organizational objectives, and social objectives.

Organizational behaviour is written with these changes as a central focus-to explain through current, often high-tech examples what students need to know about organizations as they enter employment or continue their work lives. A major goal of this book is not just to explain the fundamental theories and concepts of organizational behaviour but to help students apply those theories and concepts to their personal lives and work lives.

*Author*

# 1

# Introduction

## EVOLUTION AND NATURE

We can define the term organization as two or more individuals who are interacting with each other within a deliberately structured set up and working in an interdependent way to achieve some common objective/s. organizations play a major role in our lives. We possibly cannot think of a single moment in our lives when we are not depending on organizations in some form or the other. Right From the public transport that you use to come to your institute, the Institute itself, the class you are attending at this moment, are all examples of organizations.

So Now dear students what is Behaviour? Is it the behaviour of organization or the Behaviour of the people who are working in the organization?

Yes, it is the behaviour of the people working in an organization to achieve common goals or objectives. organization comprises of people with different attitudes, cultures, beliefs, norms and values. So now,lets understand organizational behaviour and what it exactly it means..... 'Organizational Behaviour' can be defined as the study of what people think, feel, and do in and around organizations.

The study of Organizational Behaviour facilitates the process of explaining, understanding, predicting, maintaining, and changing employee behaviour in an organizational setting. The value of organizational behaviour is that it isolates important aspects of the manager's job and offers specific perspective on the human side of mangement.

- People as organizations,
- People as resources,
- People as people.

In other words, it involves the understanding, prediction and control of human behaviour and factors affecting their performance and interaction among the organizational members. And because organizational behaviour is concerned specifically with employment – related situations, you should not be surprised to find that it emphasizes behaviour as related to concerns such as jobs, work, absenteeism, employment turnover, productivity, human performance and management

## NATURE OF ORGANIZATIONAL BEHAVIOUR (OB)

Organizational behaviour is an applied behavioural science that is built on contributions from a number of behavioural disciplines such as psychology, sociology, social psychology, anthropology and economics.

*So now students lets see how these disciplines are related to organizational behaviour*:

- *Psychology*: Psychology is the study of human behaviour which tries to identify the characteristics of individuals and provides an understanding why an individual behaves in a particular way. This thus provides us with useful insight into areas such as human motivation, perceptual processes or personality characteristics.
- *Sociology*: Sociology is the study of social behaviour, relationships among social groups and societies, and the maintenance of social order. The main focus of attention is on the social system. This helps us to appreciate the functioning of individuals within the organization which is essentially a socio-technical entity.
- *Social psychology*: Social psychology is the study of human behaviour in the context of social situations. This essentially addresses the problem of understanding the typical behavioural patterns to be expected from an individual when he takes part in a group.

- *Anthropology*: Anthropology is the science of mankind and the study of human behaviour as a whole. The main focus of attention is on the cultural system, beliefs, customs, ideas and values within a group or society and the comparison of behaviour among different cultures. In the context of today's organizational scenario. It is very important to appreciate the differences that exist among people coming from different cultural backgrounds as people are often found to work with others from the other side of the globe.
- *Economics*: Any organization to survive and sustain must be aware of the economic viability of their effort. This applies even to the non-profit and voluntary organizations as well.
- *Political Science*: Although frequently overlooked, the contributions of political scientists are significant to the understand arrangement in organizations. It studies individuals and groups within specific conditions concerning the power dynamics. Important topics under here include structuring Of Conflict, allocation of power and how people manipulate power for individual self-interest etc.

The following figure depicts to highlight the interdisciplinary nature of organizational behaviour.

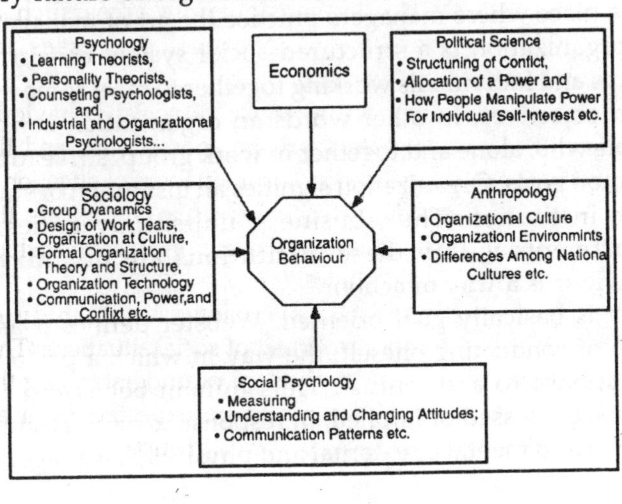

As different phases of our lives, each of us is associated with some kind of organization- a college, club, hospital or a business. These organizations differ from one another in more ways than one. Some like a giant corporation like TATA Tea or the Indian Army may be organised very formally. Others like a local football club may be less formally organised. But irrespective of their differences, all the organizations of which, each of us is a member have some common features.

Management is basically concerned with ideas, things and people. Harold Koontz defines management in a very simple form. He states that "management is the art of getting things done through and with the people in formally organised groups'. Management is a process of organised activities. Without organised activities, two groups of people won't be involved in the performance of activities. Management process suggests that all the managers in the organization perform certain functions to get things done by others. These functions include planning, organising, staffing, directing and controlling.

Organizing is the process of arranging and allocating work, authority, and resources among organizations members so they can achieve the organizations goals. The managers must match an organizations structure to its goals and resources, a process called organizational design. organization is the place where managers practice the art of management. An organization is a structured social system consisting of groups and individuals working together to meet some agreed upon objectives. In other words an organization consist of people who, alone and together in work group, strive to attain common goals. Organization signifies an institution or sub unit of an institution. Thus, business, units, universities, and departments within these institutions are organization. Behaviour is a way of action.

It is basically goal oriented. Webster defines it as 'the mode of conducting oneself; the way in which a person acts in response to a stimulus'. Thus human behaviour is his actions, expressed or implied, in response to various stimuli – internal and mental or external and physical. A manager must understand, predict and control the activities of a person at a given moment. To predict behaviour, manager must know which motives or needs of people evoke a certain action at a particular time. The field of organizational Behaviour deals with human behaviour in organizations. It is the study and application of knowledge about how people animation within organizations. OB is directly concerned with the understanding, prediction, and control of human behaviour in organizations. Stephen.P. Robbins defines Organizational Behaviour as a "filed of study that investigates the impact that individuals, groups, and structure have on behaviour within organizations for the purpose of applying such knowledge towards improving an organizations effectiveness".

Thus OB is essentially concerned with what people do in organizations. It applies the knowledge gained about individuals, groups and the effect of structure on behaviour in order to make organizations work more effectively.

## FUNDAMENTAL CONCEPTS

The subject Organizational Behaviour is based on a few fundamental concepts which revolve around the nature of people and organizations. Such fundamental concepts are not peculiar to the field of OB. Every discipline, be it a social science or a physical science, will flourish on definite assumptions.

*The subject OB is developed on the following concepts*:

- *Individual Difference*: People have much in common, but each person in the world is also individually different. Each individual is different from others in several ways. Whether it is intelligence, physique, personality or any such trait, one can find striking differences. This concept says that each person in this world is unique and individual experiences after birth make people even more different. Individual difference mean that management can get the greatest motivation among employees by treating them differently.
- *A whole person*: When an individual is appointed, his skill alone is not hired, but his social background,

likes and dislikes, pride and prejudices etc is also hired. A person's family life can't be separated from his professional life. It is for this reason that managers should try to make the office, home away from home.

- *Caused Behaviour*: Behaviour of an employee is caused and not random. Thus when a worker comes late or makes a problem with the supervisor, there is a cause behind. The manager must realise this basic principle and to solve the problems, he must discover the cause behind the behaviour.
- *Human Dignity*: This concept confirms that people are to be treated differently from other factors of production, because they are of a higher order in the universe. It recognizes human dignity because people are of a higher order, they want to be treated with respect and dignity and should be treated this way. The concept of human dignity rejects the old idea of using employees as economic tools.
- *Organizations are Social Systems*: From sociology we learn that organizations are social systems; and the activities there in are governed by the social laws as well as psychological laws. Just as people have psychological needs, they also have social roles and status. Their behaviour is influenced by their group as well as by their individual drives. Infact two type of social system exist side by side in organizations. One is the formal system and the other is the informal social system.

## CONTRIBUTING DISCIPLINE

Organizational Behaviour is an applied behavioural science. It has drawn heavily from a number of disciplines such as psychology, sociology, and anthropology.

*A brief description of each is in order*:

- *Psychology*: Psychology is understood as the science of mind. It has greatly contributed to the development of OB. Intra personal aspect of OB, like motivation, personality, perception, attitude, opinion and learning owe their study to psychology.

- *Sociology*: Sociology is the study of group behaviour. It studies the behaviour of people in relation to their fellow human beings. Sociologists have contributed to the study of inter personal dynamics like leadership, group dynamics, communication, formation of groups, formal and informal organsiations and the like.
- *Anthropology*: Anthropology is understood as the study of man and his works. In particular anthropologists study the culture. Culture has significant influence on human behaviour. It dictates what people learn and how they behave. An employee's behaviour, discretion about things good or bad, and his style of functioning are influenced by the culture of his organization.
- *Political Science*: Political science studies the behaviour of individuals and groups within a political environment. Specific topics of concern to political scientists include conflict resolution, group coalition, allocation of power, and how people manipulate power for individual self-interest.
- *Economics*: Economics helps understand the decision processes, allocation of scarce resources, and the impact of economic policies on organization. In particular it helps explain human motivation and the way people and their organizations make decisions.

## ORGANIZATIONAL PSYCHOLOGY

Organizational psychology is one of the most active and prosperous branches of modern psychological science. In most of the organizations; in the USA-, which is regarded as the home of psychology - and also in Europe, it is very common to find industrial psychologists working along with the other people. In India, also this area is of greatest importance to the psychologists.

Industrial psychology is gaining popularity because it tries to understand the human problems that have arisen as a result of tremendous expansion of industry in the last few decades. Though there is considerable dispute about the precise time of its formal beginning, it is now more or less accepted that it began as a branch of psychology in December 1901, when Doctor Walter Dill Scott, in the USA spoke on the possibilities of the application of psychological principles to the field of advertising. Many, however place the beginning of industrial psychology in the year 1930, when HUGO MUNSTERBERG published his book 'Psychology and Industrial Efficiency'.

## Meaning and Definition

Industrial psychology mans the study of the psychology of the persons working in an industrial enterprise. It is necessary to recognise that people are essential ingredients in all organizations; be they business, industrial, educational, public utility or governmental. Industrial psychology deals with the attitudes and aptitudes of the people working in the organizations. Industrial means the activities related with the production of goods and services and psychology means with the science of minds. Thus industrial psychology is a systematic study of state of minds of the people who are engaged in the production of goods and services. It is the study of the problems related with human behaviour in reference to organizations.

Industrial psychology has been defined in various ways by various psychologists. J.C.Naylor, "Industrial Psychology is simply the application or extension of psychological facts and principles to the problems concerning human beings operating within the context of business and industry." Industrial Psychology is a systematic study and analysis of the problems of behaviour of employees working in an industrial enterprise, so that their problems may be solved and the employees may work to the best of their efficiency. It also tries to improve industrial relations. Industrial psychology stresses upon the improvement of human relations in an industrial enterprise, which is helpful, in providing satisfaction to the employees; and in increasing productivity of the organization.

## IMPORTANCE AND SCOPE

The applications of psychological principles to the people working in an organization over a long period make it easier to understand the scope of typical activities of industrial psychologists working in an industry. Industrial psychology is used in all the areas of an industry. Wherever manpower is required, the importance of industrial psychology cant be under estimated.

*The scope of industrial psychology can be explained under the following heads*:

- *Personal Selection, Placement and Promotions*: Industrial psychology is used for the selection, placement and promotions of employees in an industrial enterprise. It helps in selecting the right person for the job and also for assigning right job for the right person. It also helps to develop the instruments of personal selection by conducting relevant research. These include standardised application form, scientific screening of application and use of psychological tests to test the ability and capability of candidates.
- *Education, Training and Development*: IP evaluates the efficiency and ability of the employees of an organization, so that necessary programmes for the education, training, and development of these employees may be prepared and implemented. IP develops the methods and means of the appraisal of the performance of employees. it also develops the procedures of measuring attitudes of employees.
- *Human Engineering*: IP makes a deep study and analysis of all the problems of an industry. it is particularly helpful in dealing with human problems such as suggesting changes, innovations in designs of the machines and equipment's, arranging proper working conditions to the employees and also facing labour turnover and absenteeism.
- *Motivation*: Success of organizations depends to a greater extent upon the co-operation of the employees working in the enterprise. IP makes deep and analytical study of the feelings and emotions of the employees and suggests as to which of the financial

and non-financial incentives are required to motivate the employees.

- *Productivity study*: IP also helps in lessening worker fatigue, improving environmental conditions such as lighting, ventilation, working arrangements etc with a view to maximise efficiency.
- *Determination of Wages and Salary*: IP determines the qualities, qualifications, duties and responsibilities of different jobs. Wages and salaries for different jobs are also determined on the basis of qualifications, abilities, duties and responsibilities. IP helps in the determination of wages and salaries by using the techniques of job analysis, job evaluation and merit rating.
- *Trade Union areas*: IP plays an important role in developing and maintaining harmonious relations between workers and management. Mutual negotiation, collective bargaining, grievance handling process etc are subjects of industrial psychology.
- *Employee Relation and Public Relation*: IP is a tool, which advises the management on issues of relations between employee and management. it is also helpful in improving the relations with general public and consumers.
- *Industrial Relations*: IP has been successful in changing the psychology and thinking of employers, managers and employees. The studies of IP revealed that both employers and employees have some emotions, feelings and needs, without which the organizational objectives cant be achieved. All the possible financial and non-financial incentives should be provided to the employees to encourage them to dedicate their efforts in the organization. IP motivates all the employers, managers and employees and helps in establishing cordial industrial relations.
- *Advertisement and Salesmanship*: The scope of IP is very wide. It is not limited only to increase the production and productivity of the enterprise. it is also helpful

in effective advertisement and salesmanship. IP stresses upon the study of thinking and attitudes of consumers, so that suitable programmes of advertisement and salesmanship may be developed and implemented.

## INDIVIDUAL DIFFERENCE

Individuals differ widely in their physical characteristics, temperamental qualities, mental abilities and the ways in which they behave. These differences form the very basis of organizational psychology. The significance and implications of these differences are so great that the study of individual differences and their proper evaluation assumes greater importance in organizational psychology.

Organizations are composed of individuals. Each individual is an island in himself; each subject to particular motives, aspirations, perceptions and abilities. The behaviour of each individual is influenced by several factors. No two individuals are alike in their physical characteristics like height, weight, appearance etc. This also equally true of the psychological characteristics of individuals such as their intelligence, interests and aptitudes, personal qualities like aggressiveness, honesty and so on.

These individual difference, both in physical and psychological characteristics of the individuals for the very basis of organizational psychology. The reasons for these is that only by understanding the various physical and psychological assets as well as liabilities of an individual, that we are in a better position to assign the right type of work. For example no company will ever try to select a driver or machine operator who has poor eyesight, or a salesman who is unattractive in physical features.

The study and measurement of individual difference, thus, forms the very basis of some important functions of psychologists in organizational functions such as personal selection, placement, promotions and so on. in modern times technology and industry have advanced so much that every position in a Co demands certain physical or psychological characteristics in an individual. It is for this reason that a major part of industrial psychologists efforts are directed towards investigating and understanding the differences among individuals and applying such knowledge in various areas in an organization.

## FACTORS AFFECTING INDIVIDUAL DIFFERENCE

The behaviour of each individual in an organization is different; and his behaviour is influenced by several factors.

## PSYCHOLOGICAL FACTORS

Psychological factors are an individuals mental characteristics and attributes that can affect an individuals behaviour. There are several psychological factors and more prominent among them are:

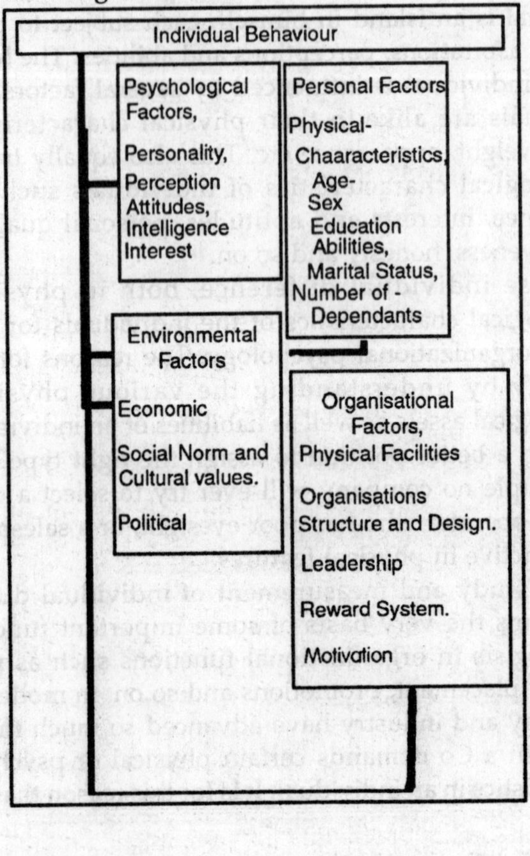

## DIFFERENCE IN INTELLIGENCE

People differ greatly in their intelligence and this affect their capacity to work. Persons intelligence is often a very good index of his ability to cope with varied problems of life. It hardly needs saying that various jobs and positions in industry require varying degrees of intelligence, if they are to be carried out effectively.

### Difference in Interest

We know that people differ greatly in their interests. Some prefer to work quietly in indoors, others like to move about, some others have great interest in music, acting, law, politics, some like repetitive type of work, others are bored by it. Organizational psychologists have found that an individual who works in the area of his interest is much more satisfied than one who has to do some work that has no relation with his interest. It is for this reason that many of organizational psychologists are concentrated in devising methods of reliable measures of an individuals interests, and making use of such measures in selecting people for various jobs.

### Difference in Personality Characteristics

People also differ very widely in their personality. The term personality as it is used in psychology, usually applies to emotional qualities of a person as well as certain uncharacteristic ways of his behaving. Most of these are learned by an individual through his own experiences in life or by imitating significant people in his surroundings. But often they are hereditary. An individuals personality make people different, and often taking in to account such differences becomes necessary in many practical work situations.

### Learning

Human beings greatest asset is their capacity to learn through their experience with the things encountered in life. People vary greatly in their capacity to learn. What a man or his behaviour is, is largely determined by the way he has learned in life. Learning acquires great importance in many situations in industry, but more directly so, when we are concerned with the problems of training. Learning has been defined in psychology as a relatively permanent change in behaviour, which occurs as a result of experience or practice. It is a key concept in psychology because humans are constantly learning:- some time without knowing and some times deliberately. It affects all aspects of human behaviour. For example a workers skill, or managers attitudes are all learned.

**Difference in Perception**

People also differ in the ways they perceive the world surrounding them. In its simple sense, perception is understood as the animation of seeing what is there to be seen. Perception refers to the unique reading of a situation. In other words what is perceived may be different from what is real. Stephen.P.Robbins defines perception as " a process by which individuals organise and interpret their sensory impressions in order to give meaning to their environments."

The perception is a complex process which, is a unique interpretation of the situation. Differences in the perceiving styles of the individuals can be of great consequence in work. The ability of a supervisor to observe defects in inspection work.

**Attitudes**

Attitude is an important factor, which affects human behaviour. It is a tendency to feel and behave in a particular way towards some objects. Individuals acquire attitudes from different sources. The most important sources of acquiring attitudes are direct experience with the object, association, family etc. Attitudes are learned, as human beings learn various other responses. At any given moment the attitude may be inactive, but when the appropriate circumstances arise, the attitude makes the individual to react in favourable, unfavourable or indifferent manner. For example a worker who has experienced considerable frustration in a Company may gradually develop an attitude of dislike towards the Co.

## PERSONNAL FACTORS

Every individual brings to the work place, a variety of personal characteristics and attributes like age, education, abilities and similar related factors.

## DIFFERENCES IN PHYSICAL CHARACTERISTICS

Physical characteristics like height, weight, strength, keenness of vision, keenness of hearing, reaction time, etc are often measured in some context or other. The study of the differences in such physical characteristics acquires great importance; because successful performance often depends upon some of these characteristics. Some heavy job require considerable physical energy, others require a very keen sense of vision or learning.

### Age

Age is an important variable because of its impact on performance turnover, productivity and satisfaction. Performance depends on age. As age advances, performance is likely to decline. Similarly ageing has impact on turnover. There is positive association between age and satisfaction level of employees.

### Sex

The issues of male and female employees has received considerable attention from academics, sociologists and researchers. There may be differences in problem solving ability, analytical skill, motivation, and leadership or learning ability.

Sex has its impact on absenteeism also. It has been proved that some times absenteeism is high among female workers due to family responsibilities.

### Education

Education has its effect upon individual difference, and behaviour, largely through the level of education received. Increased levels of education positively affect the working capacity and ability of a person. The type of education can also affect the behaviour of a person.

### Abilities

Ability refers to an individuals capacity to perform the various tasks in a job. Ability of an individual is made up of two sets of skills. - Intellectual and physical.

Intellectual abilities are needed to perform mental activities. IQ tests, for example, are designed to ascertain ones intellectual abilities. Physical abilities manifest in ones stamina, strength and the like. As each employees physical abilities are different, their performance level will also be different.

### Marital Status

Marital status has influence on people's behaviour. It affects absenteeism, turnover and satisfaction levels. As marriage imposes additional responsibility, hence the needs for steady job and steady income. The success or failure of ones marriage life also affect the behaviour of the individual.

### Number of Dependants

There is correlation between number of dependants an employee has and his behaviour in an organization. Number of children an employee has is positively related to absence, especially among females.

## ENVIRONMENTAL FACTORS

Environmental factors include such variables as economic, social, political, and the like. These factors are mainly external and will cause individual difference.

### ECONOMIC FACTORS

The economic environment is an important determinant of individual difference. All work is performed within economic framework that both directly and indirectly affects the individuals working in it. Employment opportunities will have a strong influence on behaviour. Fewer job opportunities increase the emphasis on job security and can even change the basic nature of the employee. Wages satisfy various individual needs. Money is a complex variable and its effect on individual behaviour varies tremendously. Inequalities in wages will have a negative effect on employee performance.

### Cultural Environment

The cultural environment is made up of institutions and other forces that affect the society's basic values, perceptions, work ethics, preferences and behaviour. People grow up in a particular society that shape their basic beliefs, values and behaviours. Culture varies from country to country and these variations produce different behaviours; work ethics, achievement need, effort reward expectations and values are important cultural factors which affect individuals. In the context of job, work ethic implies hard work and commitment to work. Strong work ethic ensures motivated employees. Achievement need too has influence on employee behaviour. A person with a 'high need to achieve' tends to see a high degree of personal responsibility. It is too well known that a perfect match between effort and reward will produce better performance from an individual. When the individual feels that he has been treated unfairly, the performance suffers.

### Political Factors

The political climate in which an individual lives can affect the individual behaviour through several factors. The political ideology of a country and society affects individual behaviour.

## ORGANIZATIONAL FACTORS

Individual behaviour is also influenced by physical facilities, organization structure and design, leadership and reward system in an organization.

### FACILITIES

The physical facilities such as lighting, heating, ventilation, air conditioning, space provided, equipment's etc will have their influence on employee behaviour and performance.

### Organization Structure and Design

An organization is a planned co ordination of a number of people and their activities for the achievement of some specific goals. Organization structure shows the way in which different groups and departments in the organization are set up. The behaviour and performance of an individual is influenced by where that person fits into the overall structure and design of the organization.

### Leadership

The organization establishes a system of leadership and supervision to provide direction, assistance, advise and coaching to individual members. The leader behaviour is, there fore, a potential source of influence on an individual.

### Reward Systems

Organizations establish reward systems to compensate their employees. the behaviour and performance of an individual is influenced by the reward system his organization has established.

### Motivation

Another factor which affects individual difference is motivation. One of the most important task of a management job is to identify and activate employee motives consciously and constructively towards the achievement of the objectives.

## PSYCHOLOGICAL TESTS

Psychological tests are the tests that are meant to test the ability of the candidates in a psychological manner. These tests are commonly adopted these days to select employees in a business and industrial enterprise. These tests help in testing the ability of a candidate for a particular job, their attitudes towards work, nature and mental status etc. these tests have proved very useful and helpful in various fields, such as selection, direction, training, promotion and development programme.Psychological tests are of various types. They include intelligence tests, interest tests and so on.

## INTELLIGENCE TESTS

Intelligence may be defined as the capacity of an individual of comprehension and reasoning. It may also be described as the adjustment of an individual in a given situation.

The earliest effort to measure intelligence systematically was made by French psychologists Alfred Binet and Simon, in the year 1905, when the worlds first psychological test to measure intelligence was devised. This test constituted a great land mark in the history of testing and all psychological testing that has developed later is either applications, elaboration's or refinements of original ideas of Binet.

Since Binet, a number of intelligence tests have been constructed and most of these tests measure such functions as learning memory, flexibility in thinking, speed of thinking etc. Intelligence tests are very helpful in judging the mental ability, awareness and reasoning ability of the candidate in in different situations. These tests are used for selection of employees for almost every type of jobs.

Intelligence tests may be broadly grouped in to two categories. Those which give an overall score of intelligence like Intelligence Quotient(IQ) Test, or Mental Age (MA) and those that give us some indication of persons standing in various elements or factors of intelligence.

### Intelligence Quotient Test (IQ Test)

The concept of Mental Age (MA) was first developed by Binet. It is very simple in its conception. we know that the average child of a given intelligence is able to perform certain functions, such as obeying certain commands, giving meanings to words and so on. If the tested child shows an over all ability to perform such operations, - say a 10 year old child- he is then said to have a mental age of 10 years. (ie MA=10).

If the child is also ten years old, we can say that his mental age equals his chronological age. But he may also perform the average functions, which a child of 11, 12 or 13 years could perform. such child then has higher mental age than which may follow from his chronological age. but if a ten year old is unable to pass the task set for his age, and is able to pass only for a five year old, his mental age is 5 years (MA=5) and this means he is mentally retarded. IQ is calculated as the ratio between mental age and chronological age. (MA & CA).

$$IQ = \frac{MA}{CA} \times 100.$$

In the case of an average person, the IQ will be 100. But if there is discrepancies in the MA and CA, it can be either above 100 (ie better than average intelligence) or below 100 (Lower than average intelligence).Thus by finding the IQ, we can say whether a person is of average intelligence or above or below it.

## TYPS OF INTELLIGENCE TEST

### THE STANFORD - BINET TESTS AND WESCHLER SCALES

These tests are used mostly on single individuals and require a trained person to conduct the test and to interpret the performance. These tests can be used in a number of areas. But in modern selection practice however, they are rarely used because of the time required to test a person fully.

### OTIS TEST

This test is available in two forms. - For school going children and for college students and adults. In industry the adult form of these tests have been used for almost every type of job. This type of test is found extremely useful for lower level jobs. Many adaptations of this tests are now available in Indian languages.

### WONDERLIC PERSONNEL TEST

This test is a quick test requiring only 12 minutes time to answer. The items of this test is so selected that they can distinguish between a poor worker and a good worker an a variety of industrial jobs.

### MULTI FACTOR TESTS

The present trend in testing is towards using more and

more specific tests, which can tell how an individual scores on various factors of intelligence. Most of these tests give scores on each separate factor and can be combined as a group. Some such tests are

**Chicago Test.**

Chicago Test is developed by L.L.Thurstone in the year 1941. This test include verbal meaning test, space test, reasoning, tests using numbers and word fluency.

**The DAT (Differential Aptitudes Tests)**

This test measures important abilities like verbal reasoning, numerical ability, clerical speed, language usage and so on. This test is used extensively in industrial selection. They measure different mental abilities in different proportion.

**GATB**

This test, called General Aptitude Test Battery, is specifically constructed by the US Employment Service. It is so constructed that it can test all of a persons vocational abilities. it has twelve tests and nine aptitude scores.

Most of these tests are now adapted to the Indian populations in different regions and can be used with considerably greater effectiveness because Indian norms are developed for them. It is certain that it will grow rapidly in the coming years because no industry can survive, unless it selects its personnel on scientific basis.

## USE OR UTILITY OF PSYCHOLOGICAL TESTS

Psychological tests have been an important part of selection procedure these days. These tests have proved their utility themselves. The utility and importance of such tests can be summarised as follows.

## HELPFUL IN SCIENTIFIC APPOINTMENTS

A great problem before every business these days is to get right persons for right jobs. Success of the organization depends largely upon the ability, efficiency and the sincerity of the employees. Psychological tests help in selecting appropriate persons for the enterprise by testing their ability, efficiency and interest in the particular work.

## HELPFUL IN SELECTION FOR TRAINING

In almost every organizations, training is given to workers for doing their job in most efficient manner. But everyone cant get the benefit of training. An individual can get the benefit from training, only if he has intelligence and interest required for a particular work.

Psychological tests help in testing these abilities of employees so that most suitable employees may be selected for training and both employees and the organization may get maximum benefits of training programme.

## HELPFUL IN CLASSIFICATION JUST AS TO THE LEVEL OF INTELLIGENCE

Success of a person in a particular work depends to a large extent upon his level of intelligence. on the basis of psychological test, workers can be grouped in to different categories.

Different jobs requiring different levels of intelligence and capacity can be assigned to individuals based on these classifications.

### Help in Prediction

Using psychological tests, psychologists can easily make forecast of success possibilities of an individual. They can also predict the degree of success that one is likely to achieve.

### Helpful in Diagnosis of Problems

Psychological tests are helpful in making proper diagnosis of a given problem. (that may be problem relating to an individual or a group). If the problem is properly analysed, steps may be taken to treat the problem easily.

Thus it can be concluded that psychological tests are very helpful in many areas. To ensure utility of these tests, care should be taken to see that the tests are correctly administered.

## PERSONALITY

Personality is an important determinant of employee behaviour. It influences selection of individuals to occupy various positions in an organization. The personality required for a successful sales manager is different from those required for an executive in charge of production.

The term personality has been derived from Latin name persona, which means speak through. It denotes the mask worn by actors in ancient Greece and Rome. In psychology, it is interpreted in different ways by different theorists. Gordon Allport; personality is the dynamic organization within the individual of those psychological systems that determine his unique adjustment to his environment. It is the organized set of characteristics possessed by a person that uniquely influences his or her cognitions, motivations, and behaviours in various situations.

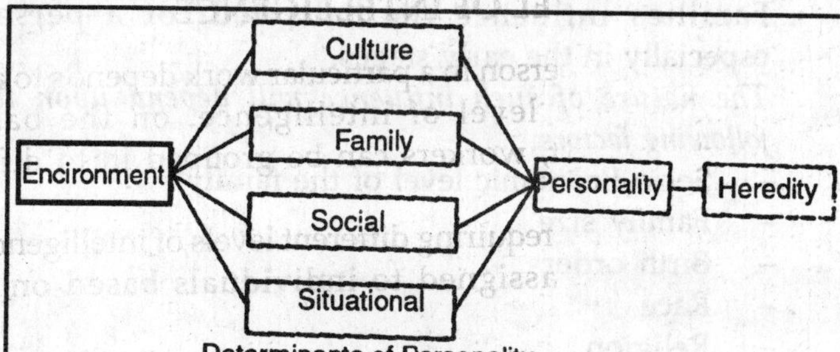

Determinants of Personality

## HEREDITY

The concept that heredity is a determinant of personality is embedded in our minds. In our day to day life, so many times we use the term "Like father like son" as "Like mother like daughter. When we use these terms we generally refer to the traits like physique, eye colour, hair colour, height, temperament, energy level, intelligence, reflexes etc. However, the importance of heredity varies from one personality trait to another.

### Environment

The personality traits are not completely dictated by

heredity, environment also plays a very important role m the development of personality of a person.

*Environment comprises of culture, family, social and situational factors:*

- *Culture: "Culture is the sum total of learned behaviour traits which are manifested and shared by the members of the society."* Culture establishes norms, attitudes and values that are passed along from generation 10 generation and create consistencies over time. Every culture expects and trains its members to behave in the ways that are acceptable to the group. Persons belonging to different cultural groups generally have different attitudes towards independence, aggression, competition, cooperation, artistic talent etc.
- *Family*: One of the very important determinants of the personality of a person is his immediate family. Families influence the behaviour of a person especially in the early stages.

  *The nature of such influence will depend upon the following factors:*
  - Socio-Economic level of the family
  - Family size
  - Birth order
  - Race
  - Religion
  - Parent's educational level
  - Geographic location.

To elaborate, a person brought up in a rich and prestigious family has a different personality as compared to the people who belong to a poor family. The family size will also affect the behaviour of a child.

The personality of a single child is different from the personality of a person who is brought up in a family of more than two siblings.

Similarly, the personality of a person brought up in a nuclear family will be different from that of a person brought up in a joint family. Studies have also shown that first born children are more responsible, rational, independent, ambitious and more sensitive to social acceptance. Empirical evidence also suggests that the home and family environment, created by the mother and the father as well as their own behaviour is highly influential on personality development of the child.

- *Social*: Socialization is a process by which an infant acquires from the enormously wide range of behavioural potentialities that are open to him at birth, those behaviour patterns that are customary and acceptable to the family and social groups. Inifially socialisation starts with the contact of the infant with the mother when he grows up. Contacts with the other members of the family and social groups influence his socialisation process. These social groups include school mates, friends, then friends or colleagues at work place, groups to which an individual belongs. Because "A man is known by the company he keeps," all these social groups influence the behaviour of the individuals.
- *Situational*: Situational factors also play a very important role in determining the personality of a person Migram s research study indicates very powerful role the situation may play in human personality On the basis of his research studv he states that "A situation exerts an important press on the individual It exercises constraints and may provide push. In certain circumstances, it is not so much the kind of person a man is, as the kind of situation in which he is placed that determines his actions. "That is why it is often said that life is a collection of experiences. Every individual goes through different type of experiences and events in his life. Some of the events and experiences can serve as important determinants of his personality

## PERSONALITY TESTS

In this connection psychologists have developed a series of tests which would help selection of right individuals for suitable jobs. Various methods of personality appraisals are used today. The most prominent among them are

## THE BELL ADJUSTMENT INVENTORY

This questionnaire is designed mainly for rapid screening of high school students for counselling purpose. It can also be used for screening of workers. It yields scores in 4 different areas - Home, Health, Social and Emotional. The items in Bell test are selected from many inventories (Questionnaires) and are then grouped in the categories. The categories used may be elaborated as follows.

| | | |
|---|---|---|
| Health | – | Extent of illness. |
| Home | – | Satisfaction with family life. |
| Social | – | Extent of shyness etc. |
| Emotion | – | Extent of depression, nervousness etc. |

## The California Test of Personality

This another very frequently used test. The basic principle underlying the test is "life adjustment", which is thought as a balance between personal and social adjustment. It evaluates areas like self reliance, sense of personal freedom, social standard, family relations etc.

## Minne Sota Multiphasic Personality Inventory.

This is the most outstanding and elaborate test ever constructed and widely used in clinical practice and research. This test was developed by Hathway and Mckinley in 1940. It is a most comprehensive instrument which gives scores on all the important areas of human personality.

The test consists of 550 affirmative statements, which the person is asked to sort out in 3 categories.– True, False and Cant say. But this test is not used extensively in industry because of the time it takes to answer, and also the clinical terminology. But it has been used by governmental agencies and often in spotting out troubled workers.

## Rorschach Ink Blot Test

This test was developed by Hermann Rorscach, a Swiss

psychiatrist in 1921. It makes use of simple materials like ' ink blots', to which the person respond by telling what things he sees in them. Rorschach first developed this test for applying to clinical cases. But now it is used widely in organizational psychology. The basic principle underlying the test is that, when faced with non conventional situations, peoples response reveal some fundamental features of his personality without his knowing. This test is used for analysing the personality and emotional aspects of an individual.

**Thematic Apperception Test (TAT)**

This method consists of thirty picture cards containing vague pictures. The person being tested is told that this is a test of imagination and that he has to make up short stories based on scenes depicted in the cards. After persons interpretation is recorded and a post test interview is arranged, in which the examiner tries to find out the origin of his stories; and how the incidents, characters, places, etc. The examiner then interprets and draws ceases regarding the workers personality.

**Situational Tests of Personality**

As the name implies, in the situational tests, the individual is confronted with a life like situation, in response to which he gives expression to his feelings and his various personality factors. In most such cases the individuals behaviour is evaluated by some trained judges.

In many jobs special situational tests can be developed. For example, it is a common practice to make an applicant of sales job to put in a sales situation to see whether he is able to convince his customers about the product. The inventories are very frequently used because of the ease with which they could be administered.

## CHALLENGES AND OPPORTUNITIES FOR OB

Global corporations such as IBM, Exxon, Texaco, McDonalds, and Hewlett Packard report deriving over 55 per cent of their revenues from international operations. In order to capitalize on these global business opportunities, organizations are continuously turning towards employee foreign assignments as a strategic human resource tactic.

*The various types of foreign assignments include*:

- Relocating an employee and family to a target country (expatriates),
- Developing management staff from the local country (inpatriates), or
- Utilizing employees in frequent short-terre assignments (flexpatriates) to transfer area-specific knowledge.

Although utilization of inpatriates and flexpatriates is increasing, most international organizations continue to pursue expatriates for foreign assignments. The costs of expatriate failure are substantial: Studies indicate failure rates for expatriate assignments of approximately 25 to 40 per cent. Estimates for expatriate relocation run from US $60,000 to US $250,000 to repatriate one executive with family prematurely. Expatriate failure is defined as either an expatriate's premature return from assignment or underperformance while on assignment.

Although there are many reasons for expatriate failure, an average of 30 per cent of US and UK expatriate placements end in failure because of a disconnect between human resource management policies and expatriate practices-a preventable cause of assignment failure. Some organizations fail to follow basic human resource practices when assigning employees and their families to international assignments. These neglected practices include failure to provide cross-cultural training, gender equity when evaluating potential assignment candidates, employment assistance to the employee's spouse, a mentor and network access to aid career development, and sufficient pre-assignment training such as language and cultural skill acquisition.

Ongoing premature repatriation of employees from international assignments also damages an organization's ability to staff its foreign operations with the best possible candidates. High levels of internal turnover dissuade employees from accepting foreign assignments. Research studies have demonstrated that expatriate job satisfaction has a distinct influence on assignment completion. We suggest that an organization might gain insight into causes of expatriate failure by evaluating how its human resource practices towards expatriates enhance job satisfaction and ultimately increase the probability of assignment completion. Rather than focus predominantly on the identification and establishment of various programmes that specifically contribute to expatriate success, global organizations stand to gain more from an evaluation of their HR practices towards expatriates using the same job satisfaction lens as used with domestic employees.

Although international assignments have specific characteristics, successful domestic and international relocations are dependent on organizational support. Additionally, many of the problems associated with relocating domestic employees are quite similar to those of international employees, namely inability of the family to adjust, family ties at the existing home location, potential impact on career, and disruption of a partner's employment/career. With the exception of foreign language and cultural training, many employee relocation challenges can be addressed by attention to job satisfaction dimensions. The incorporation of job satisfaction and utilization of domestic relocation experience will provide direction for international organizations in their establishment of expatriate programmes.

We detail the relationship between job satisfaction and employee turnover and link organization-controlled job satisfaction facets to pre-assignment preparation, assignment support, and repatriation support. Finally, we create a theoretical framework that outlines organizational best practice strategies that managers can adopt in order to enhance expatriates' levels of job satisfaction and subsequently reduce assignment turnover.

# 2

# Foundations of Individual Behaviour

Sustainable development is about creating and maintaining our options for various co-evolving elements of social-ecological systems. The need for building adaptive capacity and learning is regularly emphasised in this context. Statements such as the following appear increasingly in the literature: 'The learning process is of central importance for social-ecological capacity to build resilience' or ' ajdaptive management is based on feedback learning; it is co-evolutionary, involving two-way feedback between management policy and the state of the resource' or '... catalysing learning through discussion and debate within a global community that is striving towards sustainability'.

While these groups are heading towards a novel and constructive way of understanding and managing changes in social-ecological systems, they leave a number of important questions open: Who should be learning (individuals, groups, organizations, institutions or all of them)? What should they learn? How do these new learning processes relate to already ongoing learning processes?

How are learning processes translated between different scales? Is it always good to learn more? Learning is clearly not sufficient; how is it translated into action? Once these questions have been clarified, we can return to the question of how to incorporate learning into management practice and institutions. Surprisingly few papers have attempted to answer (some of) these questions. The development of theoretical foundations of learning processes in co-evolving systems and to draw ceases that are relevant for moving towards more sustain able development paths. The associate builds on work, but goes further in linking the emergent theory of sustainability science with theories of learning. It highlights different types of learning processes which occur in co-evolving systems, and explores learning processes on the macro-, mesoand micro-levels for moving onto more sustainable paths.

The associate sets the scene by linking the quest for more sustainable development with complex systems, co-evolution and learning. The associate includes parts which review different types of learning processes in co-evolutionary processes of social-ecological systems on different scales; parts focusing on co-evolution of the environment and governance, and on the co-evolution of human behaviour and culture. In these parts we refer to the most important learning theories from psychology, social psychology, education, evolutionary economics and political science and employ them to understand co-evolutionary processes. Each part exemplifies selected tools and methods that are useful to apply a co-evolutionary perspective on learning.

## THE ROLE OF LEARNING IN THE QUEST FOR SUSTAINABLE DEVELOPMENT

Mounting knowledge of what influences the changes of nature and societies has brought us insight that in the end as suggested, not know everything. We have to learn to live in a complex world of interdependent systems with high uncertainties and multiple interests in society.

The main challenges for sustainability science arise from the systems' characteristics (complex and evolving), indeterminancy of outcomes (comprising risk, uncertainly, ambiguity and ignorance) and the democratic resolution of the problem of unsustainability needs to account for multiple legitimate perspectives. Therefore, the focus of analyses in sustainability science has shifted away from outcomes and towards processes. Tacconi calls this move away from 'carrying out analyses of environmental issues in a snapshot approach' towards a 'process approach' one of the achievements of sustainability science. Also, the perception of a system differs by scale. Learning processes not only contribute to understand and explain the natural and societal phenomena and to explore different perceptions thereof, but also to bring opportunities for personal liberation and social transformation.

## COMPLEX SYSTEMS

A complex system is a system for which it is difficult, if not impossible, to restrict the description to a limited number of parameters or characterise variables without losing essential global functional properties. Social systems and their institutions are the main drivers to reduce complexity by making individual behaviour more predictable. Social systems provide structures of meaning; the meaning resides in knowledge, norms, values and worldviews. At the same time, social systems create or preserve complexity by offering complex organizational and functional differentiation through socialised roles.

Omnipresent change in systems causes problems for gaining knowledge about consequences. Systems theory claims that the complexity of social actions and the multitude of potential interventions, with its infinite number of possible outcomes, prevent any reliable prediction of the connections between individual choices and observed outcomes. Martinez-Alier, et aL argued that, in such systems, we can only hope for weak comparability, i.e. there is an irreducible value conflict when deciding what measure should be used to rank alternative actions.

This acknowledges that different stakeholders can exhibit different 'rational choices' when facing the same specific situation. Weak comparability does, however, not imply that 'rationality' cannot be pursued when deciding. Rather it implies that 'substantive rationality', which requires strong comparability, must be replaced by 'procedural rationality'. Procedural rationality is based on the acknowledgement of ignorance, uncertainty and the existence of multiple legitimate perspectives. The different forms of indeterminacy cause, to various degrees, problems for the ability to know consequences and thus for the role of science. Funtowicz and Ravetz argued that, if facts are uncertain, values in dispute, stakes are high and decisions urgent, then decisions need to be supported by Post-Normal Science.

'Dealing with environmental problems therefore requires opening the analytical and decision-making processes to broader categories of facts and actors than those traditionally legitimated'. This includes the introduction of extended peer communities, i.e. the involvement of lay persons through participatory processes. This creates a context where scientists and stakeholders contribute knowledge and engage with each other in an inclusive process of deliberation and decision-making. Irreducible uncertainty is a stronger motivator for these participatory decision processes.

"The extent of uncertainty seen in the scientific knowledge base is itself a subjective function of complex social and cultural factors. Scientific uncertainty can be enlarged by social uncertainties in the context of its practical interpretation, and it can be reduced by opposite social forces. Munda developed this idea further and distinguishes between social and technical uncertainty. Understanding complex and evolving social ecological systems has been aided by the theoretical development of Holling's adaptive cycle heuristic.

Holling, '... systems of nature, of humans, as well as combined human-nature systems, are interlinked in never-ending adaptive cycles of growth, accumulations, restructuring, and renewal'. These adaptive cycles of change occur at multiple scales within a nested hierarchy of faster and slower adaptive cycles. Gunderson and Holling call this multiscale perspective 'panarchy'. A funtioning system requires, therefore, that each level operates at an individual rate larger processes and revitalized from below by small, fast and innovative cycles. Holling sees the greatest potential for learning in the phase after exploitation and conservation, which he calls release. Despite being associated with 'crisis', release is not necessarily undesirable. It can be a source of renewal similar to Schumpeter's 'creative destruction," where a system's capital is reordered and reorganized. Learning can also be enhanced by crisis and renewal, as 'individuals and groups appear to do the majority of Out-of-the-box learning' or breakthrough thinking, in response to crisis'.

Hence, learning in the accumulation and conservation phases is mainly based on current paradigms and scientific and technological trajectories, also called 'single loop learning'. Learning in the release phase and - to a lesser extent - in the reorganization phase is concerned with renewal, experimentation and qualitative change ('double loop learning'). Determining if a shock causes Out-of-the-box learning' allows for the evaluation of what stage in the adaptive cycle the system lies and subsequently whether reorganization and the resultant new structures are building resilience. Evaluating learning in response to crisis across an entire system requires a multi-scale analysis. There is a need for learning among both individual actors and collectives of actors in order to achieve learning on the system level.

## MULTIPLE LEGITIMATE PERSPECTIVES

Pluralist societies are characterised by different value systems and worldviews, and increasingly so. In addition to this social and political trend, the complex nature of social systems means that they cannot be captured when using a single perspective. 'The assumptions of representative democracy have been progressively undermined by the scale and complexity of contemporary societies and their rate of change. Elected representatives can rarely capture the diverse values and social and economic interests of their constituents, while the uncertainties generated by novel threats argue for the inclusion of a wider range of knowledges in decision-making'.

Cultural theory, understanding of the world is mediated through value and belief systems and forms of social organization. Learning always takes place within a pre-existing but often dynamic context of power relations, rules, expectations, historical narratives and perceptions of group and individual interests, which affect not only what learners learn but what they think it is important to learn and why.

Wynne argued that the validity of knowledge is conditional upon the model of rationality. If knowledge creation is handled differently by each cultural bias, then the only way to create shared understanding and agreement for action is to produce meaning that lies outside of the territory of individual cultural biases. Effective policy for a society depends on successful creation of shared meaning among - not within - cultural groups.

*Two points are particularly relevant here*:

- Shared social values as well as shared meanings are created through effective social interaction, they do not exist a priori, nor are they merely the intersection of individual values, instead, they are created through social interaction;
- The only effective way to achieve this kind of interaction is through open dialogue, where social learning is necessary for forming as well as for changing shared social values.

## Co-evolution

Co-evolution is a powerful metapher for studying processes of change at various scales in socialecological systems. Co-evolution here refers to the interactive change of evolving socio-economic and biophysical systems. It differs from co-dynamic change, which does not require the systems to be evolving. The main evolutionary processes are variation and selection. In social systems they are expressed in many different ways, including regulation, communication, negotiation, cultural mediation, enforcement, retaliation and learning. The need for changing direction and for overcoming inertia in social systems makes learning a key process for moving to more sustainable development paths. Complexity, indeterminacy and the prevalence of multiple legitimate perspectives provide the reasoning for stimulating learning rather than aiming for optimising strategies.

*Over the last 30 years, there has been:*

- A growing trend to perceive not only biological, but also social systems as evolving systems;
- Growing awareness that various sub-systems are not only interdependent, but exert a interactive evolutionary influence. In biology, co-evolution is the interactive evolutionary influence between two species that become dependent on each other. Each party in a co-evolutionary relationship exerts selective pressures on the other, thereby affecting each others' evolution. When interpreting co-evolution broadly as a reciprocal process of two (or more) evolving elements whose interaction produces an evolutionary response in each of them, the natural environment as well as various sub-systems of the social system can be perceived as co-evolving. Social and natural systems are co-evolving, which means that they are characterised by qualitative change, surprises, novelty and irreversibility and their interaction produces an evolutionary response in both systems.

Learning is clearly one of the processes which play a role in evolution. But how are the two concepts related? For example, Campbell applied evolutionary thinking to ideas and cognition and argued that human learning is at the root an evolutionary process. Parson and Clark argued rightly that 'an evolutionary model cannot be equivalent to a learning model at the same level of analysis.

Evolution is based on selection among invariant forms through birth and death processes, whereas learning implies that the learning system survives its changes.... But an evolutionary model may be equivalent to a learning model at a different level of analysis.' Learning may occur at an aggregate level through selection among ideas, routines or technologies at a lower level. 'Part of an environmental manager's job is to create learning experiences to re-establish the mental connections between our actions and environments, thus creating pathways for social change'.

The co-evolutionary perspective helps to understand the processes, which has led to the present unsustainable situation and provides clues for moving onto more sustainable development paths.

*We can define three main layers of co-evolutionary processes that are relevant in the context of sustainable development*:

- Co-evolution of the environment and governance (focus on: macro-level);
- Co-evolution of technology and governance (focus on: meso-level); and
- Co-evolution of human behaviour and culture (focus on: micro-level). Between the different levels, interactions occur.

## Co-evolution on Multiple Scales

Before exploring the three levels of co-evolution and related learning theories in greater depth, we should try to group the learning theories on which as suggested, draw. In addition to the level or the discipline, we can group by their perceived main barrier to learning.

*As suggested, draw heavily on theories from group (3) and to a lesser extent on theories from the other two groups*:

(1) Rationalist theories or information deficit models of public understanding and action. The main hindrance to pro-environmental behaviour is a lack of environmental knowledge. Learners need to aquire more environmental knowledge. In a decision process stakeholders are considered as carriers of local knowledge; they can improve the knowledge base for decisionmaking.

(2) *Social structure-focussed theories*: The main hindrances to pro-environmental behaviour are social obstacles. Learners need to find ways to overcome these. Learning theories in this category are often based on critical theory and refer to concerns of social and environmental justice. In a decision process stakeholders are considered as actors who can as a group help learners to overcome some social

obstacles; it is acknowledged that stakeholders having multiple legitimate perspectives that should be accounted for in the decision; since decisions have an impact on the social reality of people, those who are affected by a decision should have an opportunity to have a say.

(3) *Evolutionary or complex systems-based theories*: The main hindrance to pro-environmental behaviour is the complexity of the sustainability issues and the resulting uncertainty. Learners need to develop ways to perceive complex problems and to address uncertainty. Learners switch between multiple forms of rationality. Problem definitions and rationality will vary depending on the context. In a decision process stakeholder involvement is considered as a way to address the problems highlighted by post-normal science.

## SOCIAL LEARNING

Adler applied evolutionary concepts to government learning, explaining two major innovations in American foreign policy through a process of idea generation, domestic selection and international diffusion. Schmid and Eder take an evolutionary approach to the explanation of social systems, norms and rules. At the social level of analysis, theories focusing on the cognitive evolution of politically salient ideas have tended to become linked with normative discussions of progress in human affairs.

In environmental management, co-evolutionary concepts are adopted to highlight the role of individual and social learning for adaptive management. Janssen et al. developed a co-evolutionary framework for identifying parts of a social-ecological system that is potentially vulnerable to internal disturbances and to identify design principles for institutions which lead to robust social-ecological systems. After reviewing a large number of historical cases, they conclude that whether or not the multi-level and multi-scale aspects of a social-ecological system provide benefits or incur costs depends delicately on the institutional arrangements, and that a diversity of adapted institutions will be necessary for fostering sustainable development. 'Social learning is the collective action and reflection that occurs among different individuals and groups as they work to improve the management of human and environmental interrelations. Social learning for improved human interrelations with the environment must ultimately include us all, because we are all part of the same system and each of us will inevitably experience the consequences of these change processes'.

Decision-making about complex and coevolving systems and under conditions of uncertainty can only be an adaptive process, where the actors involved are continuously learning. If decision-making is not simply a strategic action to satisfy individual actors alone, but rather a social learning process, this requires the stimulation of trust, identity and solidarity within the respective society. These are social phenomena and products of communication and mutual understanding. Elements of social life which require mutuality also require constant feedback in order to reach stability. They are fuelled by reciprocal actions and exchange of symbols that reaffirm shared values and convictions.

Public participation which includes deliberation and inclusion, 'can initiate social learning processes which translate uncoordinated individual actions into collective actions that support and reflect collective needs and understanding'. Fiorino and Laird emphasise that citizen participation should enhance learning.

*It should be noted here that in the literature 'social learning' is used in two fundamentally different ways*:

- Learning by individuals which takes place in social settings and/or is socially conditioned;
- Learning by social aggregates.

As suggested, employ the term in the widest possible sense including both meanings. Similarly, Hall defines social learning as a 'attempt to adjust the goals or techniques of policy in response to past experience and new information. Learning is indicated when policy changes as the result of such a process.' Generally, social learning is then a process of coordinated learning with cognitive and normative dimensions, from the individual learning in a social context to policy changes at the international level. 'Social learning refers to the process by which changes in the social condition occur - particularly changes in popular awareness and changes in how individuals see their private interests linked with the shared interests of their fellow citizens. This is a product of individuals learning how to solve their shared problems in a manner that is responsible to both, factual correctness and normative consent'.

*The two most enduring tensions in the modern debate on social learning are also central concerns in participatory decision processes*:

- The roles of the individual and of society in the creation and validation of knowledge;
- The appropriate relationship between a learning, conversing public and political or expert authority in public decision making.

In this sense we do not expect simple or unambiguous answers to questions concerning the role of social learning in sustainable development, but rather empirical studies 'all point towards a fundamentally messy, contingent and ambiguous intermingling of knowledge, power, interests, and chance in the workings of this world'.

## ORGANIZATIONAL LEARNING

Technology and governance co-evolve in development processes. This emphasises the inevitable interdependencies between technologies, institutions, values and ultimately the bio-physical environment. They highlight the possibility of path dependence, adaptive technologies and lock-in situations. In economics, the coevolutionary metaphor is probably most widely used for the interrelations between technologies with industrial structures.

Norgaard, Kemp, Minsch et al. and Rennings highlight the importance of co-evolutionary interactions between technology and the related institutional setting, which is of particular importance in the case of eco-innovation, sustainable management systems and 'green technologies'. Most of the literature refers to the co-evolution of technology and organizations, that is why we start with exploring organizational learning. Von Tunzelmann extended the co-evolutionary processes to technologies and governance systems, which we find more useful for studying development processes.

The literature on organizational learning is massive in its breadth and divergent in its aims. However, several key themes are found across all of the literature. First, many authors have highlighted the importance of converting individual knowledge to knowledge that can be transferred to the entire organization. This includes transferring tacit knowledge to explicit knowledge. In a similar vein, researchers have highlighted the need for open sharing of ideas within groups so that individuals may freely bring forth new ideas that will result in group learning. Many have also highlighted the importance of the context or environment in which learning takes place, as learning is embedded in a set of social systems and organizational structures.

The keystone concept within the organizational learning literature is the distinction between single loop and double loop learning. This has also been linked to building resilience. Single loop learning refers to the evaluation of information within a given mental model, a mental construct, or cognitive map. These shared frameworks create a context in which to view and interpret new information within an organization and, consequently, they may reduce adaptability by limiting the ability of group members to notice and interpret discordant information.

Thus, double loop learning describes the breaking of these shared frameworks in the light of new knowledge. Crossan et al. developed a model that highlights the distinction between feedback and feed-forward learning that are very similar to the concepts of single and double loop learning. Their framework posits that organizations simultaneously explore and learn new ways of doing things, while still relying on and exploiting previously acquired knowledge. Furthermore, the model argues that learning must occur at all levels of the organization. Organizational learning, therefore, can be perceived as a series of feed-forward and feedback learning processes that occur across all levels of the organization.

Sterling takes these ideas further by linking them to the challenge of sustainability, adding a third type of learning and exploring the implications of schools and universities. Learning that leaves basic values unexamined and unchanged is 'learning about sustainability.'

Learning that examines the assumptions that influence the perceptions of systems is 'learning for sustainability.' Learning that is creative, reflexive and participatory is 'learning as sustainability.' For Sterling, this last step is key to the transformative response of changing paradigms, so that we can move towards sustainble development paths. 'This position subsumes the first two responses, but emphasizes process and the quality of learning... Knowing is seen as approximate, relational and provisional, and learning is continual exploration through practice.

This shift here is towards 'learning as change' which engages the whole person and the whole learning institution. There is a keen sense of emergence and ability to work with ambiguity and uncertainty. Space and time are valued, to allow creativity, imagination, and cooperative learning to flourish'. Open sharing of information and building trust among individuals within the group have also been highlighted as vital components of group learning. For Gorz the open sharing of knowledge is essential for moving from the current 'knowledge economy' to a future 'knowledge society'.

## INDIVIDUAL-BASED LEARNING

The co-evolutionary metaphor is applied for conceptualising interrelationships between human behaviours and institutions. Actors influence each other directly or indirectly via social institutions. 'In a co-evolutionary process,... the adaptive landscape of one actor heaves and deforms as the other actors make their own adaptive moves'. However, the co-evolutionary behaviour is not 'limited to attaining point attractors which are local optima, nor is it clear that co-evolving systems must be optimising anything whatsoever'.

*Evolutionary economists such as Dosi et al. distinguish between different classes of objects of learning; agents may learn about:*

- The 'states-of-the-world';
- Other agents' behaviours;
- How to solve problems;
- One's own preferences.

While they refer to landscapes surrounding the agents, they clearly focus on the individual and their cognitive learning processes. For anthropologists, behaviours are cultural in that they are socially learned by observation and interaction in a social group. All culturally acquired behaviours, beliefs, preferences, strategies and practices are also genetic in the sense that their acquisition requires brain machinery that allows for substantial amounts of complex, highfidelity social learning. Understanding social learning is central to figuring out how, when, with whom and how much people cooperate.

While the theories discussed so far in this part focus on the conditions under which learning happens and the extent of learning that happens, Kolb focuses on the stage of the learning process. He provides a descriptive model of the adult learning process in the development of experiential learning theory. The ELT model is a useful tool as it describes how individual experience is grasped and transformed into individual learning.

The model begins with Lewin's cycle of adult learning, which consists of four stages - concrete experience, reflection on that experience, abstract conceptualisation in which general rules are developed and known theories applied to describe the experience, and finally active experimentation that allows construction of guides in creating new experiences. Two of the processes, concrete experience and abstract conceptualisation, describe modes of grasping experience, while active experimentation and reflective observation are modes of transforming experience. When learning, individuals are required to choose one type of grasping and one type of transforming mode, as each of these processes is mutually exclusive, i.e. one cannot employ both concrete and abstract learning or active and reflective learning at the same time.

Experiential learning theory posits that learning depends on the experiences of individual actors. Understanding what factors shape the experiences of actors is vital to understand if learning takes place. During the abstract conceptualisation stage of the cycle, it is necessary to have a variety of information to draw upon in order to describe the experience. Thus, creating an environment where information is abundant and readily accessible will foster learning.

Actors acquire information from multiple sources, including peers and social networks. The nature of these contacts will therefore affect the manner in which individuals learn. Lastly, competence building or formal training will also provide information and enable the experiential learning process to take place. Problems of unsustainable development are typically not well understood. Hence, the special challenge for learning for sustainable development is not to promote particular solutions to well understood problems of social and environmental policy, but rather to help establish procedures, management practices and institutions for public decision-making that support learning processes on multiple scales. A learning approach to sustainable development may enable us to understand how humans have constructed environmental problems in particular ways.

They depend on the particular contexts of governance structures and cultures and over time shape and are shaped by biophysical environments, technologies and human behaviour. Co-evolutionary processes between social and environmental systems and within these systems are ongoing whether we like them or not. For shaping co-evolutionary processes in a particular direction, we need to implement arenas and instruments for continuous learning about them. While a learning approach to sustainable development is increasingly promoted in the academic literature as well as the policy arena, the specific learning processes on the different scales are still poorly understood. We do not promote the quest for a single learning framework for sustainable development; instead they must be context- and problem-specific. Ecological economics, sustainability science and environmental management alike would benefit from borrowing from the array of learning theories in psychology, social psychology, education, evolutionary economics and political science. Different learning theories can inform, for example, the study of what stakeholders really learn in deliberative workshops and how the learning influences environmental policy decisions; how environmental technologies are promoted or hindered within organizations and by various policy instruments; and how cultures lead to certain lifestyles; how some start changing their consumption behaviours and when these start translating into changes of cultures.

A learning approach to sustainable development needs further empirical research that tries to capture learning processes and barriers to learning processes. Another area which needs much further consideration is the inter-linkage between learning processes at different scales.

# 3

# Values, Attitudes and Job Satisfaction

Many studies have found that the self-employed are more satisfied with their jobs than are wage and salary earners. However, all of this research has implicitly assumed that the self-employed are a homogeneous group. In reality, this is not the case the types of workers covered by the self-employed label include professional consultants, small family business owners, farmers, independent tradespersons, labour-only contractors, artists, and workers trying to make a living in self-employment who would otherwise be unemployed. We therefore might expect job satisfaction to vary markedly among different sub-groups of the self-employed.

This associate provides a partial test of this hypothesis. In particular, data from a survey of a representative sample of the Australian workforce are used to test for significant differences in reported job satisfaction between wage and salary earners, self-employed contractors, and other self-employed workers. The focus on self-employed contractors can be justified on at least two grounds. First, it is widely believed that the prevalence of self-employed contractors in the labour force in industrialized countries has increased markedly during the last decade or so.

While hard data with which to establish this proposition are not available, it is clear that in virtually all OECD countries, employers are moving away from the traditional pattern of full-time, permanent, waged work and instead, in their search for increased flexibility, are offering individuals a wide variety of working arrangements. Although most obvious here are permanent part-time work and temporary employment, contract employment is generally thought to have risen also in response to the same sorts of demands.

Second, it is often claimed that many contract work arrangements involve a relationship between contractor and the hiring organization which differs little from the typical employer-employee relationship. That is, similar to an employee, the contractor is heavily dependent on the hiring organization for his or her income or livelihood and, moreover, has relatively little autonomy or control over working conditions.

Thus independence one of the major advantages of self-employment is missing. At the same time, these contractors continue to bear all the risks associated with self-employment, such as poor job security and the absence of benefits typically available to employees. Self-employed contractors such as these have variously been referred to in the literature as the "fake self-employed", "bogus contractors" and "surrogate" employees.

We have chosen to label them as "dependent contractors," thus emphasizing both the tendency for such workers to be counted among self-employed contractors and their dependence on the service recipient for on-going work and income. It is expected that such workers would be unlikely to be more satisfied with their jobs than employees working in otherwise comparable jobs. Indeed, we might expect far greater dissatisfaction.

After introducing the data and methods of analyses, results from bivariate analyses are presented. Then results of a regression model of job satisfaction are detailed. The model includes controls for employment status alongside controls for other personal and industry characteristics. The analysis is then repeated after separately distinguishing "independent contractors" from "dependent contractors." The importance of the results is discussed in the ceases. The PSM is a quarterly household survey of approximately 2,000 Australian households which provides a sample representative of the vast majority of the total Australian population. Indeed, the only persons excluded from the scope of the survey are overseas visitors, diplomatic personnel of overseas governments, non-Australian service personnel stationed in Australia, and those residing in non-private dwellings or in sparsely settled areas.

Information from the selected households was collected in face-to-face interviews. Basic information concerning the composition of the household and the demographic characteristics of its members was sought from an adult member of the household. In addition, questions on a number of topics including both job satisfaction and contractor employment were asked.

In terms of response, the survey was very successful, with 83.2 per cent of the 2,752 households contacted participating. In total, the responding sample generated data on 2,799 employed persons. However, as a result of the difficulties associated with identifying contractors in the agricultural sector, we excluded workers in the agriculture, forestry, and fishing industries, reducing the sample to 2,714 workers. Of these, 1,457 were asked the questions necessary to construct measures of job satisfaction, since questions on job satisfaction were only asked of one randomly-selected adult in each household. For the purposes of this analysis, responses from employers and from a small number of workers whose employment status could not be determined were discarded, leaving a total sample numbering 1,317.

## IDENTIFYING SELF-EMPLOYED CONTRACTORS

A self-employed contractor is defined within this associate as anyone who operates his or her own enterprise or engages independently in a profession or trade and is engaged by a firm or organization for some pre-determined "all-inclusive" fee to provide a defined service for a specified period. Thus, contractors are self-employed, but unlike other self-employed workers, are predominantly involved in the provision of services to other organizations. Unfortunately, simply asking workers whether they are self-employed and whether they provide their services to other organizations is likely to lead to an undercount of the number of self-employed contractors for at least three reasons, all of which relate to the manner in which individuals classify their employment status. First, some workers who are actually employed on a contract basis may consider themselves to be employees of the firm and report themselves as such. This is especially likely where former employees are re-employed on a contract basis with little or no change in their actual work duties.

Second, employers who employ only a few family members will typically classify themselves as business owners with employees, but if they themselves do the majority of work may be more closely allied with the self-employed. Third, some business owners may classify themselves as wage and salary earners on the grounds that they draw a salary from the company they themselves own, yet in cases where they are the sole employees of that company, would be more appropriately described as self-employed. Thus for all of these reasons, a simple enumeration based on information from workers on whether or not they describe themselves as self-employed contractors would underestimate the actual number of such workers. Using this line of reasoning, we developed a series of survey questions which allowed us to reclassify certain workers to the self-employed contractor category. In short, workers were classified as self-employed contractors in this research if they indicated that their work mainly involved providing services to other organizations and if they fell into one of the four following groups:

- Persons who reported themselves to be self-employed;
- Persons who classified themselves as wage and salary earners, but who did not pay income tax on a pay-as-you-earn basis;
- Persons who classified themselves as employers who both employed only family members and had no more than two such employees;
- Persons who classified themselves as wage and salary earners but who were actually employed by their own company which had no other employees.

We further distinguish two sub-groups on the basis of the degree of dependence on the service-recipient organization, and hence their labels "independent contractors" and "dependent contractors." While distinguishing between these two groups is not straightforward, we argue that it is reasonable to suggest that self-employed contractors who provide services to only one or mainly one organization are unlikely to be independent of that organization.

We thus label these persons "dependent contractors." Further, those workers who classified themselves as employees but who were reclassified as self-employed contractors based on their income tax payment arrangements must, by definition, consider themselves to be dependent on the hiring organization and thus are also defined as dependent contractors.

In total, the data suggest that in May 1994, 7.5 per cent of the Australian non-farm workforce were self-employed contractors. Of these, 61.7 per cent were categorized as independent of the hiring organization, while 38.3 per cent were classified as dependent contractors.

## JOB SATISFACTION

When an employee joins an organization and performs his duties, he wants to satisfy his economic, social and psychological needs. When he does not feel satisfied with his job, negative attitudes towards work develop in his mind. In this case he tries to change the job. On the other hand if an employee is satisfied with his job, he will perform his duties with his wholehearted efforts. He will contribute best of his efficiency and capability towards the achievement of predetermined objectives of the enterprise. Job satisfaction of an employee is the result of many attitudes and factors.

Dale Yoder *"Job satisfaction is regarded as the composite of attitudes of individual employees towards their job and relationship they create"*.

Keith Davis defines job satisfaction as "a set of favourable or unfavourable feelings with which employees view their work".

Job satisfaction refers to ones feelings towards job. It is often determined by how well outcomes meet or exceed expectations. High job satisfaction may lead to improved productivity, decreased turnover, improved attendance and less job stress.

## FACTORS AFFECTING JOB SATISFACTION

Several job elements/ factors contribute to job satisfaction. These include the nature of job, working conditions, and capabilities and some specific attitudes developed by the circumstances prevailing in the enterprise.

## JOB FACTORS

*Following are job factors which affect job satisfaction*:

- *Wages*: Wages pay a significant role in influencing job satisfaction. This is because of two reasons. First money is an important instrument in fulfilling ones needs and employees often see pay as a reflection of managements concern for them. Employees want a pay system which is simple, fair and in line with their expectations.
- *Nature of work*: Most employees prefer intellectual challenges on jobs. Employees feel dissatisfied, if they have to do the work of similar nature for a long time. If the work of an employee is of different type, and includes moderate challenges, employees experiences pleasure and job satisfaction.
- *Supervision*: There is a positive relationship between the quality of supervision and job satisfaction. Supervisors who establish a supportive relationship contribute to their employee satisfaction. Employees prefer a supervisor who helps in personal problems, does not interfere in work and is friendly.
- *Work Group*: The work group also serve as a source of satisfaction to individual employees. It provides opportunities for interaction of group members. It is well known that for many employees work fills the need for social interaction.

- *Working condition*: Working condition that provides physical comfort to the employees and that facilitate doing a good job contribute to job satisfaction. Temperature, humidity, ventilation, lighting and heating are the features which affect job satisfaction.
- *Stability of Job*: If the employees feel stability in their jobs they feel more satisfied and if they feel their job is not stable, they will remain dissatisfied. This is due to wide spread un employment, and uncertainties in the employment market.
- *Training Arrangement*: Arrangements of training also satisfy the employees because trained employees can do work easily and more efficiently.
- *Human relations in the enterprise*: If there are cordial relations in the enterprise and if the labour problems are solved in a democratic way, it increases the feeling of job satisfaction among employees.

## INDIVIDUAL FACTORS

*Following individual factors also affect job satisfaction*:

- *Level of Education*: Level of education affects the feeling of job satisfaction. It has been seen that educated employees feel more satisfied with their jobs than the uneducated. But the Indian studies have generally shown that there is a tendency for the more educated workers to be less satisfied.
- *Intelligence*: There is a direct correlation between intelligence and satisfaction. It has been the experience that intelligent employees feel satisfied with their jobs. But the relation of intelligence to job satisfaction depends on the level and range of intelligence and challenge of the job.
- *Age*: Age also affects job satisfaction among employees. Generally it is seen that young employees do not feel satisfied with their jobs because they always try to get better job, while older employees feel more satisfied with their job.
- *Number of dependents*: Few Indian studies indicated

that, the more the number of dependents one has, the less satisfaction he has with the job. It is possible that the stress of greater financial needs, and family problems due to increase in family size create greater dissatisfaction with ones job.

Although the management cant control the personnel factors of employees, job factors are controllable by the management. The issue of wages, security, supervision etc may be given a serious consideration.

## MEASUREMENT OF JOB SATISFACTION

There are a number of ways of measuring job satisfaction. The most common way of measuring include rating scales, critical incidents and interviews.

### RATING SCALE

The most common approach for measuring job satisfaction is the use of rating scales. These scales fall in to 2 categories. Tailor made scales, which are constructed for a particular project and Standardised scales developed to establish group norms. It is the tailor made scales which are frequently used in practice. One of the most popular standardised scales is the Job Descriptive Index developed by Smith, Kendell and Hulin in 1969. the JDI has separate scales for satisfaction with pay, promotions, supervision, work and co- workers.

Requiring only 10 to 15 minutes for administer, JDI has been widely used by behaviour researchers aver the years and provides a broad picture of employee attitudes towards the major components of jobs. Another standardised scale is the 'Minnesota Satisfaction Questionnaire' which in its long form has 100 questions. It takes about 30 minutes to administer and gives a detailed picture of the specific satisfaction and dissatisfaction of employees.

### CRITICAL INCIDENTS

The critical incidents approach to the measurement of job satisfaction was developed by Herzberg and his associates in their research on the two factor theory of motivation.

Employees were asked to describe incidents on their jobs, when they were particularly satisfied or dissatisfied. These incidents were then analysed to determine which aspects were closely related to positive and negative attitudes.

## INTERVIEWS

Another method of measuring job satisfaction is the personal interview. Employees are interviewed individually and the response reveal their satisfaction or dissatisfaction.

### Use of Existing Information

Before conducting any survey, managers do well to examine two other methods of assessing employee feelings. – Daily contacts and existing data. Managers are in contact with their employees through constant interaction and communication. This is a practical and timely method of determining the job satisfaction. By analysing the data relating to labour turnover, absenteeism, performance and suggestions, a manager can find out the satisfaction level of employees.

### Survey

Surveys are also used for measuring the job satisfaction. Objective surveys using multiple choice questions and descriptive surveys which give answers in employees own words are used widely to measure employee satisfaction. The chief defect of objective survey is that management prepares the questionnaire and provide alternative answers. It does not give much chance to employees to express themselves in their own ways. In the case of descriptive survey, employees have a greater freedom of expression. The descriptive survey may be undertaken either through an individual interview or through a group discussion.

## MORALE

Morale means the attitude of a group of persons towards their jobs, their enterprise and towards their senior officers. It is a concept, which reflects the feelings and reaction of employees. It is a phenomenon of the group, which represents the state of mind of people, which arises out of their working conditions. Prof. Douglas Williams was of the opinion that morale in 'Army' means the willingness of war. The morale in industry should mean the willingness of workers to work. If the employees come to the organization at the right time, discharge their work properly, obey the orders of their supervisors and are faithful to the organization, it may be assumed that the morale of the employees is very high.

Edwin. B. Flippo defines morale as " a mental condition or attribute of individuals and groups which determine their willingness to co-operate. Dale Yoder *"morale is the combination or structure of employees attitudes towards the principal elements in the situations in which they work"*.

All managers have a constant concern for the morale of the group, which they lead. Employee's work with mutual co-operation only because of high morale. High morale of employees helps in the achievement of pre-determined objects of the enterprise and in establishing good human relations in the enterprise.

## IMPORTANCE OF MORALE

Morale is the force, which stimulates the employees of an enterprise to contribute their efforts for the accomplishment of objectives. High morale helps in effective control and supervision.

*Following are the advantages of high morale which clearly explain the importance of morale*:

- High morale increases the productivity and improves the quality of production.
- It makes the industrial atmosphere favourable.
- The employees with high morale obey the orders and instructions of their superiors, which enables the organizational activity to go on smoothly.
- High morale develops the feeling of honesty and obedience among them. Thus improves the performance of employees.
- High morale of employees helps in reducing the cost of production and labour overheads.

## ATTITUDES

Attitude is an important variable in human behaviour. Attitudes refer to feelings and beliefs of individuals or groups directed towards other people, objects or ideas. Attitudes are learned as human beings learn various other responses. When the appropriate circumstances arise, the attitude makes the individual to react in a favourable or unfavourable manner.

Joseph Reits: " *The word attitude describes a persistent tendency to feel and behave in a particular way towards some object*". Individuals acquire attitudes from several sources. The most important sources of acquiring attitudes are direct experience with the object, association, family and economic and social positions.

### Formation of Attitudes

- *Direct experience with the object*: Attitudes can develop from a personally rewarding or punishing experience with an object. Employees form attitudes about jobs from their previous experiences. For example; If every one who has held a job has been promoted within 6 months, current job holders are likely to expect a promotion within 6 months. Attitudes formed on experience are difficult to change.
- *Association*: Attitudes towards one object may develop from associating that object with another object, about which attitudes have been previously formed. E.g. A favourable or unfavourable attitude about a work will often be formed by associating it with similar other work.
- *Family and other groups*: A person may learn attitudes through imitation of parents and other family members. If parents have a positive attitude towards an object, the child is likely to adopt similar attitudes. Similarly attitudes are acquired from other close groups in which we are a member.
- *Economic status and Occupation*: Our economic and occupational positions also contribute to attitude formation. They determine our attitude towards

union and management, and our belief that certain laws are good or bad.

Attitudes of employees can be changed and it is in the best interest of the organization to try for the change. Attitudes can be changed by providing sufficient information, by using the influence of friends and others and also by giving opportunities for education.

## JOB ENRICHMENT AND JOB ENLARGEMENT

A job is a significant aspect of ones life. It is the primary institution through which the employees satisfies his primary needs. People in general spend a considerable amount of time working.

Naturally the job has become a serious subject for social scientists and practicing managers. Attempts have been made to use jobs for motivating employees in organizations. Job enrichment is an example in that direction.

## JOB ENRICHMENT

Job enrichment was developed by Herzberg on the basis of his studies indicating that the most effective way to motivate workers, was by focussing on higher order needs. Job enrichment gives workers more control, responsibility and discretion over how their job is performed. Job Enrichment simply means adding a few more motivators to a job to make it more rewarding.

As work become more challenging and workers responsibility increases, motivation and enthusiasm also increase. Job enrichment brings many benefits to an organization. It encourages growth and self actualisation. The job is built in such a way that intrinsic motivation is encouraged.

Because motivation is encouraged, performance should improve, thus providing both more a harmonised and a more productive job.

*Herzberg, job enrichment has following characteristics*:

- *Direct Feed back*: Employees should be able to get immediate knowledge of the results they are achieving. The evaluation of performance can be built in to the job or provided by a supervisor.

- *Client Relationships*: An employee, who serves a client or customer directly has an enriched job. The client can be outside the firm or inside.
- *Scheduling own work*: Freedom to schedule ones own work contributes to enrichment. Employees who perform creative work have more opportunity to schedule their work.
- *New Learning*: An enriched job allows the worker to feel that he is growing mentally.
- *Control over resources*: One approach to job enrichment is for each employee to have control over his resources and expenses. For example he must have the authority to order supplies necessary for completing the job.
- *Direct Communication*: An enriched job allows the worker to communicate directly with people who use his output such as quality control managers handling a customer complaints about quality.
- *Personal Accountability*: An enriched job holds the worker responsible for the results. He receives praise for good work and blame for poor work.

Being a direct development from Herzbergs two factor theory of motivation, job enrichment is a valuable motivational technique. A few studies conducted in US demonstrated the usefulness of job enrichment.

## JOB ENLARGEMENT

Job Enlargement is considered as an effective method for reducing monotony of overspecialised mass production jobs. It was realised by IBM USA, way back in 1943, that machine operators could save a lot of time and gain variety in their jobs by setting up their own machines and checking the results of their work.

This eliminated machine set up men and inspectors. Job enlargement means adding more different tasks to a specialised job to provide greater variety. It tackles dissatisfaction and reduces monotony by increasing the variety and scope of tasks. As job enrichment focuses on satisfying higher order needs, job enlargement concentrates on additional tasks to the workers job for greater variety.

An enlarged job motivates workers in a number of ways. It increases the number of tasks to be performed and thus reduces the level of boredom. Frequently jobs are enlarged so that one worker completes a whole unit of work, or a major portion of it. This tends to increase the satisfaction. Although the benefits of job enlargement are several, certain disadvantages cant be lost sight of. First training costs tend to rise. Workers may require additional training for the new, enlarged tasks. Trade unions often argue for increased pay because of the increased workload.

## JOB SATISFACTION MEASURES

Five questions in the PSM dealt with job satisfaction. Four of these related to specific aspects of the job - namely, job security, work-related income, control over how work is done, and hours worked each week. The fifth question provided a simple measure of overall job satisfaction. All five questions were scored on a five-point scale with response options ranging from "very dissatisfied" to "very satisfied." The use of a standard multi-item job satisfaction scale was ruled out on cost grounds, given both the large number of questions involved in constructing such scales and the fact that the PSM is administered by personal interview.

We began by considering simple bivariate cross-tabulations of employment status with responses to the different job satisfaction questions. Differences in perceived job satisfaction, however, will almost certainly be a function of a number of factors, such as age, gender, and the type of job held, which in turn may be correlated with employment status. Therefore, in addition to comparing job satisfaction levels of self-employed contractors and employees, we undertook multivariate analyses in which a range of demographic and job characteristics were held constant. Two specifications of the multivariate analysis are reported, both of which use the overall job satisfaction, item as the dependent variable. The four other job satisfaction items were not used at this stage since, in line with Kalleberg, we are primarily interested in the concept of job satisfaction as an overall affective orientation on the part of individuals towards the work roles they occupy. Thus, although it is recognized that persons may be satisfied or dissatisfied with particular aspects of their employment, the assumption made here is that the overall job satisfaction measure reflects the balance of these satisfactions and dissatisfactions.

In the first specification, a model of overall job satisfaction was tested in order to determine whether, with other factors held constant, self-employed contractors were significantly less likely to be satisfied with their jobs than both other types of self-employed workers and wage and salary earners. Since the dependent variable is ordinal but has no absolute numeric metric, the ordered logit estimation method was used. The second specification replicates the first, but with the difference that it separately distinguishes independent and dependent contractors and thus permits a test for differences in reported job satisfaction across these two sub-groups. Aside from employment status, the independent variables included in the analysis provide controls for gender, marital status, the presence of dependents, age, birthplace, educational attainment, weekly hours of paid work, occupation, and industry of employment.

In addition, we undertook simple non-parametric tests of the significance of difference in the responses of self-employed contractors as compared with wage and salary earners. Note that for this analysis all dissatisfied and neutral responses were clustered together.

The direction of that difference, however, varies with the aspect of job satisfaction being considered. Self-employed contractors were clearly not as happy with some aspects of their jobs; that is, their satisfaction with their job security and the amount of income they received was significantly lower. However, these workers were significantly more satisfied with the amount of control they had over the way in which they completed their work and the hours they worked each week. Further, these positive aspects would appear to outweigh the negative features of contract employment, with a significantly greater proportion of self-employed contractors indicating a high level of overall job satisfaction as compared with wage and salary earners 38.6 per cent of self-employed contractors were very satisfied with their job overall, whereas the corresponding figure for wage and salary earners was 29.8 per cent. These results thus suggest that, on balance, the self-employed are no less happy with their jobs than are wage and salary earners and, indeed, may well be much happier.

A comparison of job satisfaction levels of the other self-employed workers with that of the wage and salary earners reveals that these self-employed persons are also more likely to be satisfied with the amount of control they had, and less satisfied with their job security and their income. However, in contrast to the self-employed contractors, the other self-employed persons were less satisfied than the employees with the hours they worked each week. Finally, and again in contrast to the self-employed contractors, there is no significant difference in overall job satisfaction between employees and other self-employed workers.

These results thus provide support for our suggestion that there are differences in job satisfaction levels among those in the group of self-employed workers. Such results are tentative at best. It remains to be seen whether differences between the self-employed contractors and the others persist once additional factors which may also be associated with job satisfaction are taken into account. To do so, as noted earlier, we regressed responses to the overall job satisfaction measure against a range of demographic and job-related variables using the ordered logit method.

In one sense the model performs poorly. Certainly it explains very little of the total variance in the dependent variable just 5 per cent. This is not surprising since a limited number of variables describing basic personal and job characteristics could hardly be expected to explain more than a small fraction of the variance across individuals in expressed job satisfaction. However, the low level of explained variance is not a problem for our purposes, provided we have not omitted any exogenous influences of relevance to job satisfaction which are also correlated with employment status.

In other respects, the estimated model is very satisfactory. As a group, the independent variables considered are highly significant. More importantly, the variables that achieve statistical significance gender, education, age, presence of dependents, and occupation are, for the most part, variables which previous studies have found to be important. Further, in our model, the signs of these variables are generally in line with those reported in the earlier research. For example, women have frequently been found to express higher levels of satisfaction than men. This finding is supported in these data. Similarly, our finding that it is the well-educated who are most likely to express dissatisfaction with their jobs is one which is well documented.

Previous research has also found higher levels of reported job satisfaction among older workers, reflecting the existence of seniority-related benefits, lower job expectations among older workers, and self-selection effects. In our results, the oldest members of the work-force are again seen to be most satisfied with their jobs. Nevertheless, the relationship between age and job satisfaction is not found to be linear. Instead, a U-shaped quadratic relationship fits the data best, indicating that job satisfaction is relatively high among young workers, lowest for workers in their mid-thirties, and highest for workers at the end of the working-age spectrum. As with older workers, the relatively high levels of job satisfaction among young workers may reflect either low levels of expectation or selection effects.

Turning now to the variable of most interest in this research self-employed contractor status it can be seen that the coefficient for this variable, while positively signed, is insignificant. This suggests that the differences observed in the cross-tabulated data are over-stated. In other words, once other relevant factors are taken into account, the apparent differences in perceived job satisfaction between self-employed contractors and employees are no longer significant. Note also that the results suggest no significant difference in job satisfaction between employees and self-employed persons who were not contractors. Nevertheless, our results offer little support for the belief that contractor jobs are less desirable from the worker's point of view.

In our second model, we relax the assumption that self-employed contractors are a homogenous group and explicitly distinguish between independent and dependent contractors. This variation in specification has little effect on the magnitudes and signs of the coefficients of the other control variables included in the model, but contractor status now emerges as a factor significantly related to job satisfaction. As expected, job satisfaction is found to be much higher among independent contractors than among dependent contractors. More interesting, though, are the comparisons with the omitted category of wage and salary earners. Not only is job satisfaction among independent contractors higher than among dependent contractors, it is also significantly higher than among wage and salary earners. As well, it is higher than that of the other self-employed workers. Further, the expressed levels of job satisfaction among dependent contractors do not appear to be significantly different from that of wage and salary earners or the other self-employed workers.

Previous research on perceptions of job satisfaction among the self-employed has treated the self-employed as a homogenous group. We argue that due to the diversity of the types of workers classified as self-employed, job satisfaction may vary for various sub-groups of the self-employed. We partially test this argument by dividing our sample of self-employed persons into two groups self-employed contractors and other self-employed workers and then compare their job satisfaction levels with those of wage and salary earners.

Overall, when compared with wage and salary earners and while taking into account a range of job and personal characteristics which might also affect job satisfaction, self-employed contractors are no more or less satisfied with their jobs. However, when we identify separately those self-employed contractors who are "independent contractors" from those who are "dependent contractors," we find significant differences. That is, independent contractors are significantly more satisfied with their jobs than are workers in the other groups we considered. This finding suggests that the one group that may be mostly responsible for the usual finding of the higher job satisfaction among the self-employed are the independent contractors. The most likely explanation for this difference is the greater freedom and autonomy such workers have in their working lives compared with the dependent contractors. Additionally, it might also reflect differences in the ability of people to freely choose self-employment. In other words, it seems likely that many dependent contractors are confronted by a situation where the only alternative to self-employment is unemployment.

Note, however, that if dependent contractors are so constrained, they still do not appear to fare any worse, on average, than wage and salary earners. That is, our results reveal that in contrast to expectations based on the argument that dependent contractors have less desirable working conditions than wage and salary earners dependent contractors were no less satisfied with their jobs than wage and salary earners. This thus suggests that self-employed contracting, even if it involves a fair degree of dependence on one employer, need not necessarily mean a reduced quality of working life.

Note finally that the results from our research must stand as tentative. While our research is important in pointing to the need for greater recognition of the heterogeneity among the self-employed when comparing their perceptions of job satisfaction with that of other workers, we used only a single-item measure of job satisfaction at our disposal. Although our research is not unique in using such a measure, ideally a more complex measure of job satisfaction would have been used. Thus we suggest that one direction for further research in this area is the use of multi-itemed job satisfaction measures. Further, our research does not explicitly identify the source of the difference in expressed job satisfaction levels between the two types of contractors. Is the difference, for example, the result of intrinsic differences in the nature of the work performed, or does it reflect differences in the perceived range of employment alternatives? Again the answer to such questions awaits further research.

The authors wish to extend their thanks to the Australian Taxation Office, which funded the study on which this associate is based, and staff at the Australian Bureau of Statistics who coordinated the collection of data used in this associate.

- Weighted data were used for the descriptive analyses. The sample size for the weighted data numbered 1,297.
- It could be argued that business owners with family members as employees should be no different from other employers. However, given that for many small businesses there are often many advantages of having workers appear on the payroll who in fact do minimal amounts of work for the company, there is a suspicion that many of the employers who hire only a few family members to work in their contracting business are no different from the self-employed.
- Employers are required to withhold income taxation payments on a PAYE basis from all of their employees, and thus income tax arrangements can be used to distinguish between contractors and wage and salary earners.

*Cross-study differences in the contributions of work attitudes to the turnover process led us to*:

- Estimate the six relations among job satisfaction, organizational commitment, turnover intention/withdrawal cognitions, and turnover using meta-analysis;
- Assess the effects of several psychometric moderators on those relations;
- Compare the influences of satisfaction and commitment in the turnover process by applying path analysis to the meta-analytic correlations.

*Based on aggregations involving a total of 178 independent samples from 155 studies, results showed that*:

- Satisfaction and commitment each contribute independently to the prediction of intention/ cognitions;
- Intention/cognitions are predicted more strongly by satisfaction than by commitment;
- Intention/cognitions mediate nearly all of the attitudinal linkage with turnover;
- Attitudinal contributions to the turnover process vary with the use of single-versus multi-item scales, the 9-versus 15-item version of the Organizational Commitment Questionnaire, and turnover intention versus withdrawal cognition scales.

Over the last 20 years, considerable research has been devoted to developing predictive models of voluntary turnover, with job satisfaction, organizational commitment, and intent to quit among the most commonly proposed antecedents. Individual studies have generally supported hypothesized linkages among turnover and those variables. Satisfaction and commitment, for instance, have invariably been reported to be negatively related to turnover and intent to leave, and positively correlated with one another. Equally consistent is the finding that turnover intention is the strongest cognitive precursor of turnover. Important discrepancies exist, however, concerning the relative contributions of job satisfaction and organizational commitment to the withdrawal process. Three main theoretical perspectives in this area may be identified, each having distinct conceptual and research implications.

One view is that commitment to the company develops from job satisfaction such that commitment mediates the effects of satisfaction on withdrawal variables. This satisfaction-to-commitment mediation model reflects Porter, Steers, Mowday, and Boulian's claim that commitment takes longer to develop and is more stable than satisfaction, and has received considerable empirical support. The model suggests that job satisfaction has only an indirect influence on the intention and/or decision to quit, and encourages study of mechanisms through which satisfied workers become committed to their organizations. The second view holds that the direction of influence between satisfaction and commitment. The commitment-to-satisfaction mediation model suggests that commitment to the company engenders a positive attitude towards the job, possibly through a rationalization process, and people leave or stay based on how they feel about their jobs.

That commitment to the company may develop prior to entry or at least may be evident at early stages of employment, lends support to that hypothesis. The model promotes the view that changes in commitment can be expected to have only indirect effects on turnover. Several studies have provided support for the model; others, however, have not. The third perspective holds that both satisfaction and commitment contribute uniquely to the turnover process. This independent-effects model follows Porter et al.'s suggestion that job satisfaction and organizational commitment, though related, are distinct constructs. It implies no particular causality between the two attitudes, but does not rule out the possibility of reciprocal influences. More than the first two perspectives, it calls for research into how attitudes towards the job and company combine and/or interact to influence the intent and final decision to quit.

The three models noted are distinguished by the relative contributions of job satisfaction and organizational commitment to the turnover process. A related issue is the degree to which turnover intention mediates attitudinal effects on quitting. Consistent with theories stressing the importance of intent in predicting behaviour, results of some studies show that intent to leave completely mediates attitude-turnover relations; other findings, however, support direct, unique attitudinal effects on turnover independent of intention. That attitudes might influence behaviour independent of intention raises some concern over the importance of conscious deliberation in the turnover decision. Unique attitudinal effects on turnover would suggest the need to consider nonintentional aspects of work attitudes as operating on the final decision to quit or stay. Differences across studies in turnover findings impede understanding of the turnover process and may occlude identification of promising lines of further inquiry.

Sources of those differences include a variety of statistical and methodological factors. We used meta-analysis to remove both the random effects of sampling error and the more systematic distortion owing to the use of differentially unreliable measures. Then, encouraged by reasonable non-artifact variation in findings across studies, we examined the effects of four psychometric moderators on the focal relations in identifying conditions supporting certain previous findings. Finally, we applied path analysis to the meta-analytic correlations using estimates based on all samples and those for moderator subgroups.

The meta-analytic estimates provided greater power in model evaluation than in single-sample studies involving measures differing in reliability.

# 4

# Personality and Emotions

Consumers often find themselves in decision-making situations that differ in terms of the degree of novelty, change uncertainty, conflict, or complexity, and thus they often opt for maximum variety, when given the chance to select more than one item from a choice set. However, none of the explanations offered in previous studies tell us whether an individual's temporary emotional state will influence the amount of variety chosen.

This study explored whether a temporary positive or negative emotion can lead consumers to switch from their favorite item(s) when making repeated choices from a set of hedonic items. We hypothesized that, once in positive emotion, individuals will maintain or keep that positive emotion, and will take the risk to choose a variety of products more often than those who are in a negative emotion. We report here two experiments that support our predictions.

## OPTIMAL STIMULATION LEVEL

The concept of an optimal stimulation level is central to theories postulated to explain variety-seeking tendencies in consumers. The ideal level of stimulation matches the amount of stimulation a person prefers.

Previous research suggests that a person may engage in exploration of the environment to achieve a satisfactory cognitive level, or when feeling that the amount of stimulation is below an optimal stimulation level. Conversely, if a person has very high stimulation, he or she will seek a more moderate situation by reducing or simplifying input from the environment through avoidance of novelty or variety. It is suggested in this study that to maintain an optimal level of stimulation, individuals use variety-seeking behaviour as a primary motivational mechanism. For example, repeated purchasing behaviour produces a reduced stimulation level for the buyer because the behaviour is no longer novel or complex. This repeated buying leads to a perception of boredom and the consumer may then attempt to increase stimulation by switching to something different or novel in the choice of product. McAlister and Pessemier incorporate OSL into their model of variety seeking behaviour and posit that the utility derived from switching brands is positively related to consumer OSLs.

Previous research indicates that consumers often choose considerable amounts of variety when allowed to select more than one item from a choice set, even when they are given the option of repeating consumption of favored items. This variety-choosing explanation focuses on factors such as uncertainty about future preference; anticipated or experienced satiation; the belief that no one item provides the desired level of all attributes; the desire for stimulation or novelty; a decision about public consumption; and keeping oneself open to new options.

Central to each choice situation described is the idea that consumers switch back and forth among familiar items because the pleasure derived from switching exceeds the pleasure that would be derived from repeating a choice. However, previous research pays less attention to the level of risk taking as a potential factor that could impact on variety-seeking behaviour. In general, variety seeking, when consumers decide to switch among familiar items, implies that they would like to take a risk in the future with the possibility of that choice having unfavourable consequences.

Once the selected option turns out to be disappointing, this results in feelings of regret. These risks may be social, economic, and performance danger. The social risks range from losing face among family or friends, to exerting enough energy to justify a purchase to friends and associates. The economic risk is the possible loss of the monetary cost. Performance danger is the risk that the purchased item will not match expectation. When consumers are willing to take a risk in decision making, an indirect implication is that the consumer has understood the possibility of that choice having unfavourable consequences, and variety-seeking behaviour has a tendency to occur.

Therefore, understanding what factors impact on an individual's risk taking behaviour may lead to understanding of the factors that influence that individual's variety-seeking behaviour.

## THE EFFECTS OF EMOTIONAL STATES ON VARIETY SEEKING

The increasingly comprehensive literature on affect and social cognition has produced strong evidence that affective states play a major role in how people learn, remember, think, take risks, and evaluate complex social information, with associated research on emotion and risk taking carried out earlier by Isen and Patrick.

These studies found that positive moods yield risk-averse behaviour and that negative moods produce risk-taking behaviour. This finding is explained by the mood-maintenance hypothesis, which states that people with positive emotions are motivated by a desire to maintain these positive emotions and to repair any negative moods. When in a positive mood, people do not take big risks, as doing so increases the potential for large personal loss that might disrupt their positive emotional state. Similarly, it can also be asserted that, when in a negative mood, people will be willing to take higher risks to obtain higher potential gains in the hope of repairing their negative affective state.

Therefore, the influence of emotional states on a person's behaviour is explained by the desire to maintain a positive emotional state or mitigate a negative affective state. Based on the mood-maintenance hypothesis that explains the emotional influences on a person, we assert that when an individual is induced to feel a positive emotion, he or she will be unwilling to take a risk that could lessen that positive emotion, and instead will choose behaviour that is likely to restrict consumption to fewer options rather than make a decision to choose a variety of items. Conversely, when an individual is experiencing a negative emotion, variety-seeking behaviour provides the hope of repairing his/her negative affective state, and he/she will be expected to choose variety even though this choice requires the inclusion of items that the individual likes less than other items he/she could have chosen.

To examine our theoretical framework, three experiments were conducted using different emotions and measures of variety-seeking behaviour. In the experiment, the participants were induced to feel emotions that were either happy or sad by asking them to watch a 25-minute film. After eliciting these emotions, subjects were asked to respond to hypothetical questions about variety-seeking behaviour and to complete a manipulated check that rated the degree of pleasant feelings. Participants were 124 undergraduate students enrolled in a marketing management course.

Forty participants were induced to feel a happy emotion, 43 were induced to feel a sad emotion, and 41 were induced to a neutral emotion. A simple one-factor, three-level, between-subjects design was used. Emotional state was manipulated by showing participants a film. Initially, the participants were told that they would be examining the impact of various stimuli that might be used for future studies. The experimenter then showed the subjects one of two film clips.

In the positive emotional condition, a segment from the feature film Pretty Woman was shown to induce a happy mood. The clip was 20' 22" long. Previous studies had shown that this film reliably induced happy emotions. In the negative condition, a clip from the movie Ordinary People was shown to induce a sad mood. This clip was 21 '45" long, and previous studies had shown that it induced sad feelings. Participants were instructed to watch the videos as if they were watching videos at home and become fully involved in the stories. Film, as an emotion manipulator, helps exclude potential motivational and cognitive preoccupations in memory. Neutral emotional participants were not induced to positive or negative emotional condition. Immediately after the emotion was induced, subjects were asked, "How happy do you feel right now?" and "How enjoyable was it to be in this situation?", and answers were assessed with a 7-point Likert scale that ranged from 1 = extremely unhappy/bad or not enjoyable at all to 7 = extremely happy/good or extremely enjoyable. The test indicated an appropriate reliability for the scale. Participants were also asked to rate "how much do you like to take risks now?" (on a 7-point scale where 1 = do not like it at all and 7 = like it very much ). The goal was to understand whether the level of risk taking mediated in the relationship between emotion and variety seeking.

Subjects were then told to imagine that they were going to the supermarket to do their shopping, and that they intended to buy five cans of juice. Five flavours of juice were listed as being on the supermarket shelves: orange, grape, apple, star fruit, and guava. These juices were shown in a colour picture, each having the same price. The participants were instructed to enter next to each item the number of units of that item that they would buy. All subjects were also asked to rate each type of juice on a 1-5 scale (where 1 = I don't like it at all and 5 = I like it a lot). They were told that this information would be used to determine which juice would be distributed in the future.

## EFFECTS OF EMOTIONAL STATES ON VARIETY-SEEKING BEHAVIOUR

The independent variable in this analysis was whether decisions were to be made in a positive, neutral or negative manner, and the primary dependent measure was how many different flavours of juice the subjects chose. As predicted, subjects in a positive emotional condition chose significantly fewer flavours of juice than did subjects who were in a neutral emotional condition, or those who had been induced into a negative emotional condition. Consistent with the prediction the results show that subjects chose more variety when experiencing a negative emotion than when experiencing a positive emotion, even if this circumstance required them to choose items that they liked less than others they could have chosen.

## ANALYSIS OF THE MEDIATING EFFECT

We have suggested that the effect of emotion, upon which the variety-seeking behaviour depends, is a seesaw match of risk taking. If this argument proved to be true, the risk taking in this research should have statistically mediated the relationship between emotion and variety-seeking behaviour. We consider that a negative emotion may trigger higher risk taking than a positive emotion. Further, we argue that when participants are experiencing positive emotions, they tend to be more unwilling to take risk and consequently have to restrict the amount of variety-seeking behaviour they will undertake. Conversely, when subjects are experiencing negative emotions, participants tend to be willing to take a risk and venture to choose variety.

If the relationship between emotions and variety-seeking behaviour proved to be mediated by risk taking, then three regression equations must be estimated to test a mediating effect, and the following conditions must hold:

- There must be a significant effect of regressing the mediator on the independent variable.
- There must be a significant effect of regressing the dependent variable on the independent variable.
- When the dependent variable is regressed on both the mediator and the independent variable, the effect of the independent variable must be weaker than that in the second regression equation. And, when the effect of the independent variable in the third condition is zero, there is a complete mediating effect; otherwise, partial mediation exists.

A series of regression analyses provided support for our prediction. We found that emotions predicted the risk taking. We also found the relationship between emotions and variety-seeking behaviour to be significant, as well as finding that the risk taking reliably predicted the variety-seeking behaviour. A final analysis revealed that when both emotions and the risk taking were simultaneously entered as predictors for variety-seeking behaviour, the former was no longer a significant predictor, and the latter remained a significant predictor. This finding provides a direct measure for the mediation we assumed.

Specifically, we argue that risk taking may affect the relationship between emotion and variety-seeking behaviour. As we predicted, risk taking has a mediating effect on the relationship between emotions and variety-seeking behaviour. The results of the experiment indicate that a person's variety-seeking behaviour is dependent on various emotional conditions. As expected, participants chose more variety when they were induced to a negative emotional condition than when they were induced to a positive emotional condition. This study provides a new explanation that supplements earlier accounts of why a person switches away from his or her favourites before being satiated with them.

Specifically, when individuals are induced to a negative emotional condition, in order to repair or mitigate that negative mood to approach a positive mood, they may choose non-favourite items even though they would be expected to derive more enjoyment from sticking with their favourites. This result suggests that a consumer decision is influenced by temporary emotional states, namely that a consumer's negative emotion is a likely catalyst in seeking more variety; an induced positive emotion does not have the same effect.

Most studies manipulated the positive emotions by inducing happiness and the negative emotions by inducing sadness, and we followed this to make the study more robust and reliable methodologically. Nonetheless, we still wonder if joy and surprise should be categorized as positive emotions, and if fear and disgust should be categorized as negative emotions in the emotion effect. Therefore, it is worth examining whether a specific emotion is always accompanied by an exclusive emotion effect. Our theoretical framework still leaves more to be investigated.

# 5

# Perception

Job involvement has been defined as an individual's psychological identification or commitment to his/ her job. It is the degree to 'which one is cognitively preoccupied with, engaged in, and concerned with one's present job. Job involvement involves the internalisation of values about the goodness of work or the importance of work in the worth of the individual. As such individuals who display high involvement in their jobs consider their work to be a very important part of their lives and whether or not they feel good about themselves is closely related to how they perform on their jobs. In other words for highly involved individuals performing well on the job is important for their self esteem. Because of this people who are high in job involvement genuinely care for and are concerned about their work.

The construct of job involvement is somewhat similar to organizational commitment in that they are both concerned with an employee's identification with the work experience. However the constructs differ in that job involvement is more closely associated with identification with one's immediate work activities whereas organizational commitment refers to one's attachment to the organization. It is possible for example to be very involved in a specific job but not be committed to the organization or vice versa.

Research studies over the past two decades, which have explored the construct of job involvement, have approached it from two different perspectives. First when viewed as an individual difference variable, job involvement is believed to occur when the possession of certain needs, values or personal characteristics predispose individuals to become more or less involved in their jobs. For instance Rabinowitz and Hall in their review of literature on job involvement found that individual characteristics such as age, education, sex, tenure, need strength, level of control and values were linked to job involvement. The second perspective views job involvement as a response to specific work situation characteristics. In other words certain types of jobs or characteristics of the work situation influence the degree to which an individual becomes involved in his/ her job. For example research has demonstrated that job involvement has been related to job characteristics such as task autonomy, task significance, task identity, skill variety and feedback and supervisory behaviours such as leader consideration, participative decision making and amount of communication.

Fostering job involvement is an important organizational objective because many researchers consider it to be a primary determinant of organizational effectiveness and individual motivation. These links stem from the theoretical notion that being immersed in one's work increases motivational processes which in turn influence job performance and other relevant outcomes like turnover and absenteeism. Although job involvement is considered to be a key factor influencing important individual and organizational outcomes, research finding a significant impact of this construct on performance has met limited success. The general perception is that people with high levels of job involvement are likely to put more effort into their jobs and therefore tend to display higher levels of in-role performance.

Although research on job involvement provides some support for this notion, generally the results have been disappointing. For example summarizing the available empirical evidence to date, Brown's meta-analysis estimated the population correlation between overall performance and job involvement to be non-significant. Although job involvement, did have a significant estimated population correlation with 'combination measures' of performance, the coefficient was quite small. Brown and Leigh suggest that the reason for this weak relationship maybe that instead of exerting a direct influence, job involvement is more likely to affect performance indirectly through other variables like effort. Therefore the central aim of this research is to examine the relationship between job involvement and in-role and extra-role (OCB) performance. This research will not only examine the direct effect of job involvement on in-role job performance but will also study its indirect effect via organizational commitment.

More specifically this research posits that organizational commitment would mediate the relationship between job involvement and in-role performance. The second objective of this study is to find if job involvement is related to organizational citizenship behaviour. Surprisingly the relationship between job involvement and OCB has received very little empirical attention. The present study therefore aims to extend the literature by examining the effects of job involvement on OCB.

Finally this research would examine the relative effects of job involvement on in-role job performance and organizational citizenship behaviour. More specifically this study would attempt to find whether job involvement exerts a stronger impact on in-role performance or organizational citizenship behaviour.

## JOB INVOLVEMENT AND IN-ROLE JOB PERFORMANCE

In-role job performance refers to activities that are related to employees' formal role requirements. Generally it is believed that job involvement by positively affecting employees' motivation and effort, leads to higher levels of in-role job performance. Prior research has indicated some support for this claim. For instance Brown and Leigh in their study found that job involvement had both direct and indirect effects via effort on performance. More specifically they found that the modest but statistically significant relationship between job involvement and performance became non significant when effort was inserted into the model, indicating the mediating effect of effort on the relationship. Lassak et al. argued that occupation specific measures of job involvement should be created and consequently developed a measure of 'salesperson job involvement'.

Their study uncovered a significant but positive relationship between one facet of their measure, 'relationship' involvement and performance. Using a measure created by Paullay et al., to differentiate job involvement from work centrality, Diefendorff et al., found a small but significant correlation between job involvement and supervisor - rated in-role performance. Finally Rotenberry and Moberg, using the same measure of job involvement as Diefendorff et al., reported a small but significant positive correlation between job involvement and in-role performance. Although generally the results concerning the relationship between job involvement and performance have not been very encouraging there is evidence to suggest that job involvement can positively influence in-role job performance.

## THE MEDIATING ROLE OF ORGANIZATIONAL COMMITMENT

Brown and Leigh argue that one reason for the weak and inconsistent relationship between job involvement and performance may be that job involvement is more likely to affect performance indirectly through other variables. This study posits that organizational commitment would link job involvement with performance. In the present study organization commitment has been defined as the relative strength of an individual's identification with and involvement in a particular organization.

*The authors mention three characteristics of organizational commitment*:

- A strong belief in and acceptance of the organization's goals and values,
- A willingness to exert a considerable effort on behalf of the organization
- A strong intent or desire to remain with the organization. It is argued that job involvement will

first lead to commitment, which in turn will lead to higher levels of performance.

The relationship between job involvement and organizational commitment is well documented in the literature. The positive relationship between job involvement and commitment suggests that those employees who are committed to their jobs are also likely to be committed to their employing organizations.

Similarly research has indicated that organizational commitment is positively related to job performance. This finding posits that employees who are committed to their organizations are more likely not only to remain with the organization but are also likely to exert more effort on behalf of the organization and work towards its success and therefore should be better performers than the uncommitted employees.

Taken together this discussion implies that job involvement would foster organizational commitment among employees and committed employees in turn would put in extra effort on behalf of their organization, which consequently would lead to higher levels of performance. In other words organizational commitment would mediate the relationship between job involvement and performance.

- *H2*: Organizational commitment would mediate the relationship between job involvement and in-role job performance.

## JOB INVOLVEMENT AND ORGANIZATIONAL CITIZENSHIP BEHAVIOUR

Katz and Kahn, effective organizational functioning requires employees to not only perform their prescribed role, but also to engage in behaviours that go beyond these formal obligations. This aspect of performance is consistent with Organ's conceptualizations of OCBs. Organizational citizenship behaviours (or OCB's) are discretionary workplace behaviours that exceed one's basic job requirements. They are often described as behaviours that *"go above and beyond the call of duty."* OCB's have been defined as "individual behaviours that are discretionary, not directly or explicitly recognized by the formal reward system, and that in aggregate promote the effective functioning of an organization". Such behaviours are said to "lubricate the social machinery of the organization". Examples of OCB include acts of helpfulness, gestures of goodwill and cooperation among organizational members. OCB benefits organizations in a number of ways.

*Cohen and Vigoda some of the benefits of OCBs that can accrue to an organization include*:

- Improved co-worker and managerial productivity,
- Superior efficiency in resource use and allocation,
- Reduced maintenance expenses,
- Improved organizational attractiveness for high-quality new recruits.

The relationship between job involvement and OCB's has unfortunately received scant empirical attention. An examination of the literature revealed that until recently only Munene and Somers and Birnbaum had even considered this relationship. Both these authors found a significant correlation between job involvement and OCB. More recently research studies conducted by Diefendorff et al., Bolger and Somech, Chu et al and Rotenberry and Moberg have also uncovered a positive relationship between job involvement and OCB. Given the fact that OCBs are more influenced by what individuals think and feel about their jobs and that job involvement reflects a positive attitude towards the job, it follows that those high in job involvement would engage in these behaviours to a greater extent than less involved individuals.

Job involvement directly effects organizational citizenship behaviour. Thus the present study also hypothesises that there would be a direct and positive relationship between job involvement and organizational citizenship behaviours.

- *H*3: There will be a significant positive correlation between job involvement and organizational citizenship behaviours.

## THE RELATIVE EFFECTS OF JOB INVOLVEMENT

Diefendorff et al. and Somers and Birnbaum suggest that because OCB's are more discretionary than in-role prescribed duties, employees attitudes and beliefs should have a greater impact on them. Diefendorff et al. asserted that completing in-role tasks is often constrained by rules and environmental conditions at work whereas OCBs are under the volitional control of the individual employee. Because of this employee attitudes such as job involvement ought to have a larger impact upon the execution of OCBs rather than in-role performance. Consequently it is hypothesised that job involvement would have a greater impact on OCB than on in-role performance.

- *H4*: Job involvement would have a greater impact on OCB than on job performance.

For this study data was collected from full time faculty members teaching in 53 universities operating in five major cities of Pakistan: Lahore, Islamabad/ Rawalpindi, Peshawar, Karachi and Quetta. For the present study a sample of university teachers was selected because within the context of the Pakistani job market this is an under researched area and it was believed that this study would provide useful guidelines to education managers in Pakistan to increase the performance of faculty members through interventions designed to increase job involvement. The sample was taken from the five major cities of Pakistan because all the major educational institutions in the country are located within these cities.

In order to select a representative sample for this study we utilized the stratified random sampling technique. Three steps are involved in stratified random sampling. The first step requires the determination of the overall sample size. In the second step the total sample size is allocated among different strata and in the third step the required number of respondents is chosen from each strata using random sampling.

*Three factors were considered to determine the sample size*:

- The degree of variability in the population;
- Magnitude of acceptable error;
- Confidence level to ensure that the estimates would remain within the range of acceptable error.

The main problem encountered in the estimation of the sample size was the non-availability of the population standard deviation (i.e. an estimate of the degree of variability in the population). In order to find the estimate of the standard deviation, we conducted a pilot study by selecting a sample of teachers from four universities. From the results of the pilot study the estimate of the population standard deviation was calculated. By assuming a 99% confidence interval and the magnitude of acceptable error of 2 the total sample size was determined. The reason for choosing a 99% confidence interval and the magnitude of standard error of 2 was to keep the sample size within manageable limits owing to the cost and time constraints. The total sample size with these specifications came out to be 208.

Next, we divided our total population into five strata on basis of cities, with each city included in the sampling procedure considered as a separate stratum. The total sample size of 208 teachers (out of a total of 6,488 teachers) was then proportionally distributed among the five cities. Finally the required number of respondents from each stratum was selected by simple random sampling.

The required number of questionnaires and the accompanying cover letter assuring confidentiality was handed over to the research officer in the Centre for Statistics at the Lahore School of Economics. The research officer then visited the selected respondents at their respective institutions and cities and requested them to fill the questionnaires. If the respondents had the time they filled the questionnaire on the spot. In other cases the research officer dropped the questionnaire with the relevant respondents and collected the questionnaire at a mutually agreed date and time. Participation in this survey was completely voluntary. It took about eight weeks to collect the data.

Data were collected from Lecturers, Assistant Professors, Associate Professors and Full Professors teaching on a full time basis in the participating universities. Out of a total of 208 questionnaires, which were distributed, 195 were completed and returned thereby yielding a response rate of 93.8%. One reason for this high response rate was that the respondents were approached personally at their workplace by the research officer. If the questionnaires were sent through mail, it is speculated that the response rate would have been much lower. The sample of employees was 64 per cent male and 36 per cent female. The male to female ratio obtained for the present sample was quite representative of the total population of faculty members because it was found that out of a total of 6488 teachers teaching in the five cities surveyed, about 72% were male and 28% were female.

Ten per cent of the faculty members belonged to the faculty of arts, 21% per cent were from the faculty of social and environmental sciences, approximately 57% taught in the faculty of science and engineering and about 11% belo nged to the faculty of business and management. A total of 72 per cent of the sample was married. The average age and job tenure for the sample was 39 and 9 years respectively.

## ORGANIZATIONAL COMMITMENT

Organizational commitment was measured by organizational Commitment Questionnaire (OCQ) developed by Modway, Steers and Porter.

*They created the OCQ by identifying 15 factors that could be correlated with their definition of organizational commitment*:

- A strong belief i n and acceptance of the organization's goals and values;
- A willingness to exert considerable effort on behalf of the organization;
- A strong desire to maintain membership in the organization.

Each item of this instrument asked for agreement or disagreement on a seven point Likert scale ranging from "Strongly Disagree"(weighted 1) to "Strongly Agree" (weighted 7), with a statement, which tapped the organizational commitment construct. The average of the 15 items was used as the total scale score for each respondent.

The organizational commitment questionnaire has been widely used in previous studies to measure commitment and has demonstrated both convergent and discriminant validity. As a consequence this instrument was adopted in the present study to measure commitment. The value of coefficient alpha for this scale in the present sample was 0.80. Job involvement was measured by 12 items taken from the job involvement scale developed by Lodahl and Kejner. Each item was measured on a five-point scale where a value of one corresponded to "Strongly Disagree" and a value of 5 corresponded to "Strongly Agree".

The scores obtained on each of the 12 items were averaged to produce a single score for job involvement. Brown on the basis of his meta-analytic study contends that the job involvement scale developed by Lodahl and Kejner is a reliable and useful measure of job involvement and as a result this scale was utilized to measure the construct of job involvement in the present study. The value of coefficient alpha for this sample was 0.71.

## IN-ROLE PERFORMANCE

In-role performance was measured by using a self-appraisal approach. For this purpose we designed a self-appraisal form, which required the respondents to rate their performance on five dimensions, which were included on the basis of the results from preliminary interviews conducted with faculty members prior to administrating the survey. These dimensions included: teaching ability, interpersonal skills, communication skills, student advisement and consultation and personal initiative.

In North America and Europe, faculty are primarily evaluated on the basis of number of research publications and student ratings of the faculty member's teaching. However in Pakistani universities research publications is not a requirement for faculty members and as a result this dimension was not included as a measure of performance.

As far as student ratings of faculty members were concerned, the universities included in the present survey were reluctant to divulge this information and as a consequence this aspect of faculty performance could not be included in this study. Each dimension was measured by a single statement and the responses were obtained on a seven-point scale where a value of one corresponded to "Strongly Disagree" and a value of 7 corresponded to "Strongly Agree". The scores obtained on each of the five items were averaged to produce a summary score reflecting in-role performance. The method of self-appraisal has been used in research and has produced satisfactory results. The coefficient alpha of this sample was 0.78.

## ORGANIZATIONAL CITIZENSHIP BEHAVIOUR

Organizational citizenship behaviour was measured by 13 items extracted from the Chinese citizenship behaviour scale developed by Farh, Earley and Lin and the OCB scale developed by Podsakoff et al. Items from Farh et al.'s Chinese citizenship scale were included in the OCB scale for the present study because OCBs in the Chinese society seem to correspond with OCBs in the Pakistani society. This is because Pakistan is culturally close to China in the sense that like China, Pakistan is also high on collectivism and power distance.

Each item in the scale was measured on a five-point scale where a value of one corresponded to "Strongly Disagree" and a value of 5 corresponded to "Strongly Agree". The scores obtained on each of the 13 items were averaged to produce a single score for organizational citizenship behaviour. The coefficient alpha of this sample was 0.89.

### Control Variables

Two control variables included in this study were: age and gender. *These variables were measured as follows*:

### Age

The respondents were requested to report their age in years as of their last birthday.

### Gender

Respondents were asked to report their gender. In the data compilation, gender was coded as follows: male = 1 and female = 0. The reliabilities for all the multi-item scales were generally very good. All alpha values met the criterion of 0.70 proposed by Nunnaly and Bernstein. The alpha values ranged from 0.71

to 0.89 for the present sample. The correlation matrix also demonstrates that job involvement is significantly and positively correlated with self-report measures of in-role performance and OCB. These findings support hypotheses one and three.

Hypothesis two posits that organizational commitment would mediate the relationship between job involvement and in-role job performance. To test this hypothesis we followed Baron and Kenny's recommendations for examining mediating effects in regression. They argued that mediation is demonstrated if three conditions are fulfilled: The first condition stipulates that the independent variable and the proposed mediator must each be significantly related to the dependent variable when considered separately. Therefore the first condition for mediation was satisfied.

The second condition requires that the independent variable to be significantly related to the proposed mediator. Hence the second condition for mediation is also satisfied. The last condition for mediation stipulates that when both the independent variable and mediator are included in a regression equation, the direct relationship between the independent variable and the dependent variable should become significantly smaller, indicating partial mediation, or non-significant, indicating full mediation. To test this last condition we utilized the hierarchical multiple regression technique.

When in-role job performance was regressed on job involvement, it was found that job involvement was significantly and positively related to performance. In step 2 organizational commitment was added to the equation, and organizational commitment was significant, but job involvement also remained significant, although its beta weight decreased from $b = 0.295$ to $b = 0.248$. Taken together these results imply that organizational commitment partially mediated the relationship between job involvement and the self-report measure of in-role performance. Thus hypothesis two is partially supported. Finally hypothesis four states that job involvement would have a stronger impact on OCB than on in-role job performance. In order to test this hypothesis, we proceeded by examining the incremental increase in regression R2 when job involvement was entered into the regression models following the two control variables - gender and age.

For this purpose, separate two -step, hierarchical regression analyses were performed for in-role performance and OCB respectively. At step one we entered the two control variables, gender and age as a block. Both age and gender were found to be unrelated to the self-report measures of in-role performance and OCB. These demographic variables alone explained only about 1 per cent and 0.9 per cent of the variance in in-role performance and OCB respectively.

In step two we entered job involvement. With the two demographic variables controlled, job involvement accounted for an additional 8 per cent of the variance in in-role performance and an additional 18 per cent of the variance in OCB. Since the increase in the value of R2 was substantially larger for OCB when job involvement was added to the control variables, it was concluded that job involvement exerted a stronger impact on OCB than on in-role performance. Thus hypothesis four was substantiated.

This study reaffirms job involvement as a potentially important determinant of individual performance. Although studies examining the relationship between job involvement and performance have by and large produced disappointing results, the findings of this research supports the notion that highly involved employees tend to perform at higher levels. People who are highly involved in their work tend to be more motivated and consequently are likely to put in more effort into their jobs and therefore should perform better than less involved individuals.

The findings of this study show that job involvement not only affects performance directly but also indirectly by enhancing organizational commitment. The results of this study revealed that commitment partially mediated the job involvement-performance relationship. People who are very involved in their job and for whom their job is a 'central life interest' - that is the job is a major source for satisfaction of important needs - will have less of an incentive to leave their current organization and seek employment elsewhere and as a consequent would be more committed to their organizations. The relationship between job involvement and commitment is well supported in the literature.

Committed employees in turn put in extra effort to contribute towards the success of the organization, which consequently leads to higher performance. The results of this study indicate that commitment is significantly and positively related to both in-role and extra-role performance. It follows that interventions aimed at simultaneously increasing job involvement and organizational commitment can be a potent method to increase both types of performance.

The results of this study also show that job involvement is positively correlated with OCB. This result supports the findings reported by Diefendorff et al., Bolger and Somech, Chu et al and Rotenberry and Moberg, who also uncovered a positive relationship between job involvement and OCB in their respective studies. Given the fact OCBs are more influenced by what individuals think and feel about their jobs and that job involvement reflects a positive attitude towards the job, it follows that those high in job involvement would engage in these behaviours to a greater extent than less involved individuals.

In addition, the social exchange theory may also be applied to explain the relationship between job involvement and OCB. Specifically employees feel indebted for the needs satisfaction, resulting in job involvement, that their organization provides and subsequently feel obligated to reciprocate. Employees may reciprocate to this needs satisfaction by engaging in more organizational citizenship behaviours for their organizations.

Finally in this study it was found that job involvement exerted a stronger impact on OCB than on in-role performance. Rotenberry and Moberg also found the same result in their study. Somers and Brinbaum and Diefendorff et al. each argued that in-role performance is often constrained by factors outside of the employee, while engaging in citizenship behaviour is generally under the employee's control. Because of this employee attitudes such as job involvement ought to have a larger impact upon the execution of OCBs rather than in-role performance.

## IMPLICATIONS FOR MANAGERS AND ORGANIZATIONS

The findings of this research have important implications for managers and their organizations. The results of this research demonstrate that job involvement is a potent weapon to increase both in-role and extra role (OCBs) performance. In addition to having positive affects on performance, prior research has found that job involvement positively influences other attitudinal and behavioural outcomes such as organizational commitment, turnover and absenteeism. On the contrary low levels of job involvement contribute to employees' feelings of alienation of purpose, alienation in the organization or feeling of separation between what the employees see as their 'life' and the job they do.

Thus fostering high levels of job involvement is a viable option for managers to increase the competitive position of their organizations. The question is that how can managers increase the levels of employees' job involvement? Research has demonstrated that by re-designing jobs through the incorporation of job characteristics, such as autonomy, feedback, variety and task identity, management can make jobs more interesting, meaningful and challenging for job incumbents which in turn can lead to higher job involvement.

*Brown in his review of the organizational research on job involvement concludes that work environments that*:

- Provide a sense of meaningfulness to one's work,
- Offer control over the methods by which work is accomplished,
- Maintain clear and consistent behavioural norms,
- Provide feedback about the work accomplished,
- Include supportive relation with superiors and co-workers

- Offer opportunities for personal growth and development are conducive to job involvement.

Taken together this discussion implies that organizations can reap the positive benefits of job involvement by providing resources to employees at the level of the task (e.g. skill variety, task significance, task identity, autonomy and feedback), interpersonal and social relations (e.g. supervisor and co-worker support), organization of work (e.g. participation in decision making) and at the level of the organization at large (e.g. career opportunities).

## LIMITATIONS OF THE STUDY

Although the findings of this study are useful, it is limited by several factors. One limitation of this study is that it uses the self-report measures of in-role performance and OCB. If the data on in-role performance and OCB were collected from supervisors or peers of the respondents, the findings may well have turned out to be different than the ones reported in this research. Thus it is recommended that future research in this area should be conducted by using performance and OCB data, which is based on supervisory ratings of employees.

Secondly the data for this study was collected from faculty members teaching in universities across five major cities of Pakistan. The generalizability of the findings of this study to other contexts may thus be limited. In other words it could be that the findings obtained from the present sample are specific only to the context under study here. In this regard, it would be useful to replicate this study under different settings to establish the validity and generalizability of the present findings across different contexts.

Finally the data in this study was collected through self-reports, which creates the potential for common-method variance. One important concern in such cases is that common method variance may artificially inflate observed relationships between variables. This however might not be a problem because research has shown that the concern about common method bias has no empirical basis. Still we performed the Harman's single factor test to see if common method variance was a problem in the present study. If common method variance existed, a single factor would emerge from a factor analysis of all the measurement items, or one general factor that accounted for most of the variance would result. The factor analysis revealed 13 factors with eigen values greater than 1.0 that accounted for 64.2% of the total variance. The first factor accounted for only 20.3% of the variance. These results suggested that common method variance was not a serious problem in the present study.

The main aim of this research was to study the effects of job involvement on in-role and extra role performance. Generally studies attempting to uncover a positive relationship between job involvement and performance have met with limited success. This study adds to the literature by empirically demonstrating that job involvement can predict both in-role and extra role performance.

In addition, prior research has demonstrated that job involvement also leads to more positive attitudes and behaviours such as increased organizational commitment, a lower cognition to turnover and reduced absenteeism. Thus fostering high levels of job involvement among employees can be an effective strategy to increase both forms of performance and to foster more positive attitudes and behaviours. Therefore investing in conditions, which help to make employees more involved in their jobs, is likely to be important for the growth and profitability of the organizations.

# 6

# Motivation

## AN OVERVIEW

In an organization, management tries to co-ordinate various factors of production to achieve organizational goals. The efficiency of non human factors like materials, machines etc, depends on the type of technology being used and also the performance level of human factors used. Thus to make total factors efficient and effective, one has to improve the performance level of human beings in the organization. This is determined by two important factors.— Ability and Motivation.

The challenge faced by a modern manager now a days, is how to motivate employees to display behaviour consistent with organizational goals; such as reducing cost, increasing revenues and satisfying customers. Motivation is a challenge for managers, because it requires to understand 'how an employee thinks?'. Motivation arises from within employees, and motivational factors differ for each individual within an organization. When managers analyse their workers, they always discover that some people invariably out perform others of equal skill, efficiency, and ability.

A close scrutiny often reveals that in some situations a person with outstanding talents is consistently out performed by some one having lesser talents. The reason seems to be that the latter employees voluntarily put more effort, try harder, in order to accomplish their goals. These hard workers are often described as motivated workers. Since people are the most important resource of an organization, their behaviour has to be studied, analysed, and interpreted properly. Among behaviour processes, motivation is generally treated as one of strategic importance. It is because lack of motivation results in ineffective performance and high levels of absenteeism and labour turnover.

## DEFINITION

The tem 'Motivation' has come from motives, which are the expression of human needs by a human being. The activities of human beings are caused; and behind every action there is a particular motive or need. The need can be defined as feeling of lackness for some thing, and human being tries to get satisfy their needs. Motivation is the process of inducing persons to experience needs for certain desired behaviour so that the organizational efficiency is achieved. Scott has defined motivation as " a process of stimulating people to action to accomplish desired goals".

McFarland says " the concept of motivation is mainly psychological. It relates to those forces operating within the individual employees or subordinates which compel them to animation ot not to animation in certain ways." Motivation is a process, which inspires the human efforts of an organization to perform their duties in the best possible manner so that the pre- determined objectives may be achieved.

## THEORIES OF MOTIVATION

From the very beginning, when human organizations were established, people hard tried to find out the answer to what motivated people maximum. Since various people have been engaged in finding out the motivational factors, their approaches have differed resulting in to a number of theories concerning motivation.

## MASLOW'S NEED HIERARCHY THEORY

Psychologist, Abraham Maslow has developed the theory of the hierarchy of needs in 1943. There seems to be a hierarchy in to which human needs are arranged. The needs are ranked in a hierarchy in which one need is important than others until it is satisfied. Once the most important need is satisfied, the next high need becomes important, and a satisfied need can no longer motivate human behaviour. Maslow, the needs are satisfied in the following sequence.

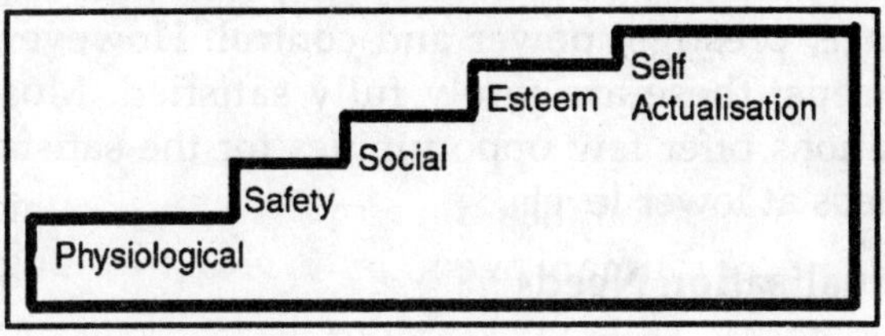


## Physiological Needs

These are shown at the top of the hierarchy because they tend to have the highest strength until they are reasonably satisfied. The primary needs consist of water, air, food, avoidance of pain etc and human beings first try to acquire necessities for survival.

The manager attempts to satisfy these needs in the workplace primarily through salary and by eliminating threats to physical safety.

## Safety and Security Needs

When physiological needs are satisfied, safety needs get most important priority as motivator. such needs get expression through employee unions, permanent job, and desires for insurance and retirement programmes.

Arbitrary management actions such as favouritism, or discrimination and unpredictable application of policies often become powerful threats to satisfy needs of any employee at any level.

## Social Needs

At this stage people desire friendship, and a place in a group. When social needs become dormant, person will strive for meaningful relations with others. If the opportunity of association with the other people is reduced, men often take vigourous action against the obstacles to social intercourse. In the organization, workers form informal group environment.

### Esteem Needs

These are concerned with self respect, self confidence, a feeling of personal worth, feeling of being unique and recognition. satisfaction of these needs produces feeling of self confidence, prestige, power and control. However, unlike lower needs, these are rarely fully satisfied. Most of the organizations offer few opportunities for the satisfaction of these needs at lower levels.

### Self Actualisation Needs

Self actualisation is the need to maximise ones abilities and potential, whatever it may be. This is necessary for continued self development. As Maslow has put it- "this need might be phrased as the desire to become more and more what one is, to become everything that one is capable of becoming". Maslows Need hierarchy theory has been highly appreciated by the managers because it offers some useful ideas for helping managers think about motivating their employees.

As a result of their familiarity with the model, the managers are more likely to identify employee needs, recognise that they may be different across employees, offer satisfaction for the particular needs, and realise that giving more of the same reward may have diminishing impact on motivation.

## HERZBERG'S TWO FACTOR THEORY

This theory is developed by Frederick Herzberg and his associates, after conducting a series of interviews with 200 engineers and accountants, focusing on factors considered to be important as sources of motivation. during the interview they were asked to describe a few job experiences in which they felt 'exceptionally good' and 'exceptionally' bad.

From the replies received, Herzberg concluded that there were two categories of needs, essentially independent of each other affecting the behaviour in different ways. There are some job conditions which operates primarily to dissatisfy employees when the conditions are absent, but their presence doesn't motivate them in a strong way. Another set of conditions operates primarily to build strong motivation and high job satisfaction, but their absence rarely proves strongly dissatisfying. The first job conditions are called as 'maintenance' or 'hygiene' factors and the second set as ' motivational factors'.

### Hygiene or Maintenance Factors

These factors are the primary cause of unhappiness on the job. When the employer is unable to provide enough of these factors to its employees, there will be job dissatisfaction. However, if they are provided in sufficient quantity, they will not necessarily animation as motivators.

They are not parts of jobs, but they are related to conditions under which a job is performed. these factors are necessary to maintain a reasonable level of satisfaction in employees. Some of these factors are - company policies and administration, Quality of supervision, interpersonal relationships, job security, working conditions, employee benefits etc.

### Motivational Factors

These factors are capable of having a positive effect on job satisfaction, often resulting in an increase in ones total output. These are achievements, recognition, advancement, work itself, possibility of growth, and responsibility. An increase in these factors will satisfy the employees, however, any decrease will not affect their level of satisfaction.

Herzberg's model is based on the fact that most of the people are able to satisfy their lowerneeds considerably. As such they are not motivated by any further addition of satisfaction of these needs. Herzberg's model has been applied in the industry and has given several new insights. One of them is job enrichment.

## MCCLELLANDS NEEDS ACHIEVEMENT THEORY

Shortly after the second world war, David McClelland of Harvard University developed achievement theory which places great emphasis on needs and individual difference. He has identified three types of basic motivating needs. They are need for power, need for affiliation and need for achievement. McClelland believes that each person has a need for all the 3 needs, but people differ in the degree to which various needs motivate their behaviour.

## POWER MOTIVE

The ability to induce or influence behaviour is power. McClelland found that people with a higher power need have a great concern for exercising influencing and control. They derive satisfaction from being in positions to influence and control. Such individuals are generally seeking positions of leadership, they involve in conversation, and they are forceful. Eg. Supervisors, Military officers etc.

## AFFILIATION MOTIVE

Since people are social animals, most individuals like to interact and be with others in situations where they feel they belong and are accepted. McClelland has suggested that people with high need for affiliation usually derive pleasure from being loved and tend to avoid the pain of being rejected. They are concerned with maintaining pleasant social relationships, enjoying a sense of intimacy and understanding. eg. Customer relations executives.

## ACHIEVEMENT MOTIVE

Some people have an intense desire to achieve. The need for achievement is a distinct human motive that can be distinguished from other needs. McClelland has identified four basic characteristics of high achievers. They take moderate risk, desire immediate feed back, find accomplishing a task satisfying and they tend to be totally pre-occupied with the task, until it is successfully completed. e.g. Sales managers with Challenging quotas.

McClelland believes that the need for achievement can be learned, and economically backward cultures can be changed by it. Although the people with a high need for achievement are often wealthy, their wealth comes from their ability to achieve goals. The research conducted by McClelland, managers show high on achievement and power and low on affiliation. Achievement motivated people can be the backbone of most organizations because they progress much faster.

## THEORY 'X' AND THEORY 'Y'

The management actions of directing human beings in the organization, McGregor, involves certain assumptions and generalisations relating to human behaviour and nature. The basic assumptions about human behaviour may differ considerably, because of the complexity of factors influencing this behaviour. McGregor has characterised these assumptions in two extreme points. Theory X and Theory Y.

### Theory X

This is the traditional theory of human behaviour. In this theory McGregor, has certain assumptions about human behaviour.

- Management is responsible for organising the elements of productive enterprise. - Money, materials, people,- in the interest of economic needs.
- With respect to people, this is a process of directing their efforts, motivating them, controlling actions, and modifying their behaviour.
- Without active intervention by the management, people would be passive to organizational needs. They must be persuaded, rewarded, punished, controlled, and directed.
- The average man works as little as possible.
- He lacks ambition, dislikes responsibility, prefers to be led.

These assumptions about human nature are negative in their approach; however much organizational process has developed on these. Mangers having these views attempt to control and closely supervise their employees. These managers feel that external control is clearly appropriate for dealing with unreliable and irresponsible persons. After describing these views, McGregor questioned these views and concluded that Theory X assumptions when universally applied, are often inaccurate and that management approaches that develop from these assumptions may fail to motivate many individuals. Management by direction and control may not succeed, because it doesn't motivate people whose physiological and safety needs are reasonably satisfied.

### Theory Y

McGregor feels that management needed practice based on more accurate understanding of human nature and motivation. Because of these feelings he developed an alternative theory called Theory Y.

*The assumptions of theory Y are*:

- The physical and mental effort in work is natural as play or rest. The average human being does not dislike work.
- Man will exercise self direction and self control in the service of objectives to which he is committed.
- The average human being learns to accept and to seek responsibility.
- The capacity to exercise high degree of imagination and creativity is widely distributed in population.
- The intellectual potentialities of the average human being are only partially utilised.

The assumptions of theory Y suggest a new approach in management. Theory Y organizations have united work force whose goals parallel organizational goals. In such organizations, there is high productivity and people come to work gladly. Both theories have certain assumptions about human nature. In fact they are the reverse side of a coin.

## THEORY Z

Theory Z describes the Japanese management practices and how these can be adopted to the environment of the United States and other countries. Ouchi; who has given Theory Z, has made a comparative study of American and Japanese management practices and has recommended that many management practices can be adopted in American context.

## FEATURES OF THEORY Z

### Trust

Trust is the most important feature of this theory and by trust Ouchi means trust between employees, supervisors, work groups, unions, management and government. Integrity and openness are closely related and these are essential ingredients of effective organizations. When an organization relies o these principles, employees tend to cooperate to the maximum extent.

### Strong Bond Between Organization and Employees

Theory Z suggests strong bond between organization and employees. Ouchi has suggested certain methods for this, including the life time employment and if there is a situation of lay off, it should not be resorted to and owners can share the resultant loss by accepting less profit or even moderate loss for a short period of time. A career planning for employees should be prepared so that every employee is suitably placed.

### Employee Involvement

Employee involvement is an important factor and this comes through meaningful participation. Any decision affecting employees in any way should be taken jointly and if there is any decision which the management wants to take individually, the employees should be informed about this so that they do not feel ignored.

### No Formal Structure

Theory Z provides no formal structure for the organization. Instead it must be a perfect teamwork with co operation along with sharing information, resources and plans. It places emphasis on rotational aspect of employee placement which provides opportunities to him to understand how his work affects others or is affected by others. This enables him to develop group spirit.

### Coordination of Human Beings

The leaders role is to coordinate people and not

technology to achieve productivity. This involves developing peoples skills and also the creation of new structures, incentives and new philosophy of management. To develop trust, there should be a complete openness in the relationships.

## ERG THEORY OF MOTIVATION

In 1969, Clayton Alderfer's revision of Abraham Maslow's Hierarchy of Needs, called the ERG Theory *"An Empirical Test of a New Theory of Human Need."* Alderfer's contribution to organizational behaviour was the ERG theory and was created to align Maslow's motivation theory more closely with empirical research.

*The letters ERG represent these three levels of needs*:

- Existence refers to our concern with basic material existence motivators.
- Relatedness refers to the motivation we have for maintaining interpersonal relationships.
- Growth refers to an intrinsic desire for personal development.

Alderfers ERG theory demonstrates that more than one need may motivate at the same time. A lower motivator need not be substantially satisfied before one can move onto higher motivators.

The ERG theory acknowledges that if a higher-order need is frustrated, an individual may regress to increase the satisfaction of a lower-order need which appears easier to satisfy. This is known as the *frustration-regression principle.*

## FINANCIAL AND NON FINANCIAL MOTIVATION

When we take human beings in organizations for analysing motivational pattern, we identify two groups of individuals. – Managers and workers. Some of the studies have focussed on the motivation of managers and some other, on workers. An analysis of these studies reveals that there is wide scope of variability in the factors of motivation. Various factors of motivation can be grouped in to two broad categories. – Financial and Non Financial.

## FINANCIAL FACTORS

There is hardly any doubt that money is an important motivator. Money not only satisfies basic needs, but also provide social position and power. Money has its special significance in the motivational plan. It can provide recognition for high performance and lead to improved goal settings. As a medium of exchange, money is the thing by which employee can buy need satisfying goods and services. It will be a powerful motivator for a person who is anxious about lack of money. Financial factors of motivation can be grouped in to two categories. Individual and collective.

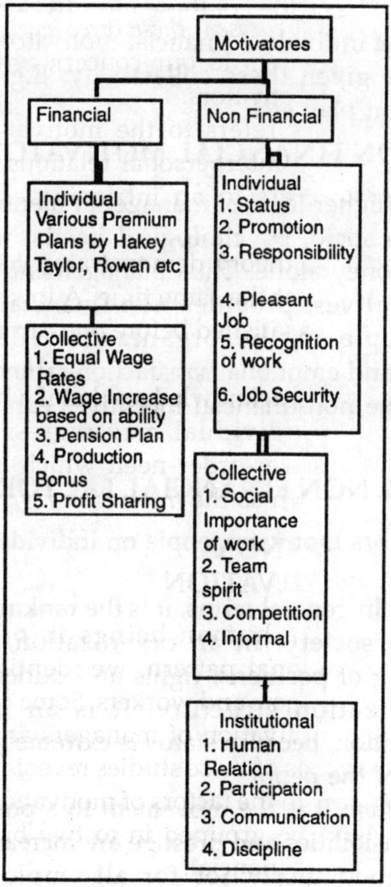

### Individual Financial Motivators

This group includes all such plans which induce an individual to achieve higher output to earn higher financial rewards. Piece rate wages, Taylors differential Piece rate system, Halseys efficiency plan etc are examples of such incentives. The basic assumption behind this is that an individual will be motivated for higher output to earn more money, which satisfies his need.

### Collective Financial Motivators

This group of motivators tries to motivate individuals collectively. The basic idea of these incentives is that the same as in the case of individual financial motivators, however the employees are given these collectively. E.g. Bonus, Profit sharing, pension plan etc.

## NON FINANCIAL MOTIVATORS

People at higher level of managerial hierarchy give more importance to socio, psychological needs, which can't be satisfied by money alone. Thus management; in addition to financial incentives, provides non-financial incentives to motivate people in the organization. These provide psychological and emotional satisfaction rather than financial satisfaction. The non-financial incentives can be grouped in to three parts.

## INDIVIDUAL NON FINANCIAL FACTORS

These factors motivate people on individual basis.
*They are*:

- *Status*: In general terms, it is the ranking of the people in the society. In an organization, status means ranking of positions, rights and duties in the formal organization structure. It is an instrument of motivation, because status is extremely important for most of the people.
- *Promotion*: It is the movement to a position in which responsibilities and prestige are increased. Promotion is a good motivator for all employees. Since it

depends upon capabilities and good performance, people will try for that, if chances of promotion exist.

- *Responsibility*: Most of the people prefer challenging and responsible jobs. If the job is a 'responsible one', it satisfies peoples natural characteristics and esteem needs, and they put more efforts for completing the work.
- *Making the job interesting*: The work can be made enjoyable and pleasant, if it is so designed that it allows the employees to satisfy their natural instincts. This creates interest in the work and employees take it as natural as play.
- *Recognition of work*: Most people feel that what they do should be recognised by others. Recognition means acknowledgement with a show of appreciation. When such appreciation is given to employees, they feel motivated to perform work at higher level.
- *Job security*: Most of the employees prefer a secure job. They want certain stability about future income and work, so that they do not feel worried on these aspects. In India this aspect is more important considering the inadequate job opportunities.

## COLLECTIVE NON FINANCIAL FACTORS.

People may be motivated in groups also. They perform their duties in groups and are affected by the group. If the group in general is effective, an individual tends to become efficient.

*Some of the collective non financial factors are:*

- *Social Importance of work*: People generally prefer a work, which is socially acceptable. If society gives importance and praise to the work, people like to perform. Some times people prefer a job of high social importance, event though the financial compensation would be less.
- *Team spirit*: The management should encourage team spirit, i.e., to work in co-operation and co-ordination.

If there is team spirit among the employees, they will try to put in maximum effort to achieve the objective.

- *Compensation*: Some times competitions are organised between different individuals or different groups in an organization. There may be a case of self competition, where an individual tries to improve his earlier performance. When a person performs well because of such competition, he should be given some advantage, not necessarily in terms of money, but it may be in terms of recognition, prestige, praise etc.
- *Informal Groups*: When people work together, they develop some sort of affiliation among themselves. These relationships are not officially prescribed, but created on the basis of some factors like personality and other social factors. Creation of these groups provide social satisfaction to employees. Management should provide the way for creation of such informal groups; so long as they are not against organizational efficiency.

## INSTITUTIONAL INCENTIVES

*These are related with the environmental factors in the organization*:

- *Human relations in an industry*: This is related with the policy to be adopted in the organization to develop a sense of belongingness in the employees, improve their efficiency, and treat them as human beings. The emphasis is on providing greater psychological and physiological satisfaction to the employees.
- *Participation*: Participation of subordinates in the decision making process will motivate an employee to take proper and prompt action on decision implementation. This will also increase his responsibility.
- *Communication*: Communication is the process of passing ideas fro one person or groups to another

person or groups. A free and adequate flow of communication is necessary for successful organizational functioning. This provides satisfaction to workers, as they want to be informed properly about the matters concerning their interest.

- *Discipline*: The quality of an organizations climate is reflected in the discipline of its employees. Discipline is the employees self control to meet organization standards and objectives. Managements maintain discipline by applying standards in a consistent, fair and flexible manner. Discipline has a positive role in satisfying employees by providing them proper atmosphere.

In an organization all these factors should be used for motivating the employees. There was an assumption that higher money would bring higher productivity. But now a day's social and psychological satisfaction is getting more importance.

- Management by objectives.
- Job Satisfaction
- Job enlargement
- Job enrichment.

## MANAGEMENT BY OBJECTIVES

Management by Objectives is a process of agreeing upon objectives within an organization so that management and employees agree to the objectives and understand what they are in the organization.

The term "management by objectives" was first popularized by Peter Drucker in his 1954 book 'The Practice of Management. The essence of MBO is participative goal setting, choosing course of actions and decision making. An important part of the MBO is the measurement and the comparison of the employee's actual performance with the standards set. Ideally, when employees themselves have been involved with the goal setting and the choosing the course of action to be followed by them, they are more likely to fulfill their responsibilities.

## ELEMENTS IN THE MBO PROCESS

### Central Goal Setting

The first step in the MBO process is to define and verify organizational objectives. These objectives are generally set by the central management and usually in consultation with the other managers.

Before setting the objectives; a detailed assessment will be made of the resources available. This detailed analysis will highlight the desirable long run as well as short run objectives. At attempt should be made to make that objectives specific and realistic.

### Departmental and Individual Goal Setting

After setting the organizational objectives, the next step is to set the departmental objectives. The top management should discuss the objectives with the departmental heads so that objectives can be mutually agreed upon. Each department sets its long range and short range objectives with the approval of the top management.

After setting the departmental goals, the subordinates work with their respective managers to set their own goals relative to the organizational goals. *Such* participative objectives are important because people become highly motivated by achieving the objectives set by them.

### Revision of Job Descriptions

Under MBO, resetting of the individual goals will call for a revision of the job descriptions of various positions which in turn, will call for the revision of the whole organizational structure.

The organizational charts and manuals will be amended to depict the changes brought in by the MBO.

### Matching Goals and Resource Allocation

Setting of objectives does not mean anything in itself unless resources and means to achieve there objectives are also provided. Thus, the subordinates must be provided necessary tools and materials by the managements, so that they can achieve their goals effectively; and efficiently.

### Establishing Check Points

MBO ensures periodic meetings between the manager and his subordinate to discuss the progress towards the accomplishment of the targets of the subordinates For this the manager must establish check points or standards of performance for evaluating the progress of the subordinate.

### Appraisal of Performance

While informal performance appraisal of a subordinate is done by his manager almost everyday, there should also be periodic review of performance. These periodic reviews are necessary since priorities and conditions are constantly changing and these must be constantly monitored.

These reviews will assist the managers and subordinates in modifying either the objectives or the methods if and when necessary. The performance review conducted at periodic intervals assesses the subordinate in improving his performance in the future. The superior will discuss with the subordinate the ways and means to remove deficiencies in performance and advise him as to how his efficiency can be improved.

### Counselling

The performance review conducted at periodic intervals assist the subordinates in improving his performance. The superior will discuss with the subordinates the ways and means to remove deficiencies in performance and advise him as to how his efficiency can be improved.

## TRANSACTIONAL ANALYSIS

When two people interact with each other, there results a social transaction. Analysis of the social transactions is called 'Transactional Analysis.' TA is the study of moves, people make in their dealings with each other. It offers a model of personality and its relationships to others. It is a method of analysing and understanding interpersonal behaviour. Transactional Analysis was originally developed by Eric Berne, a psychotherapist in 1950. He observed that it was as if several persons were inside each persons, and these various 'selves' transmitted with people in different ways.

## EGO STATES

Basic to TA is the assumption that a person has 3 ego states, namely 'Parent, Adult and Child'. *The Parent Ego state*: This represents the part of a person's personality that is authoritative, controlling, nurturing and critical. The parent ego state incorporates the attitudes and behaviour of all emotionally significant people who serve as a parent figure, when an individual was a child. The value and behaviour of these people are recorded in the mind of individual and these become the basic values of the personality. The parent ego is there fore the taught ego state.

*The Adult Ego state*: This represents the nature and rational part of a person's personality. Persons interacting with adult ego views people as equal, and reasonable human being. The adult is characterised by logical thinking and reasoning. The individual gathers relevant information, analyses it carefully, generates alternatives and makes logical choices. In dealing with other people, the adult state is characterised by fairness and objectivity.

*The Child Ego state*: This represents the childish, dependent and immature part of a persons personality. These characteristics grow out of ones childhood experiences. The child age is characterised by non-logical and immediate actions. This state has no self-direction and no ability to move out to face the life.

## SOCIAL TRANSACTIONS

When people interact, they involve in a transaction with others. Thus when a stimulus from a person is being responded by another person, a transaction is said to occur. Depending on the kinds of ego states involved, the transaction can be either complimentary, crossed or ulterior.

## COMPLIMENTARY TRANSACTIONS

These occur, when the message sent by one persons ego state receives the appropriate or expected response from other persons ego state. Here the stimulus and response patterns from one ego state to another are parallel.

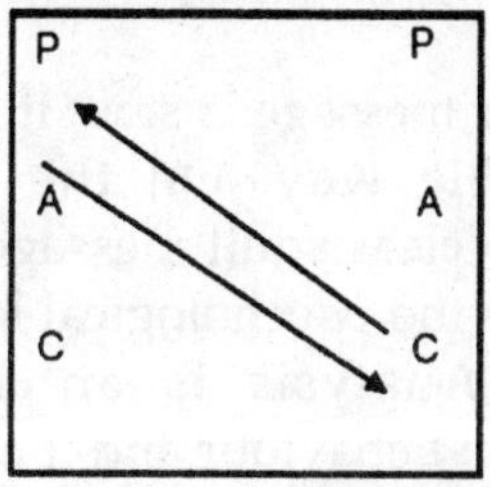


Usually in such a case both parties are satisfied and communication is complete. Since these type of transactions meet the needs and expectations of initiators communications flow freely and interpersonal relationships will improve.

## CROSSED TRANSACTIONS

In this case, the stimulus and response lines are not parallel. This happens when the person who initiates the transactions, expecting a certain response does not get it. Crossed transaction is not a satisfactory one, because the line of communication is blocked and further transaction does not take place. Crossed transactions are the source of much interpersonal conflict in an organization.

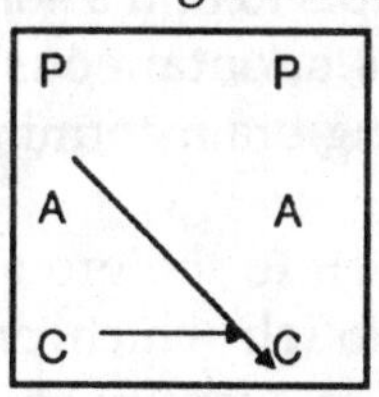


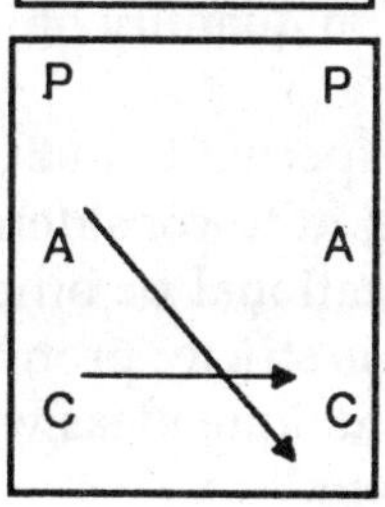

## ULTERIOR TRANSACTION

Ulterior transaction is the most complex because the communication has double meaning. This type of transaction involves at least two ego states on the part of the first person. The individual may say one thing but mean some thing quite different.

When an ulterior message is sent, it is often disguised in a socially acceptable way. On the surface level, the communication has a clear adult message, where as it carries a hidden message on the psychological level.

Transactional Analysis is an approach towards understanding human behaviour and it can be applied to any field of human interactions. It improves interpersonal relationship by providing understanding of ego states of persons involved in interaction.

## BRAINSTORMING

Brainstorming technique was developed by Alex Osborn, in 1938. The technique was used originally to develop an advertising programme, but the technique is now widely used by many Companies, educational institutions and other organizations; for building creative ideas.

Osborn has defined brainstorming simply using the brain to storm the problem. Brainstorming is a conference technique by which a group attempts to find a solution for a problem by amassing all the ideas spontaneously contributed by its members. For conducting brainstorming, a group of 10 to 15 members is constituted.

The problem is given to the group and each member is asked to give ideas through which problem can be solved. Here the importance is on quantity of ideas, and quality may follow later.

The members are expected to put their ideas for problem solution, without taking in to consideration any limitations - financial, legal, organizational or otherwise. Any criticism, judgement or comment is strictly prohibited. This encourages people to propose bold, unique ideas without worrying about what others think of them.

Brainstorming is based on the idea that critical judgement discourages people from expressing unorthodox ideas, andthese ideas may be the key to solving the problems faced by the organization.

Although brainstorming is useful for all types of decisions, it is more useful for simple, well defined problems. It encourages enthusiasm and a competitive spirit among members in generating ideas; it also prevents group members from feeling hopeless regarding the range of possibilities in a given situation.

# 7

# Foundations of Group Behaviour

Why do small-business groups in developed countries exist? Research has shown the strong economic impact of business groups throughout the world but remains heavily focused on large-business groups and on emerging economies. Theoretical approaches to explain the existence of highly diversified business groups range from market power to the resource-based view and include market failure, transaction costs, agency theory, and cultural embeddedness. These approaches, however, ate not very appropriate to explain the existence of small to medium-size firms in developed countries.

What we know is that these smaller groups exist and that they are largely the outcome of related diversification. We investigate relatively small and young-business groups organized in a holding structure. What are the perceived benefits of this kind of group for entrepreneurs and how can we explain the phenomenon theoretically? Based on case study research, we argue that the small-business group is both the outcome and the antecedent of growth. It enables, and helps to realise and manage the growth of entrepreneurial firms.

The enabling function consists in increasing reputation, attracting complementary resources that facilitate the exploitation of new opportunities, overcoming over-embeddedness, and dealing with co-opetition. The group is also the outcome of realised internationalization and related diversification. Interestingly, for the emergence of the small-business group, just as important as diversification is the integration of activities as well as the separation of closely linked activities. Finally, the small-business group corresponds to an entrepreneurial management style. The main contribution of this associate is to link organizational structure to the management and growth of entrepreneurial firms. Business groups, understood as groups of companies under common ownership, where personal and operational ties exist among the member firms, are ah important feature of the global economy.

Research has shown the strong economic impact of business groups throughout the world irrespective of context. However, three general assumptions recur in the dominant literature on business groups. First, business groups are highly diversified. Second, business groups are large firms. Third, business historians consider any organizational form other than the divisional M-form as a transitional phenomenon of inefficient organization.

Several theoretical approaches such as market failure and transaction cost theory have been used to explain the existence of highly diversified business groups especially in emerging economies. These theoretical approaches cannot adequately explain the existence and proliferation of small, young, and growing business groups in developed countries, groups that are characterized by related activities rather than by unrelated diversification.

The question of group formation is especially important, as the strong economic impact of small-business groups in Europe has been demonstrated. Khanna and Yafeh's cease is apt: "Other reasons are more likely to explain the ubiquity of business groups around the world." One missing link to better understand business groups is the role of entrepreneurial processes, but, except for the confirmed empirical fact that business groups are the outcome of diversification, it is still not understood: first, "why entrepreneurs prefer to run a group of companies rather than organizing them within the same legal boundaries," and, second, how the small-business group develops over time. When an entrepreneur is simultaneously involved in multiple activities in order to exploit new opportunities, an important question arises: What is the link between these activities and why does the entrepreneur create a new company? The literature on portfolio entrepreneurs has focused on entrepreneurs' superior human capital in detecting and exploiting opportunities. In summary, research on business groups has largely neglected small-business groups and research on portfolio entrepreneurship the organizational structure.

We focus on the facilitating effects of the small-business group organizational structure from an entrepreneurial perspective. We investigate business groups that are relatively small, young, and growing organized asa holding, in which a dominant entrepreneur has effective control. Entrepreneurship is growth. Literature on growth can be summarized in terms of antecedents and consequences of growth. Therefore, we can speak of three elements: enabling, realizing, and managing growth. The model developed by Covin and Slevin, growth increases management complexity and leads to various problems both within the firm and between the firm and its external environment, problems that need to be resolved in order to enable new growth. In other words, growth needs to be managed.

Two main dimensions are subject to growth-induced change: the organization and the entrepreneur. The organization needs to change in order to adapt to growth; the entrepreneur needs to develop stronger management competences and to adopt a different management style in order to manage the growing firm more efficiently and effectively through different stages: from birth to growth, maturity, and decline.

Common to these stage models is the assumption that firms go through crises leading to organizational change. As a consequence, growing firms will become organized in the same way through the creation of organizational subsystems in the form of departments and the development of a formal organizational structure: integrated, with functional departments or divisions. Empirical research on stage models of the film seems to partially confirm the inevitability of moving finally to the form of mature firms, involving personal and organizational changes. Interestingly, these studies have never taken into account the actual organization structure. It seems that a functional or divisional structure is simply taken for granted. In general, the entrepreneurial literature has largely neglected the impact of the choice of different organization modes on growth.

From the existing research on growth emerge distinct problem areas for enabling and managing growth. The main areas in the literature for enabling growth are increasing reputation in the firm environment; attracting highly qualified people; attracting financial resources; and increasing the number of relationships with customers, suppliers, and all other forms of inter firm relationships. Few theoretical approaches lend themselves to explaining these activities.

For the management of external relationships, empirical research has shown an association among social capital, networking activity, and growth, but we lack any knowledge as to what extent this plays a role in business groups. The main areas for managing growth are linked to coping with increasing size: how to manage an increasing number of employees, how to define roles and responsibilities, and how to coordinate the work; they concern issues of decentralization, formalization, and specialization.

In addition, the current research on stage models poses a growth paradox. Research has shown that firms increase planning, control, and formalized structures as a consequence of growth; that is, they move from an entrepreneurial type of organization to a non-entrepreneurial type of organization. However, other streams of research have shown that ah entrepreneurial management style is associated with firm growth. In this sense, entrepreneurial management would both enable and hinder further growth.

The idea that an analysis of business groups from an entrepreneurial growth perspective needs to take into account factors for enabling, realizing, and managing growth. These three aspects will guide our research. We take a qualitative theory-building approach, as entrepreneurship research has hardly established a link between organization modes and growth. We proceed in the following fashion. First, we analyse the entrepreneurial process of small-business group formation. We identify the reasons for the setting up of new companies over time as well as the establishment of a holding structure. This longitudinal view provides insights into possible development patterns and clarifies whether diversification is the sole reason for setting up business groups.

Then, we analyse in depth the reasons for setting up a small-business group: We try to understand whether and how it enables growth on the one hand and whether and how it facilitates the management of the growing firm on the other hand. A business group is a set of companies under common effective control; that is, the entrepreneurs are directly involved in the strategic decision making. The business group can be considered a firm.

A company is a legal entity mostly in the form of a partnership or limited company. In this sense, a business group is a firm made up of multiple companies. We focus on small-business groups that are relatively young and growing. By adopting the current European definition of small and medium enterprises, small-business groups have less than 250 employees. Our groups are less than 15 years old, growing as an ensemble, and controlled by a dominant entrepreneur reflecting research in entrepreneurship that often considers age, size, and growth as discriminating variables for entrepreneurial firms.

## CASE STUDY RESEARCH AS THE APPROPRIATE RESEARCH METHODOLOGY

The complex phenomenon of entrepreneurial growth and the limitations of the existing research, as well as the need to gain an in-depth understanding of the effects of the business group organizational form on firm development, led us to pursue a qualitative methodology, as recommended by other researchers. Given the exploratory nature of this study and our interest in finding out more about how and why entrepreneurs developed their companies into the organizational form of the small-business group, we decided that a case study design would be most appropriate. Dealing with a contemporary event and exploring a phenomenon that has hardly been studied, this research is inductive and theory building in nature, drawing ceases from cases to the theory. Formal hypotheses were not developed since hypothesis testing is not generally feasible, as there is little from which hypotheses can be developed.

Our objective is to compare and enrich the theoretical approaches through case studies in order to generate new propositions. We present the findings asa dialog between theory and field work, following the example of case material presentation adopted by Maurer and Ebers. We chose three extreme cases. Data were collected through a series of interviews with the CEOs of the companies. We conducted four interviews with each entrepreneur and, in order to obtain a more unbiased picture of the small-business group, also did at least one interview with each partner within the different companies that made up the small-business group. Overall, we conducted 41 interviews.

To enhance validity and reliability, we used triangulation of data sources and data collection: secondary information, company press releases, and other company information. Research faces bias from inevitable human judgments about research design and interpretation. To reduce possible bias, we proceeded in the following way: All interviews were transcribed. While the first author collected the data, the second author made initial evaluations. The first author independently made his evaluation before the evaluations were combined. If the two authors did not share the same opinion, extra data were obtained to avoid divergences in interpretation.

The data were analysed in the following way: We organized themes into emerging categories. We named the categories by moving interactively back and forth between the data and the literature. These categories are realizing, enabling, and managing growth. The main result of our case study is the drawing of ceases from cases to theory; that is, we generalize from data to theory. Therefore, the outcome of our research is the formulation of propositions.

## SHORT DESCRIPTION OF THE THREE CASES

At the outset, the three cases seemed to be very different from each other: a very small international consulting firm versus a small diversified service firm versus a medium-size integrated consumer goods firm. All three groups are organized as holdings.

Group A was founded in 1994; it is a service firm based in Paris with companies owned by the firm located throughout France. In its first year of existence, the firm made about $100,000 in sales and was already profitable in year 1. Since its foundation, the firm has had an average annual growth rate of about 16% in sales and 10% in profits. The growth rates during the last 5 years averaged 18 and 28%, respectively. Sales in 2005 were about 7.15 million, with pretax profits of about 2.2 million.

In the first year, the group had two employees. It had 25 in 2005. The majority of the capital is held by the founding entrepreneur/CEO. In 2005, the firm had eight subsidiaries. Group B was founded in 1995 in southwest France and operates in the food sector. The company produces and commercializes a variety of food products. It had sales of about $200,000 in its first year and reached break-even in its second year of existence.

Its rate of growth has averaged about 25%. During the 5-year period from 2000 to 2005, the group increased its sales from $25 million to $130 million. It currently employs about 250 people in its seven subsidiaries. The founding family holds the majority of the capital. Group C is a consulting firm and was founded in 1997 in southwest France. It specializes in consulting for high-tech industries. At its founding, the company had two employees. In 2005, it had seven subsidiaries and 18 employees who worked directly for the group. Sales in 2005 were about $3.9 million.

## SMALL-BUSINESS GROUPS: REALIZING, MANAGING, ENABLING GROWTH

### THE ENTREPRENEURIAL PROCESS AND REALIZING GROWTH

First, we wanted to understand how the group evolved over time and how this impacted both the organizational configuration and the growth of the firm. As we generally lack understanding of this entrepreneurial process, "it is important to focus attention not only on the latest ventures developed but on the overall pattern of growth, as the ventures successively established are strictly connected".

We use the categories proposed by Iacobucci and Rosa to analyse the entrepreneurial process of small-business groups. They suggest that one distinguish between different activities for realizing growth: market penetration, internationalization as the most important form of geographic diversification, expansion into new market segments within the same sector, diversification understood as the move into new sectors, and, finally, integration of activities of the value chain. While it can be argued that the latter is not necessarily the outcome of a growth strategy, we believe it an important phenomenon of group formation. We extend these categories by adding a category that emerged from the case studies: the separation of activities performed within one unit.

Group Emergence and Development Into a Holding Company. Business group formation was the result of the emergence of new opportunities. All cases are characterized by humble beginnings and, most interestingly, by the fact that-without exception-sooner or later, the initial activity was abandoned. The entrepreneurs diversified into new fields before knowing what would become the core activity of the business.

The group was not planned but emerged over time. Group A, founded by its current CEO, started as a general advertising and communication agency. The firm subsequently moved into the field of sports sponsoring and, finally, into the area of career management for athletes, focusing almost exclusively on the French market. The firm became the main competitor in France to the global market leader in this sector. The company as it is today was born out of a merger in 1997. The merger of activities, however, led to an image problem and a conflict of interest: "Clients were asking me: Who are you working for? For the athletes who are looking for a sponsor or the firms which want to sponsor a testimonial?" So the activities were separated again, and a holding structure was established. Another important factor in the separation of the activities was the competences of the CEO's main partner. While the original founder had competences in both activities, the partner only had competences in one. Group B is a small-business family group with most of the family members working in the group. When the company started in 1995, it commercialized only one type of product to large supermarket chains. This activity was later abandoned. The diversification into a different product category led to the creation of the second company.

Group C was founded by the present CEO in 1997. The firm started as a communication agency for high-tech firms in southern France. Having gained a sufficient client portfolio, Group C diversified into the field of public relations in 1998. Finally, the group entered the field of lobbying, which was considered close to the PR business. The CEO of Group C was at the time convinced that he could successfully bring in his personal networks. When the lobbying activities became more sizeable than the communication unit, the CEO entered the consulting business. The company, therefore, specialized in consulting services for a particular high-tech industry in the region. In 1999, Group C already comprised four companies that stood for the four activities of the firm. When the consulting business became the major activity, the consulting company was transformed into the central company of this small-firm holding in 2000.

## UNPLANNED EMERGENCE OF THE GROUP

- *Case A*: "I was faced with two problems: how to manage diverse clients and how to deal with the competences of my-cofounder. Finally, we ended up with a group of companies."

- *Case B*: "At the beginning we developed without any specific reason into a group structure; only later did we realise the benefits of this structure."
- *Case C*: "We were moving from activity to activity. When we launched the consulting business, we felt this was what we should be and that we needed to organize the activities."

The establishment of a legal holding structure in France can be partly explained by certain favourable economic conditions, but—at least in our cases—reasons of sense making were more important than the specific French context. There is a general feeling for defining the centre of activities, to give guidance to all partners and employees of the firm as well as to outside parties such as clients and suppliers. The entrepreneurs became aware of the group when external events forced them to think about organizational issues. While the first three ventures correspond to accumulating new activities, the creation of the holding, which took place through the creation of the fourth company for case B and the fifth for cases A and C, was somehow linked to the subsequent separation of activities into different companies, activities that were performed within the same company.

## THE CREATION OF THE HOLDING

- *Case A*: "With diversified activities, we wanted a reference point internally and for our customers. The holding was born."
- *Case B*: "With three or four companies under ownership, you feel the need to officially define a centre."
- *Case C*: "I had the vision to build a portfolio of strong sub-brands in consulting under the heading of our main brand that was the holding company."

It seems that the existence of a central company, seen as a reference point not only for third parties but also for the entrepreneur, gives some sense of stability to an otherwise fluid configuration of companies. We can conclude that nobody started out to form a group and that the emergence of the group was initially unplanned. The setting up of a holding involves different issues: fiscal and legal reasons and ease of separating activities as well as issues of sense-making internally and signaling effects externally.

The holding structure follows the initial formation of a business group once the core business of the group had been defined. The establishment of a holding structure leads to a tightly coupled group of companies favouring strategic control. The holding is the legal form of the organization; in this sense, not all business groups need to be holdings, but all our case firms adopted over time the legal form of a holding as it happened to be often the case in France.

## GROUP DEVELOPMENT OVER TIME

Over the years, the founder of Group A had developed a vision that consisted of developing new activities, becoming a majority shareholder in these new companies, helping others to develop the activity further, and developing partnerships. The entrepreneur believes that the number of companies within the group will grow as new diversification opportunities appear. Once a new activity develops good potential, it is spun off. "Cycling will be the next spin-off, we are simply waiting for the right moment".

Firm B's rapid development is directly associated with the development of the group's structure. For the first 5 years, the firm only commercialized food products. That is, the activities were limited to the packaging and branding of food products; there were no production units. In the mid-1990s, the firm had to make a decision when problems arose with its main supplier, which was located in northern France.

The management thought that changing to another supplier would be difficult and would not change the situation in the long run. Asa consequence, the firm developed into a holding company. The commercialization of one of the side products was spun out into a 100% subsidiary, and the production of the main product line was integrated into a newly founded company. "We started with a very small production line: at the beginning, we produced only one product type while buying the rest from our main supplier, then we added another product type, another product, and finally phased out the relationship with our supplier."

Shortly afterward, the firm abandoned its original founding product line by closing down the marketing company and by transferring the employees into other companies of the firm. In 1998, the firm added another major product line by creating a dedicated marketing and production company. In 2003, the firm, which had been concentrating its sales efforts on France, created a marketing company for international sales. In 2004, another product line was added, targeting a new market segment. A dedicated marketing company was created, while the production has been initially outsourced. In 2005, the firm consisted of the holding company, four marketing companies, and two production companies.

The logic of the group's organization is based on the horizontal and vertical configurations of the firm. Each product category gives rise to a category of companies: each activity within the value chain leads to the creation of a separate company. Therefore, for product category X, there is a marketing company XI and a production company. The CEO is convinced that tensions between the companies specializing in one activity are not greater than in a single firm: "There are natural tensions between different functions and product lines. This situation would not change in a single firm but capital allocation would be much more difficult to handle."

Once Group C had defined its core activities, it started to internationalize. In 1999, it created its first fully owned subsidiary in Germany. In 2002, another industry considered close to the initial industry was added to the consulting portfolio. Subsidiaries were created in Japan and Canada in 2003, followed by Spain in 2004 and Italy in 2005. The British subsidiary, which had been created in 2002 was closed down in 2004, and the Italian one at the end of 2005. In 2C05, Group C had only 18 direct employees but consisted of seven companies: a central holding company, plus one company for each activity, and one company for each country. In the same year, the CEO sold 30% of his shares to a large global consulting firm. This strategic alliance allowed the group to offer its clients reinsurance services as well as consulting services.

"When we started something new, we created a new legal entity. We have a sort of a strange matrix organizational form. The managing director for Spain, for example, is a senior consultant in the consulting company." One of the perceived advantages of this structure is the great ease with which it is possible to enter and exit activities without risking the survival of other activities. Once activities had developed a sufficient sales volume or a sufficient client base, the group diversified into new fields.

The new activities were financed separately and did not hurt the ongoing activities in other fields. Additionally, a side aspect of separating activities into different companies was performance control measures. "You do not expect immediate results from a new firm. Therefore, the performance criteria are different. Sometimes within units, there are little incentives to add new activities because they will hurt the unit's results over the short term." Third, as a consequence, motivation to enter into new activities is supposed to be higher in a new company than within an existing company.

## THE GROWTH DRIVERS

The question of where the growth comes from in business groups is an important one. In our cases, we see two common patterns: first, a trial-and-error process in which the entrepreneurs jump onto different activities until they find one or two core activities; these core activities allow for significant growth through further market penetration.

The two main businesses of Group A are responsible for 70% of sales. Group B's main marketing activity captures 70% of sales. Group C's initial consulting business accounts still for about 50% of sales. The groups realised substantial growth through their core businesses, which are still contributing in absolute terms to the overall growth of the firm. However, the most recent diversification or new market segment activities are those that show the highest relative growth rates and are perceived as the future growth drivers of the firm. At the current stage, growth is driven both by growth in the core business and the creation of new businesses.

In all cases, diversification of the activities can be characterized as related diversification. This finding contrasts hypotheses about large-business groups where the group is understood as a result of unrelated diversification and confirms findings about small-business groups, suggesting that the logic of these two types are different. The small-business group develops around certain core competences: These core competences are the basis for related diversification but also limit the effective control of companies in the periphery of the group, if those companies have important new competences relative to the existing ones within the group. As the CEO of Group A explained: "When the resources and competences that the rest of the group can contribute to a particular company are minimal, we need to think about spinning out the activity. It's a flexible structure."

The group also facilitates the divestment of activities, which increases the flexibility of the company and reduces risk. "When you are small, and your brand declines, for whatever reason, the firm is dead. Having different companies and different brands, lowers our mortality risk. 'Different' also means 'different identities.'" The history of the groups shows strong dynamics in which change happens frequently. Change involves not only the creation of new companies but also the closing down and spinning off of existing companies.

Complementary to existing empirical research, the small-business group is the outcome not only of diversification but also of separation and integration of activities. In particular, the separation of activities seems to be very important in structuring the business group around a holding company. This result needs further investigation since, once again, the main question emerges: "Why do entrepreneurs prefer to run a group of companies rather than organizing them within the same legal boundaries?" While this question is already puzzling for the case of related diversification, it is still more puzzling for activities that have been handled within one unit and that subsequently were separated into different companies. Overall, the group facilitates the diversification and integration of activities without having to change the organization of the existing structure.

## MANAGING GROWTH

Stage models, the first crisis the entrepreneur has to face is a management crisis if the firm wants to grow and prosper. This means that entrepreneurial firms need to abandon the entrepreneurial management style, which is to be perceived as different from the management style of established companies. The way a company is managed influences the way work is performed.

One of the key differences between entrepreneurial management style and established firm management is that entrepreneurial management is driven by opportunities and not by the resources currently controlled, by flar organizational structures, by informal planning systems, by loose job descriptions, by little formalization, by uncertain reward systems, by unsophisticated control systems, and by multitasking employees who ate not particularly specialized in a specific area. Employees in small firms have a certain versatility because they must be able to handle very different tasks. Our cases have not been subject to transition crises. The impression emerges from our cases that the group structure helps to delay transitions and to prolong the maintenance of an entrepreneurial management style.

The small-business group seems to be a means of replicating a known structure and, therefore, a means of facilitating the management of the growing firm, which helps to overcome the problem of managing a larger structure without having to formalize and specify the tasks. The case entrepreneurs who were unfamiliar with managing larger structures prefer to replicate known structures to pursue both diversification and integration strategies.

## Management Style

- *Case A*: "The whole structure can be managed like a start-up and the structure is very transparent. There is clear direction within the firm: one company—one project."
- "Personally, we prefer to head a few companies and not one large unit."
- *Case B*: *"I am an entrepreneur. I had been working for two years in a large firm before starting my first firm. I do not like working in large firms."*
- *"From my first venture, I learned how to manage a small firm. I feel more comfortable managing eight small companies instead of one larger company."*
- *Case C*: *"When I talk about company x with an employee, we talk about their consulting activities, when we talk about company y, we talk about their business development activities. I think it is more transparent than if I had to handle this within one company."*

The group structure facilitates management and control of the firm. Lack of management and industry experience can be overcome by the organization structure. The entrepreneurs can replicate a structure that they know how to manage. Their role is not in question, and they are hardly subject to change, contrary to the assumptions of entrepreneurial growth models. The small-business group seems to be the small firm's alternative to the large firms' divisional structure.

Another factor linked to the replication of known structures is competence building. The small-business group allows for the specialization of individual companies, especially through the competences of the respective CEOs or cofounders. It facilitates the development of broad competences in its employees, in contrast to the specialization promoted by the task division of large firms.

In this sense, the firms remain more entrepreneurial, less formalized, less centralized, etc. The small-business group allows the entrepreneur to keep their entrepreneurial management style without sacrificing the growth of the firm. The firms will, therefore, differ in their management system.

*Proposition* 1a: Small-business groups are associated with high degrees of decentralization, low degrees of formalization with little precise job descriptions.

*Proposition* 1b: Low management or industry experience is positively associated with business group formation.

## ENABLING GROWTH

### Reputation

Entrepreneurial firms are characterized by liability of newness and smallness. One form these liabilities take is the lack of credibility and legitimacy and the uncertainty of third parties about the quality of products and services, which we can summarize as lack of reputation. Larson, reputation is a precondition for economic exchange.

Reputation leads to social and economic trust in capabilities. Increased reputation should facilitate access to other stakeholders, such as suppliers and clients who are willing to engage with the young firm, since the perceived risk of an exchange relationship is lower. Gaining reputation is an effective means of overcoming liability of newness and increasing firm performance.

Research has shown that certain forms of endorsement have positive effects on venture development. In addition, it has been suggested that mimicry, acting as if a company were bigger or older than it in fact is, could be a means to overcome problems linked to missing reputation.

### Reputation

- *Case A*: "Being the head of a division in a company with a small number of people is not very credible. And furthermore, to manage everyone together in one entity would lead to confusion."
- *Case B*: "Distribution channels think that we are bigger than we are: for them, we are a house of brands with different companies for each brand."
- *Case C*: "When you have a holding company with a specialized company for a particular service, people

> think that you are a real champion in the field and they do not immediately ask how many people ate working in the firm. If we had only one company offering different services, people would think that we were not capable of delivering these services."

The existence of a group structure seems to signal reputation. The group structure gives an impression of bigger size, specialized competences, and stability. Clients and suppliers seem to have greater trust in a small firm that is composed of many companies instead of only one.

The group appears as a sort of second-best alternative for reputation, which is effectively gained through relationships with clients and suppliers. The group structure seems to influence the perception of clients and suppliers. The signaling effects should positively influence firm development. In this sense, the mimicry effect should be even stronger for very small firms.

*Proposition* 2a: Small-business groups will have positive signaling effects on reputation thus positively influencing firm growth.

*Proposition* 2b: The smaller the size of the group, the greater the signaling effect of group structure on reputation.

## Attraction of Firm Resources

Entrepreneurship is also understood as seizing opportunities independent of the resources currently controlled. This understanding of entrepreneurship implies that the entrepreneur does not yet control all the resources necessary to run, maintain, and develop the business. We make a distinction between the acquisition of resources and the attraction of resources. Acquisition of resources means that an entrepreneur can exchange existing resources for other resources; attraction of resources means that entrepreneurs can control resources without having to acquire any.

It has been argued that the difference between large-firm management and entrepreneurship is the capacity to attract resources rather than acquire them. Attraction of financial, human, and other productive resources is seen as a primary factor for enabling growth. In our case studies, the small-business group facilitated, through the creation of new companies, the attraction of complementary competences via the hiring of specialists and the attraction of financial resources.

## ATTRACTION AND CONTROL OF RESOURCES

- Case A: "When I had an idea but not all the competences, I was looking for partners inside or outside the firm to develop the activity. So I decided to give them the activity upfront, invest in the company and take a stake in it."

"You cannot compete with X, the largest global competitor, in terms of attracting top talent, even if we have a strong position in France. You only can attract top people if you give them real responsibility, a stake in the project, and a buy-out option for the future."

- *Case B*: "We partially financed production through the holding company and partially through banks. Bankers like the concept, one activity, one company, dedicated results.

And finally, you add another money stream and can partially guarantee the sales for the new firm. It is much more difficult to attract financing for the development of a single company."

- Case C: "It's better to be managing director and a major shareholder of C-Japan than being an employee of a large consulting firm."

"Consulting is our basic business for which employees receive a salary; business development is a result-based activity."

Entrepreneurial firms cannot compete using the same means as large firms; they have to offer a different package to attract resources. To be the managing director with a significant stake in a company, to participate directly in its development, and to be one's own boss can be a worthwhile package. The creation of a new company makes hiring top talent possible, which is an attraction of superior human capital. Third-party equity resources, other financial resources and superior human resources enable firms to diversify or to integrate activities. The small-business group and the creation of new companies are considered a means to attract complementary competences by hiring specialists.

While some research investigated reasons for entry and exit of the initial founder team and showed that increasing task diversity after the start-up phase was linked to member entry, we show how the creation of new companies within the small-business group kept the initial founder team unchanged and effectively enabled the attraction of new, key personnel and facilitated financing. In this sense, business group development can be seen as a process of resource allocation, as argued by Rosa, as well as a process of resource attraction leading to entrepreneurial opportunities.

The organizational form facilitates the exploitation of entrepreneurial opportunities and addresses problems associated with resource attraction. It seems that the business group facilitates the access to exterual financing as well as the attraction of diverse resources.

*Proposition* 3: Small-business group organization has a positive influence on the attraction of resources in terms of time, scale, and scope.

## Management of External Relationships

Engaging and managing relations with other people, groups, or entities are based on social capital, i.e., on the capacity of people to connect. "Social capital is the sum of the resources, actual or virtual, that accrue to an individual or group by virtue of possessing a durable network of more or less institutionalized relationships of mutual acquaintance and recognition". For many entrepreneurial research questions, it is interesting to understand the ability of a person of a firm to manage external relations. Firms are constrained by their relational capability, i.e., the capability to establish, maintain, and develop relationships. Two areas of investigation emerged from our case studies: network overembeddedness and managing relationships with competitors.

## Embeddedness

The theory of structural embeddedness considers network structure and a firm's network position as both opportunities and constraints. Favourable positions are regarded as network resources; over-embeddedness, however, can lead to inability to act. Social overembeddedness can, at a certain point, become a development barrier for firms. Often, young companies have to offer customised products for clients in order to win first contracts, which can lead to almost exclusive relationships.

The literature has proposed various models to deal with overembeddedness and the limits of relational capability. One is network restructuring, i.e., the cutting of redundant ties and the adding of new nonredundant ones, leading to a network in which the core is stable but, as a whole, evolves. Another model is network hierarchy, i.e., the structuring of networks into different layers, thereby reducing the direct relationships a firm has to deal with.

A third model is the integration of activities: Once firms organized as networks have reached a medium size, they tend to hire over-proportionally and increasingly integrate activities performed externally. These are the three established models. In our cases emerged a fourth alternative model: the small-business group that facilitates relationship building through setting up new companies.

## Overembeddedness

- *Case A*: "We work for C and manage their sponsoring programme but we are also the manager of P. Now the folks at C will tell us that they will not work with us because we also manage P. By having different companies with different CEOs, we could convince them that this is another business, another company, with different people responsible for managing the business and the relationships."
- *Case B*: "It was clear to us that we had to integrate production activities: we created the production company. Our main supplier had already begun to sell us lower quality while he sold a superior quality

to our clients in the south in order to take over our market share."

"Private labeling is a similar issue: we produce for the same clients their private labels and sell them our brand."

"The relationship would be almost impossible to handle within a single company. It reduces tensions between units."

- Case C: "We created the Italian consulting company, mainly because one of our Spanish clients did not want us to work with a particular company in Italy. I did consider the Italian market attractive, but the impetus for setting up the company came from the problems we experienced in handling a particular client."

The small-business group can be understood as a strategic network with multiple centres that can engage independently in interfirm relations. Old relationships sometimes hinder the formation of new ones. People will not work with the firm because the firm works with certain other companies.

Dividing up the firm into separate companies by creating a small-business group thus enables the firm to address this problem and thereby to position itself to create new relationships. By adding new companies to the firm, the small-business group overcomes overembeddedness, and, by hiring top talent as CEOs for the new company, the firm can acquire superior human resources and additional social capital that extends the relational capability of the firm. In this sense, it is the separation of activities that facilitates the management of external relationships—a key issue for growing firms. The group structure is therefore partially an outcome of external pressure.

*Proposition* 4: Small-business group organization has a positive influence on the development of new relationships and, therefore, for the building of interfirm networks.

## Co-opetition

Co-opetition is a situation in which a company has at the same time both cooperative and competitive relationships with another company. The management literature generally considers industries to be collections of firms bound together by rivalry, therefore questioning the value of relationships with competitors.

However, it has been shown that co-opetiton is a common phenomenon both for large and small firms even if the management of these complex relationships has only been studied for large companies.

*Co-opetition*:

- *Case A*: "At the moment, we cooperate in the cycling business with a big group who is our competitor in the football business. Without separate companies, we could not deal with this kind of situation."
- *Case B*: "Occasionally, we produce some special lines for competitors. If we had integrated all activities into one firm, it would not work. Our sales team would really lose their motivation."
- *Case C*: "We have partners in the space sector who ate competitors in aeronautics. Separation helps."

Two of the main strategies employed by large firms to deal with co-opetition are dissolution and decentralization. Dissolution of the relationship means avoiding co-opetition. Decentralization of the management means that each division treats its relationships independently.

The cases suggest that divisionalization is not an option for small firms but that the group structure and the existence of different companies are an effective means of handling situations of co-opetition. The cases also suggest that co-opetition is seen by the firms as a necessity. In Case A, co-opetition seems to help overcome size or competence constraints; in Case B, to stabilize sales by occasionally producing for other firms as well as gaining entry into distribution channels.

In Case C, it is a means to increase the number of clients. Overall, relationships with competitors can give access to temporarily needed resources or lead to the temporary pooling of resources; this should positively influence firm performance, especially in the years after foundation, when sales tend to grow discontinuously. Entrepreneurial firms that view competitors not only as pure rivals but also as a potential resource should therefore be more successful. However, the major problem of how to manage these relationships has not been addressed in the current literature. The creation of new companies and the separation of activities seem to be an effective means to deal with co-opetition. Similarly, we can also argue that the group structure is partially a result of co-opetition.

*Proposition* 5: Co-opetition is positively associated with small-business group formation.

## LIMITS OF THE SMALL-BUSINESS GROUP MODEL

An interesting phenomenon concerns the activities within the small-business group that the firm decides to spin out. Why do entrepreneurs spin out companies? Entrepreneur A explained the decision between taking a majority stake in the new company and linking it to the test of the group or simply spinning out the activity by maintaining a minority stake in the following way: The most desirable process is to bring in a partner who will become the CEO of the new company and then to develop the new activity.

The entrepreneur and/or the holding company takes a majority stake in this new company and finances the development activities; this is especially the case if important competences ate held by the existing structure and if the activity is close to the core businesses. A second possibility is that the firm develops an activity and takes a significant stake in the company, while the partner brings in new and decisive competences.

A last possibility is that the firm takes only a minority stake, but the partner, who benefits from the image and infrastructure of the holding company, has chief responsibility for developing the activity. Therefore, if the competences of a specific company happen to become more important than the core competences of the group, the management of the group might have to reconsider the legal and financial relationships. One of the main advantages of the group, i.e., the capacity to attract considerable complementary resources, might actually decrease the control function of the group since the CEOs in the companies could, in time, acquire sufficient experience, competences, and reputation and financial resources to be able to start a company on their own, outside the group, especially if the corporate added value is considered negligible. In this case, the financial relationships might not be sufficient to maintain and control the whole group structure.

Unlike in large corporations, it would seem that the control potential of the small-business group depends on financial relationships on the one hand and on the division of competences within the group on the other hand, or more specifically between the competences of one individual company and the rest of the group, i.e., on the value added of other parts of the group to a specific company within the group.

Effective control of the companies forming the small-business group is, therefore, also a function of the ability to make a relevant contribution to the companies. Limited competences within the group will lead—in the case of a further increase of activities within the small-business group—to an externalization of activities and the transition from a pure small-business group towards a network model of organization.

We could consider the small-business group as an elastic organizational form, a loosely coupled system. The small-business group might be characterized as a process of constitution and reconstitution around certain core businesses through the entry and exit of activities. The small-business group seems to constitute an organizational and strategic paradox, insofar as it is a possible growth strategy for an entrepreneurial firm through structural replication and through a process of resource attraction, but, at the same time, it leads almost naturally to a mechanism that limits its replication, i.e., the number of its subsidiaries.

The empirical evidence of the small-business group in developed countries opens a new field for analyzing growth strategies and the structural development of entrepreneurial firms. Our research question was "why does the small-business group exist?" in developed countries. Given that the theories used to explain large-business groups in emerging and transitional economies were ill suited to answer this question, we took an entrepreneurial perspective. The small-business group helps to realise, enable, and manage growth. It seems that the organizational form plays an important role in the exploitation of new opportunities through the attraction of superior complementary resources. Entrepreneurship research has highlighted the importance of identifying and acquiring resources at the early stage of a company's life. We found that the small-business group is able to call upon and mobilize resources, especially superior human and social resources, without having to acquire them or without having to possess them right from the beginning.

Entrepreneurship is about growth, and our case studies are growing firms with an organizational model that facilitates realizing, enabling, and managing growth. Where does the entrepreneurial behaviour come from? In our cases, there was a dominant entrepreneur that used the benefits of the business group structure not only to seize new opportunities for growth but also to grow the existing activities. We cannot answer the question of whether the business group form is particularly suited to the growth intentions of individual or dominant entrepreneurs, since we did not have a case with a founding team.

We could also consider that the partners brought in the newly formed companies as entrepreneurs, but this consideration would be beyond the scope of this associate, even if our cases strongly suggest that the small-business group promotes an entrepreneurial orientation throughout the firm. Entrepreneurs are obsessed with opportunities, and our cases suggest that they create new companies because they see new opportunities.

These new opportunities are linked to their existing competences and those developed in companies, but the emergence of the group structure is unplanned. Only after the creation of several companies did the entrepreneurs try to make sense of what they had carried out, which, in our cases, led to the creation of a holding structure. Other companies emerge because of the necessity to separate activities. Over time, entrepreneurs started to use the business group structure consciously as a tool to enable, realise, and manage growth. While it has been argued that the small-business group is a model for diversification strategies, we found that it is an effective structure for implementing the vertical and horizontal configuration of the firm.

The small-business group is a means for diversification, integration, and separation of activities. The small-business group seems at least to delay, if not avoid, the typical management crises that entrepreneurs face as outlined in the stage development models of entrepreneurial firms. By replicating known structures, entrepreneurs are able to manage a larger aggregated structure without having to radically change their management style.

In this sense, the organizational structure partially compensates for lack of management and/or industry experience and helps to at least temporarily delay growth transitions, maintaining an entrepreneurial management style. The cases suggest that the small-business group as an organizational form is a means of overcoming over embeddedness and dealing with co-opetition.

This is a very interesting finding since it means that the organizational form helps to overcome growth barriers, in our cases, the ability to develop new relationships with other firms or clients. The small-business group, however, poses an important question: Does it, at some point, limit the development of the firm? Our cases seem to suggest that the small-business group evolves around certain core competences and spin-out activities.

Therefore, the firm periodically reduces the scope of its current activities while adding new ones subsequently, leading to continuous entrepreneurship and evolution towards a network model. In this sense, the small-business group is a truly competence-driven firm model that stimulates entrepreneurship through the exploitation of new opportunities within the group of within the evolving network. The relationships between the different companies, i.e., the structure of the small-business group, should be analysed in a dynamic perspective rather than a static one.

The case studies suggest that entrepreneurs have a limited capacity to control the periphery of the group. The development of the group depends heavily on the development of the individual companies: The potential for action on the periphery of the group is dependent on the strengthening of the competences of the core.

The latter might pose definitional problems: To what extend do we need to take into account the spin-out businesses that were once controlled financially and effectively by a dominant entrepreneur but that still might benefit from the small-business group in terms of reputation, possible utilization of brand names, and other group resources?

In this associate, we have developed a series of unique propositions that should stimulate further research. Our study, of course, has its limits. It is based on only a few cases, and the main goal is to extend existing theory. We need more in-depth case studies on the development of the small-business group as well as quantitative and hypothesis-testing research endeavors.

A replication of our study in other settings would be very useful for advancing theory. While there are no particular incentives, e.g., from a legal or tax point of view, to set up such an organizational form in France, in other countries, the specific context might favour this particular organizational form. Lazerson found, for example, that the frequent occurrence of the network model in Italy was favoured by legal and tax incentives that limited the size of the firm in terms of number of direct employees.

In these cases, it would be interesting to see if the propositions we developed apply. Many questions for future research arise: Does the organizational form actually limit the size of the firm? Does structural instability finally mark the difference between entrepreneurial and established firms' development? What competences are most appropriate for preventing the departure of individual companies towards the periphery? We also believe that the linkage to the resource and dynamic capabilities debates needs to be explored further. What resource hurdles do holding companies have to address? What learning is required and exhibited?

What is the linkage between resources/capabilities and opportunity recognition, pursuit, and exploitation? The main impulses for further research arising out of our study would be to consider the outcome of habitual entrepreneurship and to direct more attention to an organizational perspective.

# 8

# Interpersonal Skill

One of the primary means to promote effective interpersonal relations in the workplace is through formal classroom training. Despite widespread investments in interpersonal skills training, however, the desired impact may not be realised.

Some researchers have questioned whether trainees fully develop interpersonal skill proficiency during formal training and whether trainees successfully apply, or transfer, these skills on the job. It has been argued that formal classroom training produces individuals who are only able to perform crude and forced imitations of target behaviours. Further, meta-analytic evidence suggests that the posttraining impact of interpersonal skills training is modest.

A potentially viable means of increasing the impact of interpersonal skills training is through supplements beyond the formal classroom environment. Fundamentally, training effectiveness is grounded in the proper design of the formal learning experience. However, researchers have argued that training should not be an isolated classroom activity if the benefits of training are to be fully realised. Pretraining supplements may motivate and prepare individuals for learning within the classroom, whereas posttraining supplements may motivate transfer and promote further skill development.

This study extends research on training interventions beyond the classroom by examining the impact of posttraining supplements in the context of interpersonal skill development. Building on a corporate training programme focused on developing the supervisory skills of newly hired managers from multiple units of a national restaurant chain, this study examined the effectiveness of two supplements. One supplement was a self-coaching programme, and a second was upward feedback. Both were designed to reinforce training content, provide relevant performance feedback, and direct skill application and further development when the trainee managers returned to the field.

## PRIOR RESEARCH ON POSTTRAINING SUPPLEMENTS

Two general types of posttraining supplements have often been examined in research. One is goal-setting supplements that aim to promote transfer by focusing trainees on the implementation of training content. The rationale for utilizing such supplements is that competing demands and interests inhibit transfer, and thus, mechanisms are necessary to direct skill application.

Goal-setting supplements have addressed the importance of transfer, characteristics of effective goals, and specific implementation priorities. Some goal-setting supplements have been implemented within the classroom, whereas others have involved meetings with trainers or supervisors after training has been complemented. On the whole, goal-setting supplements have been found to have a favourable impact on transfer beyond the effects of classroom training only. Self-management training is a second commonly researched supplement to promote transfer. This training is related to goal-setting with a focus on the implementation of training content. However, self-management training specifically aims to equip individuals with skills to overcome obstacles to transfer.

Proponents of self-management training assume that trainees will encounter obstacles on the job, such as time pressure or lack of social support, and then relapse into patterns of behaviour. This training is implemented within the classroom, and it typically focuses on identifying obstacles to transfer, establishing performance maintenance goals, identifying strategies to overcome obstacles, monitoring progress towards goal attainment, and self-administering rewards and punishments. Support for this posttraining supplement has been mixed. Although some research has demonstrated a posttraining impact for self-management training in comparison to classroom training only, other studies have not.

Despite the degree of support for the supplements examined, examination of alternatives is warranted. In one respect, research is necessary to examine supplements that address not only the implementation of training content but also further skill development, as interpersonal skills are not necessarily fully developed within the formal classroom. In another respect, research is warranted to examine additional supplements appropriate for individuals who work largely autonomously and where structured guidance from others is not administratively feasible.

Yelon and Ford have argued that a key consideration in designing transfer supports is the degree of trainee autonomy on the job. Even though the benefits for posttraining goal setting supplements have been demonstrated, these activities usually involved the active participation of trainers and/or supervisors to facilitate goal setting. Self-management training could be appropriate for autonomous trainees, but this type of supplement has not always been effective.

Selfmanagement training may place too much emphasis on trainee control in the work environment, whereas more structured on-the-job supplements could have a stronger impact on transfer.

## SELF-COACHING AND UPWARD FEEDBACK

The effectiveness of two on-the-job posttraining supplements to enhance the impact of interpersonal skills training are examined in this study, specifically training focused on supervisory skills for new managers. One supplement is a self-coaching programme that is a new supplement that has not been examined in prior research. The second is upward feedback, which has been studied in research as a means to enhance interpersonal skills but not as a posttraining supplement directly linked to formal training content.

## Self-coaching

The self-coaching programme is an autonomously managed supplement in which trainees reflect on their performance and establish transfer enhancement goals for several weeks upon completion of training. The programme comprises three components. The first is an assessment in which trainees examine the extent to which they engaged in desired behaviours addressed in training through a standardized checklist.

For example, trainees reflect on how often they established clear and specific goals for subordinates, praised performance improvements, and worked with subordinates to develop performance improvement strategies. In turn, the second component is an assessment in which trainees reflect on specific interpersonal incidents by answering open-ended questions.

These open-ended questions are included to facilitate deeper-level processing. The final component is a goal-setting module, in which trainees establish performance maintenance and performance improvement goals to translate trainee insight into successful future performance. In sum, the self-coaching programme represents a regular self-appraisal linked to on-the-job performance expectations addressed in training. The medium for the self-coaching programme is a workbook with written assessments and exercises to facilitate the self-reflective and goalsetting efforts.

This instructional medium may be effective for several reasons. First, written analysis helps individuals to distance themselves from their daily routines and focus on personal growth and development. Second, the animation of writing helps individuals become more conscious of their strengths and areas for improvement. Third, written documentation allows individuals to monitor their progress over time. Although individuals may engage in activities to facilitate performance improvement informally, a workbook provides structure for doing so. The self-coaching programme is distinct from researched supplements. Compared to goal-setting supplements, the programme differs with its focus on autonomy and corresponding emphasis on self-reflection to facilitate independent goal-setting.

The programme is thus well suited for autonomous employees. Compared to self-management training, the self-coaching programme differs in two aspects. First, the self-coaching programme is implemented on the job, whereas self-management training occurs within the classroom. The self-coaching programme could provide greater control over post-training behaviour.

Second, the self-coaching programme is broader with an emphasis on performance assessment, identification of strengths and weaknesses, and the development of performance improvement goals; whereas self-management training is focused on overcoming obstacles to transfer. Consequently, the self-coaching programme is thought to be a more effective means to promote further development and successful transfer.

The second supplement examined is upward feedback, a variant of multi-source feedback, in which individuals receive feedback from subordinates. Multisource feedback has been widely used to enhance interpersonal skills, and a number of studies have examined the effectiveness of multisource feedback in facilitating a variety of performance outcomes. Smither and colleagues' meta-analysis found that multisource feedback facilitated improvement on such outcomes as behavioural change, objective performance measures, and subordinate attitudes.

The largest, although modest, effect sizes were found for the impact of upward and supervisor feedback. The corrected mean effect sizes were.15 for both forms of feedback. The corrected mean effect sizes for peer and self-ratings were.05 and -.04, respectively. Two arguments support the use of multisource feedback systems. One, different raters and raters beyond an employee's supervisor, the traditional rater in the appraisal process, have valid insights into an individual's performance. Two, a formal system, in which raters provide written feedback under conditions of anonymity, facilitates the sharing of information that might not otherwise be communicated.

Given that interpersonal feedback may be perceived as "personal," individuals may not share this feedback informally. Further, in the context of supervisorsubordinate interactions, subordinates may be less likely to provide feedback due to the legitimate authority and reward power supervisors possess. Structured assessments, though, provide a medium for feedback to be provided, and providing feedback anonymously allows information to be shared with less fear of negative repercussions.

Multisource feedback has typically been used and researched as a stand-alone development tool. A notable exception was the work of Seifert, Yukl, and McDonald, where the impact of formal training after receiving multisource feedback was examined. This training focused on the interpretation of feedback reports, discussion of key behaviours, presentation of video models, and exercises to practice key behaviours.

In contrast to individuals who received no formal training and no feedback and those who only received a feedback report, individuals who received formal training after feedback exhibited significant positive behavioural change. Although this work suggested that multisource feedback coupled with formal learning was superior to multisource feedback only, research is needed to examine whether formal training coupled with multisource feedback has a favourable impact on performance outcomes beyond formal training alone. This study aims to answer this question. A key consideration in rater selection in multisource feedback systems is a potential rater's opportunity to observe a ratee's performance on focal dimensions.

Given that the formal training in this study focuses on supervisors' interpersonal skills directed towards subordinates, subordinates are the primary raters. Hence, the multisource feedback system examined herein is an upward feedback system. The upward feedback supplement examined herein involves three primary components. First, the trainees are provided with data regarding the frequency in which they engaged in behaviours addressed during training. Second, they are provided with written comments from subordinates on their performance.

Third, and parallel to the self-coaching programme, trainees are directed to establish performance maintenance and performance enhancement goals to translate insight gained from the feedback received into future performance.

## Operating Mechanisms

The self-coaching and upward feedback supplements may facilitate post training interpersonal skill performance in several respects. On a general level, post training supplements may serve as an organizational signal to denote the importance of transfer and thus motivate the application of training content. Rouiller and Goldstein highlighted the importance of trainees' perceptions of cues in the work environment to promote transfer.

In an interpersonal context, supplemental cues are important as such performance may not be "hard coded" into individuals' work and may be perceived as discretionary. In the absence of such cues, individuals may neglect interpersonal responsibilities and focus on what is perceived to be more central aspects of their work.

The posttraining supplements are also argued to enhance the impact of interpersonal skills training by reinforcing content addressed in the formal classroom. Research has highlighted that knowledge and skill decay may occur over time, suggesting the need for "refresher" training. Reflecting on performance expectations via self-coaching and upward feedback serves as a form of refresher training and could thus favourably impact posttraining performance.

The self-coaching and upward feedback supplements are also believed to promote further skill development in a natural learning environment. Practice opportunities within the classroom, such as role-playing exercises, are limited in promoting full skill acquisition because trainees are not confronted with the same pressures and consequences for their actions that they face on the job. As such, trainees may not always perceive these exercises as serious learning endeavors, or they may not experience the difficulties and complexities that might otherwise impact their performance. In either case, trainees might not perform as they otherwise would in a natural context and receive meaningful developmental feedback. However, posttraining supplements provide opportunities to develop focal skills more completely by adding realism to the learning experience.

Given that successful interpersonal performance requires adaptive expertise, or skill in adapting one's performance to novel situations, the challenge of achieving proficiency in the classroom is compounded. There is often no exact standardized approach to manage interpersonal interactions. In many situations, individuals must adapt their behaviour based on different situational demands and choose from a variety of alternatives.

For example, there are a number of ways to manage the performance of a substandard employee. The approach one adopts could be contingent upon the severity of the problem, the frequency with which the problem has occurred, and characteristics of the employee. Achieving interpersonal skill proficiency may require trial and error over time as individuals learn to adapt general principles from the classroom to specific applied contexts.

With respect to self-regulation, the self-coaching and upward feedback supplements may facilitate improved posttraining performance by directing trainees to engage in specific transfer enhancement strategies. Such strategies include practicing focal skills, reflecting on one's performance, establishing performance enhancement goals, and developing strategies to achieve performance success.

The supplements are believed to direct engagement in such activities as trainees review and complete their respective materials, and the content of the supplements may direct trainees' engagement in these activities throughout their regular workdays. Finally, the self-coaching and upward feedback supplements could improve posttraining performance by enhancing trainees' self-efficacy beliefs. Defined as individuals' judgments of their capabilities to organize and execute specific courses of action, self-efficacy is a central motivational variable in employee performance.

Self-efficacy influences individuals' choices regarding which behaviours to undertake, how much effort to expend, how long to persist in overcoming obstacles, and, ultimately, levels of performance. The supplements may enhance task-specific self-efficacy beliefs as the trainees may perceive the supplements as providing the resources to execute superior performance.

Further, the supplements may enhance task-specific self-efficacy as a result of realizing better performance throughout the course of the study period. It has been argued that mastery experiences, or performance accomplishments, are the strongest contributors to enhanced self-efficacy beliefs.

## HYPOTHESES

The first hypothesis asserts that trainees who participate in either supplement beyond formal training will demonstrate better posttraining performance than those who attend classroom training only.

*Hypothesis* 1: Participation in self-coaching or upward feedback will have a more favourable impact on posttraining performance than formal classroom training only.

The second hypothesis examines which supplement has a stronger performance impact. Answering this question is useful in determining whether self-coaching or upward feedback is the better single supplement. Self-coaching and upward feedback differ in certain respects that may lead to a different performance impact.

For example, self-coaching spans a longer duration and therefore extends development over a greater period. The self-coaching programme involves completing assessments and goal-setting activities for several weeks on the job, whereas upward feedback involves the receipt of feedback and goal setting at one point in time. In turn, upward feedback involves the receipt of feedback from others beyond the trainees themselves. Individuals may be somewhat blind to their strengths and areas for improvement and may require feedback from others to facilitate interpersonal growth. The supplements' strengths may offset each other and lead to similar performance effects, but one supplement's strengths could be more effective in facilitating posttraining than the other's.

*Hypothesis* 2: One supplement may be superior to the other in facilitating posttraining performance.

A final question to be answered is the impact of combining selfcoaching and upward feedback as a posttraining supplement. Because selfcoaching and upward feedback include shared and distinct features, the supplements could provide mutual reinforcement, while also enhancing performance through unique means. However, utilizing two posttraining supplements could provide no additional benefit over utilizing one. This alternative would be likely when skills have already been close to fully developed. However, because the focal training is targeted towards new managers and the challenge of fully developing interpersonal skill proficiency, combining self-coaching and upward feedback is argued to have a superior posttraining impact.

*Hypothesis* 3: Participation in a combined supplement will have a more favourable posttraining impact than either selfcoaching or upward feedback.

In addition to assessing the direct influences of self-coaching and upward feedback on posttraining performance, the mediating influences of trainees' engagement in transfer enhancement strategies and self-efficacy in facilitating the impact of the supplements on posttraining performance are assessed.

As discussed beforehand, the supplements may facilitate better posttraining performance by directing individuals to engage in specific activities to improve transfer and by enhancing their beliefs in their abilities to execute successful performance.

*Hypothesis* 4: The relationship between the posttraining supplements and posttraining performance will be mediated by engagement in transfer enhancement strategies.

*Hypothesis* 5: The relationship between the posttraining supplements and posttraining performance will be mediated by selfefficacy beliefs.

The research sponsor for this study was an organization that owns and operates approximately 120 casual-theme restaurants in the United States. Each restaurant employs 56 individuals on average and has an annual turnover of 108%. The trainees were new managers who worked in a restaurant management team of three to five people. The management team for each restaurant includes a general manager, an assistant general manager, and one to three entry-level managers. Regardless of qualifications, all new managers enter the organization as entry-level managers. All new managers in the organization during the study period participated in this research. Nine managers left the organization prior to the completion of the study, yielding a sample of 87 trainees from 75 restaurants. Of the valid sample, the average age was 31 years, and the trainees averaged 7 years of experience. Seventy-six of the trainees were male. Seventy-two trainees were Caucasian, eight were African-American/Black, four were Hispanic/Latino, and one trainee was Asian/East Indian. Two trainees reported their ethnic background as "other."

## FOCAL TRAINING

An established programme conducted in the organization's centralized corporate training centre focused on developing supervision skills was the foundation for this study.

*Through this training, the organization aimed to develop five general skill sets*:

- Clarifying expectations;
- Monitoring;
- Rewarding;
- Correcting;
- Inspiring.

The formal training spanned approximately 8 hours and included lectures, discussions, video, and role-playing activities. One, these items reflect the learning points used during training to guide classroom discussion and practice activities. Two, they provide the foundation for the standardized behavioural assessment in the self-coaching programme. Three, they serve as one component in the upward feedback assessments. Four, they comprise the posttraining performance dependent variable. The items for four of the dimensions-clarifying expectations, monitoring, rewarding, and inspiring-are based on the work of Yukl, Wall, and Lepsinger. Slight wording modifications were made to reflect the specific training objectives and organizational context. Items for the correcting dimension were developed for this study and corresponded to the training program's objectives. This research employed a quasi-experimental posttest-only, control group design to examine the impact of the posttraining supplements on trainees' performance.

A posttest-only design was employed because pretraining performance measures could not be obtained for the newly hired trainees. A quasi-experimental design was used, in which blocks of trainees rather than individuals were assigned to treatment conditions, to simplify administrative and coordination efforts. The research sponsor conducted formal training sessions once approximately every 2 months.

*Four groups were used over a 7-month period, and each group was randomly assigned to one of the following conditions*:

- Classroom training only,
- Classroom training with self-coaching,
- Classroom training with upward feedback,
- Classroom training with self-coaching and upward feedback.

A trainee's start date within the organization was the only criterion for his or her assignment to a training condition; an individual attended the first available session following his or her start date. The first training group served as the control. Subsequent groups were assigned to the upward feedback, self-coaching, and combined supplements, respectively. The number of trainees per treatment condition was 21, 22, 23, and 21. Analyses of variance demonstrated no significant differences across the groups regarding age and years of management experience. Further, chi-square analyses demonstrated no differences across groups with respect to gender and ethnic background.

There was limited potential for trainees to have had knowledge of other trainees' participation in the alternative designs. Thus, compensatory rivalry, where individuals in different treatments knowingly "compete", was not expected to bias the results of this study. Trainees participating in later training designs likely were not influenced by designs because they were not yet employed as managers in the organization. Further, the trainees were distributed in different restaurants. Sixty-three of the 87 trainees were employed in different restaurants across the country. Four pairs from the same restaurants participated in the same treatment condition concurrently. Sixteen trainees were employed in the same restaurant as another trainee but participated in a different treatment condition at a different time.

This research focused on a 10-week posttraining period on the job. The self-coaching trainees received their workbooks during the first week and completed their materials over the following 5 weeks. The upward feedback trainees received a packet for administering their feedback assessments during the third week. These trainees were required to complete survey administration within a week's time and return the assessments to the researchers via prepaid overnight express delivery for compilation of their feedback reports. The upward feedback trainees received their feedback reports approximately during the fifth week via overnight express delivery. Final measures for all trainees were assessed at the end of the 10-week period.

## TREATMENT ADMINISTRATION AND DESIGN

### Self-coaching

The self-coaching programme spanned 5 weeks and included four parts. The first part of the workbook was the standardized behavioural assessment with the five performance dimensions in which the trainees assessed their own performance from the week. The second part included four open-ended questions to facilitate self-reflection. The third part was a development plan worksheet in which the trainees were directed to establish three goals for the following week.

*This worksheet instructed trainees to establish*:

- A "continuance" goal,
- A "stop" goal,
- A "start" goal.

The final part was a development plan follow-up worksheet to help trainees assess the extent to which their goals from part 3 were achieved.

*The materials were identical from week to week with two exceptions*:

- Week 1 did not include a development plan follow-up worksheet because trainees had just begun the programme;
- Week 5 did not include a development plan because it was the final week of the programme. To help ensure compliance, every week each trainee was required to obtain his or her general manager's signature on a verification form that confirmed that the trainee completed that week's materials. The form was then faxed to the corporate office to track each trainee's progress.

## Upward Feedback Assessment

The upward feedback assessment packet included the feedback assessments, materials for returning the assessments to the researchers and an accompanying cover letter from the vice president of Human Resources and Training detailing administration procedures. The feedback assessments included one self-report survey, seven surveys for dining room staff, and seven surveys for kitchen staff.

*Specifically, the subordinates were instructed to provide examples of*:

- Behaviours the trainee performs well and should continue,

- Behaviours the trainee should start engaging in,
- Behaviours the trainee should engage in less frequently.

The subordinates returned their assessments to the trainees in sealed envelopes, which were then returned to the researchers. The trainees were requested to obtain at least five assessments for both dining room and kitchen staff members. An average of 12 usable subordinate surveys was obtained per trainee, yielding a response rate of 86% and reflecting on average 21% of the employees in a restaurant.

## Upward Feedback Report

The upward feedback report included five parts. The first three parts presented data on the five performance dimensions, including the self-report ratings, average subordinate ratings, and self-subordinate gaps. The first part provided composite scores for the five dimensions, and the second part provided scores for the individual items. The third part identified the five highest and lowest self-report ratings, average subordinate ratings, and self-subordinate gaps. The fourth part presented the subordinates' comments. The fifth part was a development plan worksheet. Parallel to the self-coaching workbook, the trainees were directed to establish "continuance," "stop," and "start" goals. The sixth part was a development plan follow-up worksheet to later assess goal attainment.

## Organizational Support

The research sponsor instituted several supports to help ensure compliance with the post-training supplements. The sponsoring organization's vice president of Human Resources and Training strongly supported the implementation of the supplements. He conducted the formal classroom training sessions. At the end of which, he introduced the post-training supplements and emphasized the value of extending development beyond the classroom. In addition, he conducted conference calls with general managers across the country to educate them on the supplements so they could ensure trainee compliance. Moreover, corporate administrative staff monitored trainee compliance and followed up with trainees via e-mail and telephone in the event materials were not submitted in a timely fashion.

**Control Variables**

Several variables were included in the analyses to enhance control in this quasi-experimental design. These variables were general mental ability, the Big Five personality dimensions, pretraining self-efficacy, and management experience. General mental ability measures were obtained from personnel records, and measures of personality, management experience, and self-efficacy were obtained at the beginning of the formal training sessions.

- *General mental ability*: General mental ability was assessed with the 126-item Thurstone Test of Mental Alertness. The test was administered under the standard 20-minute, timed protocol.
- *Personality*: The Big Five were measured with the NEO Five-Factor Personality Inventory, Form S. Twelve items comprised each dimension, and respondents indicated the extent to which the items described themselves. Response choices ranged from = strongly disagree to = strongly agree. Chronbach's alphas for the Neuroticism, Extraversion, Openness to Experience, Agreeableness, and Conscientiousness dimensions were.86,.73,.72,.69, and.84, respectively.
- *Management experience*: Trainees indicated their years and months of previous experience managing others.
- *Self-efficacy*: Pretraining self-efficacy beliefs were assessed with a seven-item measure adapted from Martocchio and Webster. A sample item includes: "I feel confident in my ability to manage the performance of employees." Response choices ranged from = strongly disagree to = strongly agree (a =.80).

**POSTTREATMENT ASSESSMENT**

Posttreatment data were obtained following administration guidelines similar to the upward feedback assessments. Trainees provided ratings of engagement in transfer enhancement strategies and self-efficacy. Subordinates provided ratings of the trainee performance. An average of 11 usable subordinate assessments was obtained per trainee, yielding a response rate of 79% and reflecting on average 20% of the employees in a restaurant.

Transfer enhancement strategies. The trainees' engagement in transfer enhancement strategies was assessed with an 11-item measure based on the work of Machin and Fogarty. Specific strategies include: "I spent time thinking about how to use my people management skills in my daily work" and "I discussed with my coworkers ways to develop my people management skills." Response choices ranged from 1 = never to 5 = daily (a =.83).

Following the CFA results, which indicated a single higher-order performance dimension, a single dependent variable was constructed for subsequent analyses. To determine weights for the five dimensions in creating the composite measure, principal components analysis was performed.

The five dimensions were subjected to PCA, yielding a single factor. This factor explained 72.53% of the variance with an eigenvalue of 3.62. The overall performance measure was computed as an average of the product of the dimension scores and their respective factor weights. Multiple regression was used to test the hypotheses.

Regression was used rather than analysis of covariance to more parsimoniously assess the impact of the supplements and control variables. Participation in self-coaching, upward feedback, or the combined supplement was indicated with three dummy variables, in which "1" represented participation in a supplement and "0" did not.

Regression coefficients for the supplements provided estimates for their magnitude and direction beyond classroom training only. A similar coding plan in ANCOVA would have provided an F-statistic for each supplement with no indication of effect size or direction. Similarly, with respect to the control variables, regression coefficients provided an estimate of the magnitude and direction for the effect of each, whereas ANCOVA would have provided a general F-statistic.

*Variables were entered into the regression model in three steps:*

- Control variables,
- Posttraining supplements,
- Transfer enhancement strategies and self-efficacy. For the final model predicting trainee performance, R2 was.33 and the F-statistic was 2.72.

*Hypothesis* 1, which proposed that participation in self-coaching or upward feedback would have a positive impact on posttraining performance beyond classroom training only, was supported. The standardized regression coefficient was.22 for self-coaching and.43 for upward feedback.

*Hypothesis* 2, which proposed a difference in the effectiveness of selfcoaching and upward feedback, was not supported. This hypothesis was examined by assessing the significance of the difference between the selfcoaching and upward feedback regression coefficients utilizing the formula outlined by Paternoster, Brame, Mazerolle, and Piquero for testing the equality of regression coefficients. A two-tailed significance test was executed because it was not articulated a priori which supplement would be more effective; competing arguments were presented why each supplement could be superior. Although the upward feedback coefficient was larger, the difference between the coefficients was not statistically significant.

*Hypothesis* 3, which proposed that participating in the combined supplement would be better than participating in one posttraining supplement, was partially supported. Following the formula from Paternoster et al., participating in the combined supplement was superior to self-coaching. However, a statistically significant difference in posttraining performance between the combined supplement and upward feedback was not demonstrated.

*Hypotheses* 4 and 5, which proposed mediating influences of engagement in transfer enhancement strategies and self-efficacy, respectively, in the relationships between the supplements and post-training performance, were not supported.

*These relationships were assessed by examining the extent to which four requirements set forth by James and Brett and Baron and Kenny were met:*

- Significant relationships between the initial independent and dependent variables,
- Significant relationships between the initial independent variables and proposed mediators,
- Significant relationships between the proposed mediators and dependent variables with the inclusion of the independent variables,
- Nonsignificant or reduced relationships between the initial independent and dependent variables with the inclusion of the proposed mediators.

All four criteria were not met for either Hypothesis 4 or 5; thus, neither hypothesis was supported. The supplements were related to posttraining performance. However, no significant relationships between the supplements and engagement in transfer enhancement strategies were found, and only self-coaching was significantly related to self-efficacy. Finally, the point estimate for the impact of upward feedback on posttraining performance remained constant when the proposed mediators were included, whereas the point estimates for self-coaching and the combined supplement fell modestly.

This study has contributed in several ways to training research. One, this study examined supplements in the applied work environment not previously examined as posttraining supplements. The self-coaching programme represented a unique supplement, and upward feedback had not been examined previously as a direct extension of formal training. Two, this research validated the utility of the focal supplements within an experimental design framework, overcoming limitations of some work that utilized cross-sectional survey designs to examine posttraining support.

Three, this study specified posttraining supplements appropriate for a specific skill set and context-interpersonal skills performed under autonomous working conditions. This research has helped address the need for more context-dependent transfer enhancement systems. The self-coaching and upward supplements were designed to further develop and enhance the transfer of interpersonal skills, and the data demonstrated that both supplements were successful in achieving this end. Trainees who participated in either supplement exhibited better performance than those who attended classroom training only.

Further, trainees participating in both supplements as a combined intervention were more effective performers than the self-coaching trainees. However, trainees participating in the combined supplement were not found to be significantly better performers than the upward feedback trainers, despite the positive point estimate.

The results indicate that self-coaching and upward feedback are similar in their posttraining impact. Although the point estimate for upward feedback was almost twice as large the self-coaching estimate, a statistically significant difference was not found. The supplements do share a common framework for evaluating performance and goal-setting to direct performance enhancement efforts.

Further, the supplements' relative strengths (i.e., the longer duration of the self-coaching programme and the receipt of feedback from key constituents with upward feedback) may offset each other. To more fully determine whether the supplements are equivalent or whether one is superior to the other, additional research is necessary using larger samples to obtain effect sizes with less sampling error and to assess potential differences with greater statistical power.

Beyond considering the impact of the supplements, practitioners should consider available resources when electing to adopt either self-coaching or upward feedback. For example, consideration should be paid to the degree of expertise within an organization to design and implement a posttraining supplement. An upward feedback system requires more expertise than a self-coaching programme. Among other things, implementing an upward feedback system requires skill in survey design and administration, data collection and analysis, and developing systems to efficiently return results. Implementing a self-coaching programme also requires expertise, yet such expertise is limited to the initial design of the programme. In addition, attention should be paid to trainee effort required and necessary administrative follow-up. The upward feedback supplement required less effort by the trainees and less administrative follow-up than the self-coaching programme.

The upward feedback trainees were required to complete self-assessments and obtain feedback from their subordinates at one point in time. In comparison, the self-coaching programme required more trainee effort and administrative follow-up as the trainees were required to complete and submit materials on a weekly basis.

Further research is necessary to examine the mechanisms by which the supplements do not operate to improve post-training performance, as neither engagement in transfer enhancement strategies nor self-efficacy was demonstrated to have an impact. The inability to demonstrate these mediating influences could be attributed to limitations of the measures because they were obtained at the end of the study period. Due to imperfect recall or self-serving biases, these measures may not have reflected trainees' true use of such strategies and self-efficacy beliefs during the intervention period.

In future work, it is recommended to assess these variables on a regular basis over a shorter duration, such as through an experience sampling procedure where subjects respond to questions on a palmtop computer at random intervals throughout a workday. Further, to overcome self-report biases with respect to engagement in transfer enhancement strategies, it may be advantageous to obtain measures of observable strategies from others (e.g., discussing with supervisors, coworkers, and subordinate employees ways to facilitate skill enhancement).

Interestingly, the self-coaching programme, but not upward feedback, was related to enhanced self-efficacy beliefs at the end of the study. A non-significant impact for upward feedback is noteworthy given that the upward feedback trainees' performance was demonstrated to be better than those who attended classroom training only. It is possible that the feedback may have initially had a negative impact on trainees' beliefs in their competence. For example, any corrective feedback or feedback revealing inflated self-report ratings could have lowered such beliefs.

The trainees may have improved their performance based on the feedback and perceived themselves as more competent. However, self-efficacy improvements may not have been detected because early self-efficacy beliefs initially declined. Further, the upward feedback trainees may have lacked sufficient positive feedback on their performance improvements prior to the assessment of post treatment self-efficacy beliefs.

Two strategies might prove effective in enhancing self-efficacy beliefs in upward feedback systems. One strategy is to provide feedback at regular intervals, highlighting performance improvements, as opposed to limiting upward feedback to a one-time intervention. As such, individuals could monitor performance improvement over time. A second strategy is supplementing upward feedback with self-coaching after, rather than before, individuals receive feedback. In the absence of additional feedback from others, a self-coaching programme could be a resource for individuals to provide themselves with self-generated positive reinforcement.

One primary limitation of this study was the lack of random assignment of trainees to the treatment conditions and their posttraining restaurants. Ideally, all individuals would have attended formal classroom training at one point in time, each trainee would have been randomly assigned to one of the four treatment groups, and the trainees would have been randomly assigned to one of the organization's restaurant units. Cohort effects are possible where the trainees may have differed in their pretraining levels of interpersonal skill proficiency. However, the research sponsor maintained consistent selection standards when hiring the new managers, and several variables were used to help control for potential differences in interpersonal proficiency.

## FUTURE DIRECTIONS

One avenue for future research is examining the impact of the supplements over time. This research provided support for the impact of selfcoaching and upward feedback on performance assessed several weeks after completion of these training supplements.

However, their impact over time is unknown. Although they may have had long-term effects, trainees' skills and motivation to apply training content may have decayed over time. Research has found that skill decay does occur over time in a variety of cognitive and physical skill domains, but the degree of skill decay with respect to interpersonal skills has not been a topic of concerted research attention. An understanding of the rate of such decay would provide guidance for determining how often supplements should be implemented as a form of refresher training.

Examining self-coaching and upward feedback pretraining supplements to enhance motivation to learn and skill development within the classroom is another opportunity for research attention. Self-coaching and upward feedback prior to training could familiarize individuals with programme content, instill within trainees the need for continued development, and provide a resource for assessing training needs based on applied experience. As such, pretraining developmental exercises could make the formal learning experience more effective.

The generalizability of the supplements could be also examined for different skill sets and contexts. For example, self-coaching and upward feedback could be examined as supplements to enhance the effectiveness of team-training efforts, a growing area of interest in the training and development domain. In addition, it may be valuable to examine skill sets where posttraining supplements may not be necessary. Such supplements may not be necessary for interpersonal skills that are more explicitly in-role dimensions of performance, such as customer service skills, or where interpersonal skills are more closely supervised by others. In such circumstances, individuals may be more motivated to apply their skills on the job and receive relevant feedback to facilitate performance improvement. By knowing where posttraining supplements are most beneficial, they may be judiciously implemented.

A final research recommendation is examining the impact of additional context-dependent transfer enhancement systems. One size does not fit all, and continued research is necessary to validate more refined systems of training interventions.

Such work will continue to enhance the theoretical basis for training design and will provide clearer guidance for applied practice. As this study examined supplements appropriate for interpersonal skills performed under autonomous working conditions, future research should examine interventions appropriate for other knowledge and skill domains and working environments.

# 9

# Leadership

"Systematic development of global leaders requires an even stronger, more focused commitment than does a domestic effort. You have to know what you are doing, why you are doing it, and what you want to get out of it. Without the clarity of commitment, the complexity of the global environment will swamp the effort." One of the fundamental questions asked by scholars and business leaders today is, "How can a company prepare to effectively compete in the hypercompetitive, complex, global environment of the 21st Century?" One of the central precepts in the management literature is the necessity to have a well developed, experienced management team at the helm, or in other words, experienced, well prepared executives.

However, what constitutes an executive with the "right stuff" is defined in a variety of ways. There is reasonable agreement that much of what tomorrow's executives need to know can be learned yet, how they gain that knowledge is another matter and is not a simple 'cookie cutter' formula. Each person has individual talents and strengths that have to be amalgamated into finely tuned organizational and market skills set.

It is necessary to continuously assess the transformation from a good executive to a great executive, as well as how to develop leaders that are able to insure that organizations survive in today's multi-faceted multicultural global marketplace. To gain insight into what it takes to be 'great' involves comparing past strategies for developing executives with the espoused formula for success today. In 1938 Chester

Barnard put forth his thoughts on the traits and skills of the executive in a 'cooperative system' in order to be successful. Recently, after completing an empirical qualitative worldwide study, McCall and Hollenbeck (2002) described their vision of the uintessential 'global executive' and the necessary skills needed to retain a competitive edge in today's complex global business world.

The purpose of this associate is twofold. The first objective is to provide a brief historical review and draw a parallel of some of the more prominent changes in the management environment across the last 70 years. As we enter the 21st Century, it would seem to be an appropriate time to examine the evolution of desirable characteristics of managers compared to the past. Barnard's seminal work in the 1930s provides the backdrop for the historic representation of what was thought to be the necessary qualities of 'successful' managers.

Secondly, we develop a comparative analysis of Barnard's 'successful manager' of the early 20th Century with that of McCall and Hollenbeck's (2002) 'global executive' of the 21st Century. Their empirical research can serve as the foundation of what is thought to be needed for success in the global marketplace of the 21st Century and therefore, be used to foreshadow what qualities are necessary to succeed in the future.

It is important to continue to look at current phenomena through the lens of the past; thus the use of the comparison of the two perspectives should be helpful in linking the 70 years of change and development in the management conceptualized by Barnard with the expectations developed by McCall and Hollenbeck about developing executives to meet the challenges in managing in the global marketplace.

## MANAGEMENT DEVELOPMENT

Discussion about what makes a good manager/executive/ leader and how to develop such archetypes of commandership has been an ongoing debate for millenniums. As early as 400 BC, Socrates noted that management skills were transferable from one setting to another; it was just a matter of understanding the key areas of needs by a given group. In the year 1513, Machiavelli penned the first 'how to' book for rulers (executives) and listed his 'must knows' for the aspiring ruler. Even though the content was technical and procedural in nature, in 1836 James Montgomery wrote what is considered by some as the first text book on management. In 1908, Henri Fayol responded to a call for a theory of management by developing his now universal 'principles of management' that allowed for what was thought to be an art (management) to be studied as a discipline in the classroom.

A glance back through the pages of management history emphasizes that many management gurus of the early 20th Century had their beliefs about what constituted the qualities of a top notch manager. Each writer supported the viewpoint that management as a philosophy and practice, which helped to provide a backdrop of executive education throughout the decades. Perhaps ahead of her time, Mary Parker Follet believed in the communities of creative practice and suggested that employees be considered an intrinsic part of the organization that allowed it to be more productive.

Nobel prizewinner Herbert Simon held strong beliefs about the decision-making process of executives and firms in general as he espoused his ideas about "bounded rationality". Simon believed that no one person, including the executive, could make the complicated decisions of running an organization in isolation. He defined the organization as "the pattern of communications and relations among a group of human beings, including the processes for making and implement decisions". And, not to be forgotten; Ralph C. Davis wrote "Management is defined as the function of executive leadership".

Fayol, Follet, Simon, Davis, and many others made important contributions to our understanding of management skills and competencies. But, it is the belief of many that one name prominently emerges from the early part of the 20th Century as having a significant impact on shaping the business landscape of his era and defining the roles that executives play in creating viable thriving organizations. Chester Barnard, as a great scholar, a notable successful businessman, and a consultant, through his imagery of the chief executive of the 1930's set the foundation for many to view the development of a world class leader. Barnard attended Harvard Business School where he studied economics, but through out his life he earned seven honourary doctorates for his contribution to the understanding of organizations.

During his presidency of New Jersey Bell, he was noted for his 'unbounded' enthusiasm and concern for his employees. As a consultant, Barnard assisted such organizations as the Atomic Energy Commission, the New Jersey Reformatory, and the United Service organization, just to mention a few. Barnard was known for his belief that the executive "carried out his functions in a cooperative and democratic manner rather than in a unilateral autocratic way".

Having acknowledged the contributions of a few of the pioneers of management thought, it is useful to assess the picture as it is presented today. A review of the recent literature on developing executives revealed many prominent names, too many to capture in this brief note. Individuals who will no doubt go down in the history books as having left interesting and monumental footprints in the sands of management development include: Peter Drucker, Michael Porter, and Victor Vroom, just to name a few.

Drucker, the author of 30 books, touted as being a candidate for being one of the most influential observers in modem business history was an advocate of giving employees responsibility and not empowerment. Porter (1980) outlined the 'Five Factor Analysis' that gave a clearer picture of the forces that impact profitability in an industry. Vroom promoted participative management and matching decision processes to the nature of the problem.

However, McCall and Hollenbeck completed an extensive, qualitative, multi-country study in 2002 that generated an all-inclusive list of the competencies of the global executive. Their list was chosen for our basis of the discussion of the 21st Century executive, because of the comprehensiveness of their methodology, the amount of data collected for the study, and the attention given to the holistic global executive.

## MANAGERIAL AND SOCIETAL TRANSITIONS ACROSS THE 20TH CENTURY

Perhaps a constructive first step would be to examine changes in society in general, and the business world specifically, to better understand how and why current conceptions of management might different from those of the early scholars.

For clarity and to draw distinctions between various stages in the development of management thought, we have divided the 20th Century into five basic eras, between which paradigm shifts occurred in both the business arena and more specifically in the conventional wisdom among management scholars as to what constituted the practice of management and what managers needed to be successful:

- Era I, 1900-1945;
- Era II, 1945-1970;
- Era III, 1971-1991;
- Era IV, 1991-2001;
- Era V, 2001+.

Harvey and Buckley (2002) synthesized many of the changes in the economy and management philosophy very effectively over the 70 plus years.

Our objective is to tie their observations of changes to these specific eras as they emerged as an impetus of change in the management arena.

## ERA I: 1900-1945

In the early part of the last century, the United States experienced a major transition from a basic agrarian economy to an industrialized society.

Technology focused on the mechanization and the production of goods, the business and economic sectors became contributors to critical societal issues (i.e., employee rights, child labour, health/safety in the workplace, taxation of corporate entities and the role of corporation in a society), and improvements in communications and transportation broadened external perspectives from local to national and indeed, international concerns. Making things with machines became known by a large segment of the society, as consumers demanded goods in a quicker time frame.

How to make money by borrowing to maintain and grow businesses was discovered, creating capital markets. America discovered that unregulated markets could lead to monopolies and unfair business practices, and also fought two World Wars. Business organizations grew in wealth and size, management and ownership separated, and working for a wage became the norm in the United States.

Unrestrained competition led to monopolies, unfair business, poor labour practices, and massive debt accumulated by organizations. As a result, society demanded reforms and the resulting legislation increased the constraints on business practices. And the theories of economics taught managers important topics in the Great Depression of the 1930s. New Deal programmes formed by the government began to restore the faith in the power of government to help individuals as Social Security and many other work programmes were established.

Management's view of its world was broadened somewhat to include societal issues external to the business organization. This era of dominance by the organization also spawned the growth and importance of the trade unions in the United States. This trend of organizing by labour provided the appropriate countervailing power to the economic strength of the corporate world. This position was strengthen even more during the depression of the 1930s where the rights of laborers was abused in many cases due to the magnitude of need of those out of work/looking for work during the depression.

From a management perspective the growing size and complexity of organizations, and the need to create a skilled labour force, led to Fayol's theories of structure and division of labour. While many theorists were impressed with industrial technology and mechanization, management discovered that human assets (largely focused on individuals) were also important. Management theories and development began to focus on improving the productivity of those human assets. The acknowledged founder of a body of knowledge known as scientific management, Frederick Taylor, stated that training needed to be a part of the corporation's responsibility to its employees, yet he felt the best teacher for managers was experience. Taylor also postulated that the principal objective of management was to secure the maximum prosperity for the employer and the employee.

The 1920's brought the end of World War I and the onslaught of more studies of the employee and his/her reaction to task and work environments called the human relations movement. Chief among these studies were those conducted at the Hawthorne facility of Western Electric in Chicago between 1924 and 1933 by a group headed by Elton Mayo. The results highlighted the importance of understanding the social interaction of workers and the existence of informal organizational social systems.

Kaufman characterized the human relations focus as "the incorporation of the human factor into scientific management." Lewin introduced a theory that human behaviour is a function of both person and environment. This led to the thought that the work environment needed to give the individual a sense of belonging for him to function at maximum capacity and popularized the term group dynamics.

**ERA II: 1946-1970**

In the three decades following World War II, large American corporations benefited from the weakened economies of other nations such as Germany and Japan. The United States economy was strong, stable, and experienced unparalleled prosperity.

Producers benefited not only from the demand from American consumers, but also from the demand created when the United States government committed to rebuild war-torn Europe, as well as the Philippines and Japan. United States corporations grew into mega-corporations that started exploring international holdings to meet both worldwide demand and to locate closer to new markets created. Two wars and the continuing cold-war arms race continued to fuel the economy whenever recessions threatened. The tremendous economic growth and prosperity of these three decades, while beneficial to the industrial sector of the economy, led to a shift away from reliance on this sector to an emphasis on the development and delivery of services. Two factors explain this shift. First, as Americans enjoyed high earnings and prosperity, they began to add services to the 'goods' demanded on a daily basis. Second, technology born in the war efforts and space race began to pervade the economy. The computer was born during WW II and greatly perfected during the space race of the late 1950's and throughout the 1960's. While the computer was a product, its effectiveness was determined by the software developed to make it useful as a data processor, as a reporting system, and in an increasing number of situations as a data repository.

While the industrial world was in full development mode, the philosophers and psychologists were in the 'academic wings' analyzing the changes from the worker's perspective. Team or group dynamics became the focus of management interest. Deutsch suggested that cooperation and competitive spirit are ever present and demonstrated that developing cooperative groups increased production. Trist and Bamforth indicated that it was important to allow the social dynamics of the group to exist and that the technical aspects of the job need not denominate the success of the workflow. Management continued to place increasing emphasis on its human assets/capital, now visualized in group or team dimensions, rather than as individuals. The advent of the civil rights movement also highlighted the disparity among social/ethnic groups as to opportunities in the workforce. The movement continues to this day having a direct as well as an indirect impact on the diversity and vitality of businesses.

While the computer clearly had a role in business organizations, it also made significant contributions to the development of management theories and practice. Computers made it possible to process larger amounts of data and coupled with a growing body of statistical techniques, management researchers turned to empirical studies with greater frequency. Moreover, as a data repository, computers made it possible to collect and store large volumes of data on economic transactions, which complemented research needs and theory development.

## ERA III: 1971-1991

The years from the early 1970's through 1991 were a period of economic adjustment for the United States and much of Western Europe. The oil and gas crisis of the 1970's played a major role as the increased cost of energy made the United States and many European companies less competitive in the manufacturing arena worldwide. Companies in the United States faced an increasingly competitive and rough economic environment laced with technology advancements, government interventions, and many international dynamics. Struggles to survive became the mantra of many boards-of-directors. Casio reported that in the 1980's United States based manufacturing firms cut more than two million workers with a seventeen per cent of the dismissals being from middle management.

However, the demand for services grew exponentially, and as technology spread globally, an increasing number of enterprises from countries other than the United States became "best in the world" in various industries. And, because the United States' consumer market was the world's largest, many of these foreign enterprises entered the United States market and experienced phenomenal success. Domestic consumers, ever egalitarian in their purchasing choices and experiencing some belt-tightening of their own, bought foreign goods and services because they were less expensive and in many cases of higher quality.

Companies in the United States faced an increasingly competitive and difficult economic environment laced with dramatically changing industry boundaries, increasingly rapid technology advancements, government interventions, and many international dynamics. Companies in all sectors faced tough strategic decisions such as downsizing, restructuring, and rightsizing as well as adopting new employment philosophies. During this time, diversity increased due to the increase in women and minorities in the main stream of management.

This increased diversity provide the foundation for improving the skill set and management capabilities of the organization but also created a tension and in some cases a conflict among those in the organization. Michael Porter argued that business organizations needed to focus on their value-chain, which led many to create interorganizational alliances with suppliers and buyers to increase competitiveness. TQM and business process re-engineering tools were used to drive out costs and improve quality, speed, and responsiveness. Many companies turned more to global markets in an effort to expand markets and gain added competencies.

Working dynamics were also changing. Teamwork and the subsequent social facilitation were recognized as important features, but negative behaviours were also being identified. Social facilitation highlighted the point that the presence of others could sometimes motivate individuals and spur them to greater efforts. However, the opposite pattern was also found in that sometimes individuals worked less hard in the presence of others than they did alone. This effect became known as social loafing. Two primary reasons were given for social loafing 1) feeling of anonymity and 2) perception of easy or not challenging task.

The 1980's presented a change in philosophy and organizations found that it was important to foster a sense of mutuality and trust in the relations between management and workers, to develop employees as assets with the view of increasing competitiveness, and to assist the organizations' compliance with the increased government regulations. The influence of the Japanese management style was being felt through out the American corporate landscape. The successful application of the Theory Z concept contributed to the recognition that employees represented a vital resource just as important as capital and should be managed to facilitate competitive advantages.

## ERA IV: 1992-2002

The economy of the 1990's could best be summed-up by a statement made by Larry Chimerine, former Managing Director and Chief Economist at the Economic Strategy Institute in an address to the Fibre Box Association's 63rd Annual Membership Meeting on April 27, 2003 in Phoenix, AZ. "The 1990s was the longest period of uninterrupted growth in United States history, with no inflation, low unemployment, and record corporate profits. Inflation has been taken-off the counter for a very long time. We're in a permanent disinflationary economy now."

The need to increase speed and responsiveness led to increasing use of virtual teams, new forms of organization, virtual offices, and more adaptive policies and procedures. As gaining a competitive edge became increasingly important throughout the 1990's management researchers began to rethink old theories and reframe them in a modern context. Pfeffer argued that gaining the skill to effectively manage people was one of the most competitive tools. Corporate strategy theorists argued that the core competencies of organizations rest in the human assets and knowledge base of the organization. Throughout this period, management organizations and specifically the human resource management function within them changed their philosophy and turned to a more incorporative mindset.

Pfeffer argued that gaining the skill to effectively manage people was one of the most competitive tools. But, with a diverse workforce that faced more complex problems and group dynamics than ever before it was not an easy task. Diverse workforces brought opportunity and advantage along with considerable challenges. The need for organizations to more proactively use cooperative and self managed teams to improve their competitive position was recognized by many managers. Those teams were being drawn from across functions, from various business units, and even from external market sources. Rodrigues posited that, "United States based organizations rely more heavily on the multi-boss, ad hoc organization than in the past." Teams-the size of teams, the kinds of teams, the dynamics of teams, the member diversity of teams, and the processes of teams-became the central focus of training initiatives for employees and managers. Marks, Matthieu, and Zaccaro created the team process taxonomy to try and assist in the research on teams.

One of the primary methods of growth utilized by organizations is that of employing an acquisition strategy. This mode of gaining market power, diversifying risks, and gaining a broader consumer base has been an inordinately popular corporate strategy over the last several decades. In 2005, it was an estimated $2.9 trillion worth of acquisitions made globally. In what appears to be an unrelenting quest for limited resources; the need to capture unique combinations of human resources to gain competitive advantage; the necessary speed of getting products to a market to remain competitive; the growing importance of relational marketing efforts and the resulting synergistic marketing channel strategies, an ever increasing number of firms are focusing on acquisitions to address these marketplace challenges more than ever before.

## ERA V: 2002-DATE

The dawn of the 21st Century found the United States facing more economic uncertainty and increased government regulation. The Sarbanes Oxley act, terrorist attacks, and the subsequent war on terrorism have left executives of this new day concerned and very cognizant of the fact they are facing new tumultuous times.

Kiechel and Sacha listed the following as trends that will reshape the workplace throughout the next decade.

- The average company will become smaller, employing fewer people.
- The traditional hierarchical organization will give way to a variety of organizational forms, the network of specialists foremost among these.
- Technicians, ranging from computer repairmen to

radiation therapists, will replace manufacturing operatives as the worker elite.
- The vertical division of labour will be replaced by a horizontal division.
- The paradigm of doing business will {continue} to shift from making a product to providing a service.
- Work itself will be redefined: constant learning, more high-order thinking, less nine-to-five.

It is obvious that the role of the future CEO will be riddled with surprises, seven major issues will dominate to Porter, Lorsch, and Nohria.

*These authors listed the following as possible pitfalls for future executives*:
- You can't run the company solo;
- Giving orders is very costly;
- Hard to know what is really going on;
- Always sending a message;
- You are not the boss;
- Pleasing shareholders is not the goal;
- Recognizing that managers/leaders are still only human.

These seven tenets speak to the dynamic changes of the multi dimensional environment in which future executives must operate. Bums and Stalker would argue that the movement has been from a 'mechanistic' management to an 'organic' management.

While Harvey and Buckley would postulate that it is time to recognize those changes and make some tough decisions about what still works for the manager of today and discard the concepts that no longer apply. With that thought a look at a comparative model of the two executives that reside at the polar ends of the time continuum is in order.

## 20TH CENTURY MANAGER/EXECUTIVE

Chester Barnard developed his concept of what a manager/executive needed to learn to remain a viable part of the organization and to guide those for which he was responsible. He outlined five key competencies that every executive of 'the future' needed to brace themselves with beyond their formal institutional instruction:

- *Broad interest and wide imagination*: Barnard felt that having a well-rounded liberal arts education beyond business made managers/executives more 'flexible and adaptable' in their thinking. While in his role as company president, he arranged a series of lectures and readings that were non business related and lasted up to six non consecutive weeks for all of the top management, many of who had college degrees. His position was that education could not be overemphasized.
- *Superior intellectual capacities*: Having survived the Great Depression, World War I, and World War II, Barnard saw the future of businesses to be a 'closer integration of social activity'. Moreover, he felt "without education the supply of leaders of organization competent for conditions of the modern world would be wholly inadequate". He drew on that advance understanding when he spoke to the concept of intellectual capacities. There is no doubt in my mind that training in the more logical disciplines tends to foreclose the minds of many to the proper appreciation of human beings. Nevertheless, for executives, as well as many others, the world of the future is one of complex technologies and intricate techniques that cannot be adequately comprehended for practical working purposes except by formal and conscious intellectual processes.... to deal appropriately with combinations of technological, economic, financial, social, and legal elements; and to explain them to others so manifestly call for ability in making accurate distinctions, in classification, in logical reasoning an analysis.... This means that the student needs rigorous training in subjects of intellectual difficulty, thereby to provide himself with the tools and mental habits for dealing with important problems.

- *Human Relations*: Barnard was clear on his position of understanding social systems and recognizing formal organizations as 'organic and evolving social systems'. He used the analogy of organizations not being like machines, static and fixed; instead they were compilations of employees who would be different from location to location. Interaction and experiences with a given group of people is needed to fully understand their physical and psychological needs. This too requires constant and consistent communication to get to 'know your people'.
- *Persuasion*: Barnard's belief s that one important managerial function was the process of explaining their actions and beliefs about company activities. The art of persuasion is paramount in getting others to accept and even agree with management perceptions. He expressed the need to for adequate written and oral persuasion skills when dealing in human affairs.
- *Rational behaviour*: Perhaps the more difficult of his concepts to understand or that might be misinterpreted is the last; 'an understanding of what constitutes rational behaviour towards the unknown and the unknowable'. After having waxed on so eloquently about the need for superior intellect, here he adds the intuitive piece. The business world is full of unknowns and many situations are faced with incomplete knowledge of all the facts and thus require the executive to takes leaps of faith based on past experiences, signals from the business environment, or just gut instinct. Barnard prophesized that it is just as important to be able to exercise wisdom and instinct as well as intellect.

He definitely was a man of vision and saw dimensions of the future that many of his time could not comprehend. All five of his competencies are still needed today, as will be demonstrated in a subsequent section of this associate as parallels are drawn between Barnard's list and the more modern interpretation of what competencies are needed by modern global leaders.

## 21ST CENTURY GLOBAL LEADER/EXECUTIVE

As stated earlier it was hard to choose one set of leader characteristics from the list of noted scholars. However, the McCall and Hollenbeck empirically based qualitative study conducted interviews with over 100 global executives stationed throughout the world. The insight of such seasoned leaders was thought to add to the richness and insights derived from their research efforts.

*Their extensive interviews lead to the following list of competencies*:

- Open-minded and flexible in thought and tactics;
- Cultural interest and sensitivity;
- Able to deal with complexity;
- Resilient, resourceful, optimistic, and energetic;
- Honest and authentic;
- Possess stable personal life;
- Value-added technical or business skills.

McCall and Hollenbeck would be the first to say that no one list can depict a universal set of competencies as there is no 'universal global job.' "Global competencies, like global jobs, must be thought of as a mix, depending on the job". The world is just too complex and multi-dimensional. However, their list is comprehensive, thought provoking, and empirically created.

One additional interesting and apparently new facet to the development of the global executive is the importance of personal responsibility for their career paths. They seem to agree with Peter Drucker who advocates learning 'personal management' is as important as learning to manage other people. McCall and Hollenbeck address the organizational and personal responsibilities in the development of the 21st Century leader.

A close look at the list reveals a number of parallels between the way Barnard described the 20th Century

Executive and how today's leaders of the 21st Century depict their roles as articulated by McCall and Hollenbeck. First, broad interest and wide imagination seems to be another way to say open minded and flexible. Barnard realised in 1948 that the market place was getting more competitive and changes would come more quickly. He spoke of staying flexible and adaptable to allow for the changes that were occurring in the marketplace. The global leader of today is faced with changes at a faster pace and has more information to deal with than any manager in history. Technology puts more information at their finger tips than the average person can process. Therefore 21st Century leaders must also remain alert and responsive to the hyper competitiveness and fast changes of today's global business arena.

Second, Barnard spoke of superior intellectual capacities, where the leaders of today reference value-added technical and business skills. It would appear that getting an education and additional training as a foundation to success is still a must. Both sets of authors speak extensively about honing intellectual abilities by continuously pursuing diverse educational opportunities. While it is clear that computer and technical skills are more of a necessity in the 21st Century, that does note preclude other forms of education. Life long learning seems to be their motto, which they allude to being as much an attitudinal issue as it is as it is a skill.

Third, perhaps the human relations in Barnard's day were framed in a more domestic backdrop and focused on respecting employee and employer relations. Yet he still realised that each organization was unique by virtue of the set of employees that happen to make up the employee base. He spoke of organic and ever evolving systems because of the human element.

The same is true today, however the multinational multi-cultural dimensionality of today's organization requires global leaders to be sensitive to respecting people from around the world from very diverse backgrounds, beliefs, and mores. The fourth comparison evolves around personal attitude, both the manager of the 20th Century and the leader of the 21st Century need to understand the importance of persuasion, optimism, and resourcefulness in dealing with others. Good communication skills, both oral and written, are a necessity as the executive is always acting as a spoke person for the organization and must be able to persuade others to accept and support organizational objectives. Both sets of authors also stress the need to be optimistic and caring when dealing with others in order to have true relationships with constitutes.

The fifth and last direct parallel between the authors addresses the need for dealing with ambiguity. McCall and Hollenbeck speak to the issue of complexity distorting the facts that leaders have to deal with on a daily basis. Barnard talked about how the executive needs to understand that the facts needed for decision making is not in 'black and white,' clearly spelled out.

He explains there will be times where intuition is needed to make decisions because executives have to deal with the 'unknown and the unknowable.' It is interesting that two additional characteristics are explicitly discussed when describing the leader of the 21st Century and yet were not given as descriptives for the 20th.

*Century manager/executive*:

- Stable personal life
- Honesty and integrity.

Perhaps, Barnard felt these two items were innate or such essential characteristics that he did not find it necessary to put them on paper. Whereas the authors of today may have recognized the changing demographic trends of blended families such as 'dual—earner lifestyles', and situations where both marital partners are sharing the burden and responsibility for family care. There is an emerging stream of literature that discusses the stress issues related to work-family conflict.

When addressing the issues of honesty and integrity, McCall and Hollenbeck stated that is necessary for the leader of today to not only possess these characteristics, moreover to 'engender' them in others. Furthermore, they found in their research that consistent authenticity was crucial for one to stimulate honesty and integrity in others. There is evidence that Barnard believed in and promoted an authentic approach to leadership and that was an important concept when leaders were faced with ethical decisions. However, he did not list it as one of his competencies. Again, perhaps he felt it was so basic it was expected. It still leaves one to wonder if these personal dimensions are just talked about more today or are they seen as fading standards that need to be recaptured.

## Common Themes

Two common themes run through the two lists. First, both executive images capture the value of and the human relational skills needed to succeed. Each seems to echo the Dale Carnegie philosophy of understanding your fellow man and mastering the art of influence and persuasion. A second commonality that ties the two together is the thought that first-hand experience in the lead role as CEO is still the most helpful step in the development of an executive.

It appears that nothing can replace being in the trenches. People learn to be global from doing global work. The 21st Century global leader lives and operates in a more complex, faster paced, culturally diverse business arena. Yet he/she should start with the principles that Barnard's 20th Century manager/executive lived by and then add a keen understanding of the traits and competencies that ensure success today as expressed by McCall and Hollenbeck. Moreover, this associate suggests that it is necessary to use today's profile as a basis for growth for tomorrow.

Human beings are the most precious part of an organization. Effective utilisation of the capacity of human resources depends upon management. Management can get the results from the people in two ways. (A)- By exercising authority and (B)- By winning the support of the people. Out of these the second method has a lasting effect over the peoples motivation. However it is only possible when a manager becomes their leader in the real sense to influence their behaviour in the desired direction. Effective leadership is of great importance in an enterprise to enable to enable that organization in achieving its objectives.

Leadership is a process by which an executive directs his subordinates and influences the work and behaviour of others for the common benefit of the organization as well as its members. An effective leader directs the activities of his followers and integrates their activities for the accomplishment of some predetermined objectives.

The term leadership has been defined by many authorities. Keith Davis: *"Leadership is the ability to persuade others to seek defined objectives enthusiastically. It is the human factor which binds a group together and motivates it towards a goal."*

Bernard: *" Leadership refers to the quality of the behaviour of the individuals where by they guide people on their activities in an organization"*.

Leadership is a quality which enables a person to direct other persons of the organization and they become his followers. A leader directs and guides the activities of his followers and influence them to contribute their whole hearted efforts to achieve the common objectives of the enterprise.

## TYPES/ STYLES OF LEADERSHIP

These are the pattern of behaviour which a leader adopts in influencing the behaviour of his followers in the organizational context. There are many dimensions of leadership styles. Following are the types of leadership which may be found in an enterprise.

### AUTOCRATIC LEADERSHIP

In this style a manger centralises the decision making power in himself. He structures the complete work situation for his subordinates and they do what they are told. Autocratic leadership is based on the principle of centralisation of power. Under this type of leadership all the important functions are performed by the autocratic leader himself, like to take decisions, to plan, to make the allotment of work etc. He wants to concentrate all the powers in himself. The subordinates are not free to take decision or to do any work on their own. Autocratic leadership is based on the assumption that the employees are not capable to take decision; and they do not want to work by their nature. They can only be compelled to work if they are closely supervised and controlled.

*There are 3 categories of autocratic leadership*:

1. *Strict Autocrat*: He follows autocratic styles in a very strict sense. His method of influencing subordinates behaviour is through negative motivation; ie, by criticising subordinates, imposing penalty etc.
2. *Benevolent Autocrat.*: he also concentrates decision making power in him, but his motivation style is positive. He can be effective in getting efficiency in many situations.
3. *Incompetent Autocrat*: Sometimes, superiors adopt autocratic leadership styles just to hide their incompetence.; because in other styles they may be exposed before their subordinates. However this cant be used for a long time.

## DEMOCRATIC LEADERSHIP/ PARTICIPATIVE LEADERSHIP

This type of leader believes in the co-operation and co-ordination of the group. He permits his subordinates to participate in the process of decision making. He believes in the decentralisation of authority, two way communication and joint participation in decision making process.

A democratic leader takes his decisions just as to the opinion of majority and he makes his best efforts to improve the job satisfaction and morale of his followers. This is the most popular form of leadership these days and is most successful because it gets full co-operation and integration in group activities.

## FREE- REIN LEADERSHIP

Under this style of leadership, the leader doesn't direct the activities of his followers. This style gives complete freedom to subordinates. In this style, manager determines policy, programmes and limitations for action and the entire process is left to subordinates. Group members perform everything and the manager usually maintains contacts with outside persons to bring the information and materials which the group needs. This type of leadership is based on he assumption that all the subordinates are competent, willing to work and self motivated. There is no need to direct their activities. It is believed that they will perform better if they are free to decide and do on their own.

## PERSONAL LEADER

A personal leader is a person, who becomes a leader in the enterprise on the basis of personal relations. Such leader influences his followers in his personal capacity only. This type of leader influences the followers only because of his personality, personal abilities and character.

# THEORIES OF LEADERSHIP

Various theories have been developed to describe, analyse and explain the leadership function. Each theory has its own contributions, limitations assumptions and frame work of analysis.

## TRAIT APPROACH

This approach was one of the first attempt to explain leader behaviour, or attempts to influence subordinates. This approach focused on certain characteristics that separate leader from others. Trait approach leadership studies were quite popular between 1930's and 1950. The method of study was to select successful leaders; and their traits were studied. This theory assumes that such traits cause them to rise above their followers. The basic traits are ones energy, looks, knowledge, courage etc. The underlying logic of trait theory is that an individual possessing such traits is usually able to influence others. Leadership traits are of two types. They are innate qualities and acquirable qualities. Innate qualities are those which are possessed by various individuals since their birth.

- *Physical features*: Physical features of a man are determined by hereditary factors. To some extent height, weight, health and appearance are important for leadership.

- *Intelligence*: For leadership higher level of intelligence is required. Intelligence is generally expressed in terms of mental ability. Intelligence, to a very great extent, is a natural quality in the individuals because it is directly related with brain.

Acquirable qualities are those which can be acquired and increased through various processes. Many of these traits can be increased through training programme.

- *Emotional stability*: A leader should have high level of emotional stability. He should be free from bias, is consistent in action, and refrains from anger.
- *Human relations*: A successful leader should have adequate knowledge of human relations. ie how he should deal with human beings. Since an important part of a leaders job is to develop people and get their co-operation for achieving work, he should have intimate knowledge of people and their relationship to each other.
- *Objectivity*: Objectivity implies that what a leader does, should be based on relevant facts and information. He must assess these without any bias or prejudice.
- *Motivating skills*: A leader must acquire the quality to motivate his employees. Though there are many external forces which motivate a person, there is inner drive in people also for motivation to work. The leader can play active role in stimulating these inner drives.
- *Technical skill*: The leading of people requires adherence to definite principles which must be understood and followed for greater success. The ability to plan, organise, delegate, analyse, make decisions and control requires the use of important abilities which constitute technical competence of leadership.
- *Communication skill*: A successful leader knows how to communicate effectively. Communication has great force in getting the acceptance from the receivers of communication.

There are some obvious limitations of the trait theory. Firstly it is very difficult to find out a particular leadership trait in the greatest leaders of the world all times. Secondly while all of the traits might be desirable in leaders, none seems to be absolutely essential. There have been many people with the traits specified for leader, but they were not good leaders.

## SITUATIONAL THEORY

The prime attention in situational theory of leadership is given to the situation in which leadership is exercised. Therefore effectiveness of leadership will be affected by the factors associated with the leader and factors associated with the situation.

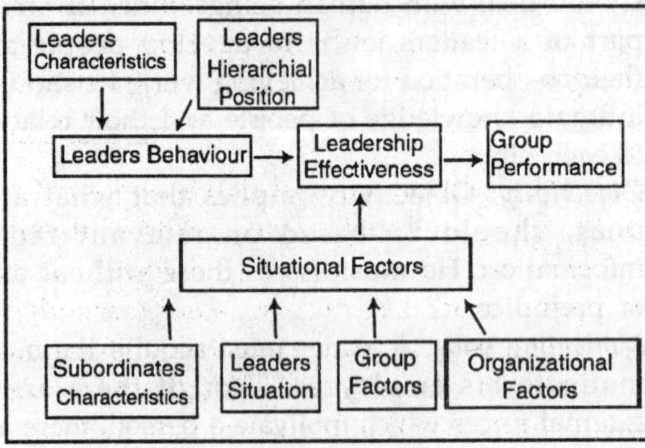


The various factors affecting leadership effectiveness may be broadly classified in to two categories; leaders behaviour and situational factors. Leaders behaviour is affected by his characteristics and his hierarchical position. Situational factors include subordinates characteristics; Leaders situation; Group factors and organizational factors like organizational culture, climate etc. This theory has wide implications for managers in the sense that it offers clues why a manager who is successful in one situation, fails when there is change in the situation.

## EMPLOYEE COUNSELLING

In every organization, a large number of employees work together. Their attitudes, feelings and needs differ from each other. Such individual difference cause different problems in an enterprise. These problems may relate to the organization, working condition, supervision, remuneration, or technical aspect. Some times these problems may result in emotional conflicts. Such conflicts may arise between employee and employee, employee and supervisor, employee and employer, supervisor and manager or between supervisor and supervisor. Such conflicts are against the interest of all, and the enterprise. So the need is to get rid of these conflicts and the best way is to counsel the concerned parties.

Employee counselling is a discussion with the concerned employee on an emotional problem so that the problem may be solved. Under this technique the problem is listened carefully and the suggestions are given to him to reduce the problem. In the words of Keith Davis, "counselling is defined as discussion of an emotional problem with an employee, with general objective of decreasing it."

Emotional problems cause tension and confusion in the minds of an employee. He may find it difficult to discharge his duties properly due to such tensions. Emotional upsets can reduce the productivity, or it may make them leave the Co. it may lower the morale of the department they belong to. Such tensions should be removed at any cost because these adversely affect the achievement of organizational objectives.

## TYPES OF EMPLOYEE COUNSELLING

The objective of counselling is to help reduce emotional problems of employees. A reduction of such problems will benefit every one- the employee, his family, supervisor and the organization.

## BASICALLY THERE ARE THREE FORMS OF COUNSELLING

- *Directive counselling*: This is the process of hearing a persons emotional problems, deciding what he should do, and then telling and motivating him to do it. Under this method the counsellor listens to the problems of the employee very patiently and analyses this problem in his mind. Then he advises the employee, what he should do. Thus this method of counselling stresses upon the suggestions by counsellor to the employee. Directive counselling mostly accomplishes the counselling function of advise, but it may also communicate, give emotional release and to a minor extent clarify thinking.

*But this method is subject to certain limitations such as*:

- The counsellor may not be able to in understanding the problem of the employees
- The employee may or may not agree with the advise
- The success of this method depends upon the ability and efficiency of counsellor.

- *Non Directive Counselling*: Under this method, the counsellor listens to the problems of employees. The employee is encouraged to explain his problem in detail. This method concentrates upon the employee rather than the counsellor. Under this method the employee himself controls the direction of discussion and he himself tries to find out the solution of his problem. The counsellor does not give his suggestions. This method is more effective because the employee gets the status equal to the counsellor. He feels complete freedom, and tries to find out the solution of his problem. But this method takes more time and can be effective only when the employee have self confidence.
- *Co-operative Counselling*: This method is a combination of both directive and non directive method of counselling. Under this method, both the employee and counsellor co-operate each other finding a solution of the problem. Here both discuss their views on the problem in detail and try to find out the solutions based on mutual consent and co-operation.

This form of counselling is worth a serious notice as this appears to b more practically applicable and more readily suitable to managerial attitude and temperament in Indian organizational situations than the other two.

# 10

# Power and Politics in Organization

In many ways power is a unifying thread by which we can connect and rationalize the history of mankind. Of course other, more traditional perspectives like economic events, wars, ideology, and religion provide important and needed perspectives on our evolution as a society. But, certainly understanding how leaders as well as followers used power will help in understanding our history. It will be equally useful in helping us determine how people will relate to each other in the twenty-first century.

Viewing our leaders, our literature, our government, our philosophy, and our religion in power terms helps us understand each other better. These social systems record our history of competition, conflict, struggle, violence, and war. In a word, they record our fascination with power and the politics of power use. Perhaps there is no single concept of human relationship of more gut importance than how we get our way in the group. It is central to both who and what we are as individuals and as group members.

We engage in power activity in group settings. It is logical, therefore, that psychology, political science, anthropology, and the rest of the social disciplines should have interest in power. Each has something to add to our understanding of power and its use. Each discipline, almost each writer, has added specific definitions to the lexicon of power. The resulting confusion has done little to clarify concepts, or to reduce the trauma many feel when someone introduces the word power into a discussion. The study of power dates from the earliest efforts to define a social science. However, most of the modern work on power in organizational contexts had its beginnings in the 1930s. Since then, the focus of research has varied widely. Some focus on sociological underpinnings. Some see power as political. Others give it a behavioural twist. A few researchers give power a psychological thrust. And finally, some discuss power in organizational and structural terms.

Power continues to be a difficult subject to surround. Disciplinary foci have helped, but have left about as much confusion as they have added insight into the subject. Analytical studies, while relatively few, have helped to clarify elements of power, its sources, and constituent parts. This work has added needed insights into specific dimensions of power, but has not delimited the central essence of power. Indeed, most work on power adds to the ambiguity rather than diminishes it.

Power is a part of life. It is manifestly a part of interpersonal behaviour in most social situations. People are always interacting in group settings to secure goals and desired results. All interactive communication is purposeful, and to achieve this purpose, the individual engages in power activity. Because of the ambiguity of the power concept in life, it is not hard to understand the existence of its multiple definitions. It becomes the foundation for the following discussion about power in formal organizations and in other issues raised hereafter.

## POWER IN FORMAL ORGANIZATIONS

When analysed from the perspective of the individual in a structured organizational setting, we see some interesting insights on power. Achieving desired organizational results is dependent on our capacity to influence others to our point of view. The mechanism often is one of offering desired rewards to followers as inducement to desired behaviour. In effect, we say, as suggested, provide you with physical or psychological results that will meet your needs or be instrumental in achieving one or more of your desires. In this sense power use is a kind of political exchange transaction. It is instrumental to task accomplishment. Power is also a process by which we induce change in another's behaviour or attitudes. It is in this sense, then, that one can define power as the basis of all organized action. As a social structure of human interrelationships, the organization controls the action of individuals; and control over others is power. We organize for power. Control in the organization rests on power. Delegation is a power relationship. Negotiation is an exercise in power. Leadership is power in action.

Organizationally, we can describe power as the ability to make something happen-the essence of the causal relationship. Power defined in these terms becomes the basis of the "power relationship." Power relationships are interactive, interpersonal processes where one gets power from and uses it in interaction with others in the group.

## POWER AND FORMAL AUTHORITY

The literature equates the opportunity to progress within the group with a getting of more authority than other group members. We see it in action when the group places more of the total so-called "group power" on one individual. Authority is a divisible commodity that managers ration among themselves via the process of delegation. In this sense it is the basis for organizational order, logic, and control. It is the basis of status and hierarchy in the organization.

A view of power in authority terms connotes a system of dependencies; and, in this situation, distribution is the key issue. Each member of the organization relates to others in a power role relationship that constrains each member. If one gains power, it is at the expense of others in the group. If one gains, others lose. Mary Parker Follett defined this "face" of power as "power over" others.

## POWER AND SELF-ESTEEM

Power is central to defining individual self-esteem within the organization. It is part of the pursuit of personal goals. Gaining power allows the individual to place himself in the group context in specific terms, in a specific relationship to others. Adler says that power does much to explain the behaviour of exceptional people. He claims that it, more than the sex drive propounded by Freud, is the dominant determinant of personality. Weber also ascribes to power a dominant role in social organization.

The word "power" derives from the same root as the word possibility. The Roman root "possess" literally means "I can." The Latin verb "potere" means "to be able." Both words connote the central function of affecting something or someone. The word power entered the English language from this Roman/ Latin foundation at the time of the Norman conquest of England. Over time, power has come to connote personal capacity in our English heritage. Power is a capacity, a talent, a skill resident in all of us, but held in larger quantities by specific individuals.

Power is the ability or capacity to induce others to behave in desired ways in human interaction. All individuals can control or influence other people and, in turn, can be under another's influence. Power is part of all organized group activity that results in enhancement or limitation of our ability to do. Thus, power is a part of concepts like organization, authority, control direction, competition, conflict, coordination, planning, budgeting, staffing, or other administrative functions.

## POWER IN LEADERSHIP

Power is the essence of leadership. It is the extra element in interpersonal relations that allows the leader to effect others and secure their willing compliance. Rollo May defines power as the ability to cause or prevent change. Kaplin calls it the process of effecting the policies of others.

Bertrand Russell defines it as the "production of intended effects." Power allows people to alter the behaviour of others in ways they—the power users—want. Power lets anyone be a leader. The source may vary but the object appears universal. Power allows the individual to effect, to sway, others' behaviour in desired ways; in a word, to lead them. At one level, all interpersonal relationships are leader-follower relationships. We are constantly moving from a directive position to a follower one in our contacts with others. At times we engage in persuading others to do something we want them to do. It may be to follow our orders, to get us something, to laugh at our jokes, or to understand and respect out ideas and values.

At one level, all interpersonal relationships are leader-follower relationships. We are constantly moving from a directive position to a follower one in our contacts with others. At times we engage in persuading others to do something we want them to do. It may be to follow our orders, to get us something, to laugh at our jokes, or to understand and respect out ideas and values.

At other times—often in the same conversation—we persuade them to laugh, or induce them to do something that we want them to do. We see power in leadership contexts in a much larger dimension. It is a personal, rather than merely a positional, concept. The operative characteristic of leadership is its intimacy. It is a personal power relationship between one leader and one follower reiterated in a series of one-to-one relationships. These power relationships are constituent parts of organizational life.

## POWER IN USE IN ORGANIZATIONAL CONTEXTS

Few ideas are more basic to the study of organizations than power. It is an important and active reality in all dimensions of organizational life. Indeed, power interactivity is, perhaps, humankind's most pervasive dimension. We experience the result of power use at all levels in the organization and by all participants.

It is a constituent part of informal as well as formal organization. As Dahl said, it is as "ancient and ubiquitous as any that social theory can boast." Power is central to both leadership theory and practice. It is a core element of human interaction. organization and management of the environment predate recorded history. It is a primary activity of human organization. Administration and the desire to order our immediate situation have inspired the classics in literature. Certainly, we must count Machiavelli *The Prince* and Plato *Republic* among those classics. They typify a literature that carry our search for order and organization of our immediate environment into everyday life.

Power is central to man's continuing concern for administration and organization. How people organize and relate to each other to get planned goals accomplished is central to organization and administrative theory. The overreaching problem of organization life is securing follower compliance. This compliance, however, must come without losing the long-term amicable relationship between the person desiring compliance and the person whose behaviour change we seek. And this must be done with an eye on conserving scarce resources.

Machiavelli *The Prince* provides extensive advice to rulers on how to extend and combine their power and capacity to direct compliance. Similarly the libraries of the world are full of books to help us to influence subordinates, raise our children, make friends, and influence others.

Few concepts are more crucial or more central to the understanding of behaviour in organizations. We may treat it as a prime aim or as instrumental to other, strategic aims. Nevertheless, power is a necessary part of the interaction of people. Power is a cornerstone of both leadership and management theory and practice. It is the essence of leader behaviour. It is central to subordinate-to superior interaction. It helps explain the myriad relationships we experience with the many peers and external contacts that make up the fabric of organizational interaction.

On another dimension, most organization members influence others and are, in turn, influenced by them. Power use dominates not only management and leadership perspectives, but those of ordinary workers, suppliers, consumers, and other stakeholders also. People in all kinds of work or in any social or hierarchical relationship share the goal of getting others to behave in ways they want them to. We want others to like us, to work for us, to think the way we want them to think. We want them to go where we think they ought to go, to be what we think they ought to be. Seen in this light, power is a political transaction process.

In agrarian societies our power usage was more personal, immediate, and limited in scope and domain. In industrial societies, complexity has affected power use as well as other elements of life. Power use now is more impersonal, anonymous, and institutionalized. In real ways it is the primary measure of our value to the group—be it the work organization or the social group. Hobbes, as early as the seventeenth century, listed power as the measure of our social status. Today, power is in many ways the measure of position. Money or possessions, while instrumental, are less significant in assessing social position than is power. We are a power-oriented society: one particularized by institutions.

Using these ideas, we can see that many managerial and leadership concepts have power connotations. For example, we can define authority as a manifestation of power characterized by position and relationship within the formal, hierarchical system. Authority connotes the legitimate right of the holder to command, decide, or determine the way the organization will go. It is an obvious manifestation of power, one connoting the formally granted rights inherent in the organizational position held.

Personal influence, an integral part of leadership, is a form power takes. Influence is a form of power, often subtle and indirect, by which we impact the situations and behaviours of others. We can understand influence best as a mechanism of attitude change. It uses esteem and respect to accomplish the task of changing the behaviour of another. Using a power connotation helps us interpret competition and its companion concept, conflict.

In competition settings both participants exercise power in trying to achieve their purpose at the expense of the other person. Competition becomes conflict when we include emotions. Conflict, too, is a power relationship. Power has a direct connection to many of the underlying functions of management. For example, power is a constituent part of organizational control systems. As individuals exert energy towards activating others to behave in organizationally useful ways, they are exercising power. Direction, control, planning, coordination, and correlation are all manifestations of power used in organizations to accomplish intended results. The process is an impact one; the capacity is power.

In fact, we can understand all of a manager's tasks-execution of authority, personal interaction, control, direction, planning, conflict resolution, and so on-better from a power perspective. While often masked, ignored, and even denied, power is central in understanding organizational participant behaviour. In budgeting, planning, staffing, controlling, and directing, individuals constantly engage in power relationships and power exchanges. They negotiate schedules, compromise goals, marshal support, and compete for available resources. Implicit in each of these traditionally accepted managerial activities is an element of power use, of producing intended behaviours in others. Every animation of interpersonal behaviour directed towards goal accomplishment results in actual or potential power use.

Using power allows us to affect another's behaviour in ways we want. This effect can result regardless of the will of the target of power. Leadership implies the inducement of followers to do something that the follower would not do without the leader's intervention. At some levels, at some times, for some leaders, the operative words may be persuasion, opening of opportunity, or facilitation of the work of followers. At other times the focus may be on coercion, force, or control. Whether the connotation is positive or negative, we are in the business of getting others to do what they would not done if left alone.

## ORGANIZATIONAL POLITICS

An obvious cease from this analysis is that management is a political activity. It involves us in all interactions aimed at reserving resources to our special needs. Much of existing literature on management and organizations, in fact, describes aspects of power acquisition, legitimization, and maintenance functions. Even limited experience in organizational life will leave us with a realization of the importance of political negotiation in organizational systems. Our organizational laws, rules, standards, policy, and regulations are manifestations of political influence-that is, power. Power is at the heart of what Mayes and Allen call the "management of influence" throughout the organization.

Organizational politics has been a largely undiscussed phenomenon in organization and management theory and practice. It has only recently found its way into the formal literature of organizational behaviour. Earlier writers also have made significant contributions to our understanding. Hobbes, over 300 years ago, helped distinguish political power. He pointed out that the power of the subject impacts the sovereign as well. Since then, the debate has ranged from concern with the instrumental nature of power to its resource qualities to its operating impacts in group situations. Definitions of organizational politics typically include several factors.

*Organizational politics involve*:

- Actions taken by individuals throughout the organization
- Any influence of one actor towards another.
- Effort by one party to promote self-interest over that of another and, therefore, threaten the second party's self interest.
- Actions typically not sanctioned by the host organization or results sought that it does not sanction.
- Some kind of exchange process with a zero-sum outcome.

Much of the literature suggests that organizational politics concerns itself with influence and control relationships of this kind. Many definitions place organizational politics in this kind of control-of-others light.

Pfeffer suggests that many definitions ascribe "sinfulness" or "illegality" to this social phenomenon. Porter, Allen, and Angle see organizational politics in self-interest terms. Martin and Sims tie organizational politics to control. We also can see another construction of organizational politics. Operationally, organizational politics is a ubiquitous fact of organizational life. Allen, Madison, Porter, Renwick, and Mayes suggest that it is an important social influence process. It has a potential of being both functional and dysfunctional to organizations and individuals.

Organizational politics is a solid part of organizational life. Its use conforms with current research suggesting that all group interaction has specific change purposes. organizational politics is, therefore, a part of social interaction. Its positive or negative face is dependent on factors other than the mere fact of interaction for influence purposes. Our experience with power places it in the centre of all social intercourse. Organizational politics is merely a structured, purposeful, organized group version of this universal social practice. An operationally useful definition of organization politics may include elements that Mayes and Allen called the management of influence.

For them, organizational politics is a process that involves formulating political goals, decision strategies, and tactics. It entails executing those tactics and setting up feedback loops to ensure effective results. Organizational power politics is also defined in terms of a process of change. Defined in this way we can say that organizational politics is the essence of leadership.

Organizational politics therefore includes actions taken to gain and use power to control organizational resources to achieve our preferred results instead of those of others. This definition places organizational politics in the classroom when a teacher "teaches." It is in the home as a father asks his child to do something. It is in the office as the subordinate "manages" his or her boss by couching interaction upward in ways calculated to induce the boss to respond favourably. And it is present when the manager orders employees to adopt a new procedure. David Bell emphasizes the "talk" aspect of organizational politics. He says traditional definitions of politics as who gets what, when, where, and how is not helpful.

Getting control over needed resources can be, and often is, an intensely personal and private affair, not a public one. Talk, on the other hand, always involves others and more consistently conforms to the definition of politics. Talk effects others, and to that extent it is power. To the widest extent possible, organizational politics concerns how people affect each other.

## POLITICAL BEHAVIOUR

Given our definition of organizational politics, it is a commonplace activity in organizations. Research by Madison and others supports the idea that organizational politics is fully a part of organizational life. Sixty per cent of managers he surveyed averred that it was "frequently" or "very frequently" a part of organizational life. Most managers see organizational politics as a part of work life at the middle and upper management levels and less so at the lower levels.

Engaging in the politics of the organization may be helpful to the individual. Madison's research report that 95 per cent of respondents agreed that office politics is necessary in achieving individual goals. They also were unanimous in saying that it could harm them. For Madison, engaging in organizational politics is a "crucial path" to success in the organization. We use political action in the organization in situations of uncertainty, importance, and salience to either the individual or the unit concerned.

It is an old and hoary behaviour pattern in groups. People in groups interact in a power struggle and to limit the exercise of power in others. Individuals behave politically in all facets of organizational life. They use power to secure promotion, salary increases, or job transfers. It is part of the interplay of activity involved in resource allocation and delegation of authority and responsibility.

It is intrinsic to policy development and policy change, performance appraisal, grievances, and intra-organizational coordination. Politics is part of the process of rule making and decision making in all aspects of organizational activity. Gandz and Murray ranked perceptions of political action of various common organizational activities and concluded that politics was instrumental in determining interdepartmental harmony. Other areas of organizational activity where politics was a significant factor included promotions and transfers, delegation of authority, facilities and equipment allocation, and work appraisals. Less significant arenas for the exercise of organizational politics were such activities as assessing penalties, hiring, employee development, policymaking, setting pay rates, and budgeting. Analysis of these data suggests that people use organizational politics most often in areas where individuals have some discretion in the actions open to them. We see less political behaviour in those activity areas where formalized rules and systems are commonly in place.

Madison and others explored the positive or negative impacts of the use of organizational politics. His research emphasizes that organizational politics can be useful in helping the organization reach its goals and cope with survival and organizational health concerns. It confirms also that organizational politics is helpful in coordinating staff and units, developing esprit de corps, and decision making. It is useful in organizational goal achievement. It can result in inappropriate use of scarce resources, cause divisiveness, create tension, allow less fully qualified people to advance, and reduce communication flows. And, finally, it can damage the image of the organization and sully its reputation.

Madison also assessed the positive and negative impacts of the use of organizational politics on the individuals concerned. Engaging in organizational politics can aid significantly in career advancement, getting recognition, and status in the organization, and increasing our power position. It also helps us accomplish personal goals and is helpful in allowing us to get our jobs done. Engaging in organizational politics can help individuals feel positive about their achievement and their ability to be in control of their organizational life. There are risks involved, however. Engaging in political activity may result in reducing perceived or actual power in the group. It can result in removal from the organization. It can accentuate negative feelings about us by others. And, political activity can result in loss of promotion or increased feelings of guilt and interference with job performance.

Political activity can have both positive and negative results. Its use, however, is not in doubt. It is a ubiquitous part of organizational life. Older group members use it more than those newly inducted into the organization. This is the case also with middle and upper levels of the organization. They engage in organizational politics more than do those in lower-level positions. It is beyond doubt an instrument for securing organizational rewards.

Allen, Madison, Porter, Renwick, and Mayes assessed personal skills and traits common to politically active people in organizations. They conclude that effective political actors, all share some common characteristics. They are articulate, sensitive, and socially adept. They are competent, popular, extroverted, and self confident. They exhibit aggressive tendencies, are ambitious, can be devious, and are clearly "organization men." They are also "highly intelligent and logical people." The politically adept individual in the organization is outgoing, competent, and effective in interacting with others. They are seeking, energetic advocates of their desired results. They are willing to engage others in competition for available resources and for the dominance of their ideas and ideologies.

## POLITICAL BEHAVIOUR VERSUS ADMINISTRATIVE BEHAVIOUR

We can distinguish organizational politics from administrative behaviour in several significant dimensions. Most view administrative behaviour by organizational participants as consensus behaviour. Group members agree that the behaviour in question is legitimate, that it flows from recognized "right," and that it fits the terms of the exchange. On the other hand, people resist political action and behaviours, if power targets recognize their intent. There is a consensus feeling that such behaviour is illegitimate.

All members of the organization participate in power use. Senior executives, middle managers, informal leaders, and rank and file employees all use power. Madison's work shows that politics is more in the superior's mind and actions than in that of lower-level employees. While this may be true, it does not lessen the fact that all employees have some power. No one is powerless, even if it is only the power to withhold talent or energy. They use power to secure their desired results in the same ways that higher-level participants use their capacities.

It is a thesis of this book that power politics is a central activity of life. We can define much of life activity as the exercise of power. Our success, in part, is a function of our ability to use power in our interrelationships. Success requires that we develop power skills along with, or perhaps in preference to, functional and task skills. Power is basic to effective living in the same way that energy is basic to physics. It is a foundation element of human interaction. Power is the ability to activate human and material resources to get work done.

# 11

# Conflict Management

When individuals and groups interact, there is always a potential for conflict. Conflict is disagreement or opposition between or among persons regarding goals, issues, perceptions and so on, whenever there is some interaction between or among these persons. David.L Austin, *"conflict is the disagreement between two or more individuals or groups, with each individual or group trying to gain acceptance of its views or objectives over the other"*. Because people differ in their attitudes, values and goals, conflict among them becomes unavoidable. The earlier traditional view of conflict considered it harmful, destructive and unnecessary.

The existence of conflict was regarded as a sign that something had gone wrong and it needed to be corrected. It was believed that the existence of conflict reflected poor management and the deliberate efforts of troublemakers. Since conflict involves disagreement on such factors as allocation of resources, nature of goals and objectives, organizational policies and procedures, the conflict at its worst can lead to unnecessary stress, blockage in communication, lack of co operation, and this results in reduced organizational effectiveness. In recent years, however, management scholars have shifted their view of conflict.

The current view, also known as "inter-actionist" view holds that some degree of conflict is not only inevitable but also necessary for organizational health. It proposes that because people differ in their attitudes values and goals, conflict is a natural outcome in any group of people and that it can be helpful and constructive if it is handled properly.

*Some Positive consequences of conflict are*:

- *It helps in analytical thinking*: It provides an individual and companies a chance to critically analyse views, opinions, rules policies, goals and plans and to make such changes that may be required.
- *It helps in increased cohesion*: Conflict between organizations and groups develops loyalty within the organization or group and loyalty results in cohesive efforts in order to compete with outsiders.
- *Conflicts promote competition, which results in increased efforts*: Some individuals are highly motivated by conflict and severe competition. For example a manager who is turned down for a promotion due to conflict within the organization may work harder to prove that he is more capable and deserves a promotion.
- *It serves as a foundation for organizational development*: Conflict with the status quo is a pre requisite to change. Creative and innovative people are always looking for grounds to challenge the status quo. These challenges lead to search for alternatives to existing patterns, which lead to organizational change and development.
- *Conflict when expressed can clear the air and reduce tension*: Some disagreements, if unexpressed, can lead to frustration and tension resulting in fear and distrust.

However, when it is expressed, openly and honestly, it may show the cause of conflict to be a minor one resulting in co-operation and compromise.

## TYPES OF CONFLICT SITUATIONS

Since conflict has both positive and negative consequences, it must be looked into and managed for organizational benefit.

Management must survey the situation to decide whether to stimulate conflict or resolve it. There are five basic types of conflict.

## CONFLICT WITHIN AN INDIVIDUAL

These are usually value related, where role-playing expected of the individual does not conform with the values and beliefs held by the individual. For example, a secretary may have to lie on instructions that her boss is not in the office to avoid an unwanted visitor. This may cause a conflict in her mind. Conflict within an individual can also arise when a person has to choose between two equally desirable alternatives or between two equally undesirable goals.

## INTERPERSONAL CONFLICT

This involves conflict between two or more individuals and is probably the most common and most recognised conflict. This may involve conflict between two managers who are competing for limited capital and manpower resources. This conflict can become further acute when the scarce resources cannot be shared and must be obtained. Another type of interpersonal conflict can relate to disagreements over goals and objectives of the organization.

For example, some members of the board of directors of a college may propose open admission policy where the college follows a policy of admitting only top quality students. In addition to conflicts over the nature and substance of goals and objectives, the conflicts can also arise over the means for achieving these goals and objectives. For example two marketing executives may argue as to which promotional methods would result in higher sales.

These interpersonal conflicts are often the results of personality clashes. People with widely different characteristics and attitudes are bound to have views and aims that are inconsistent with the laws and aims of others.

## CONFLICT BETWEEN THE INDIVIDUAL AND GROUP

All formal and informal groups in an organization may have certain norms of behaviour and operational standards, which all members are expected to adhere to. Individual members may want to remain within the group for social needs but may disagree with the group goals and the methods to achieve such goals. For example if a group is going on strike for some reasons, some members may not agree with these reasons, thus causing conflict within the group. This type of conflict may also arise between the manager and a group or between the leader and followers. A manager may take disciplinary action against a member causing conflict with the group and this may result in reduced productivity.

## INTER GROUP CONFLICT

An organization is an interlocking network of groups, departments, parts or work teams. The inter group conflicts are not so much personal in nature as they are due to factors inherent in the organizational structure. For example there is active and continuous conflict between the management and union. One of the most common conflicts is between the line and the staff members of the organization.

These types of conflicts can also be caused in consistent rewards and differing performance criteria for different units and groups. For example sales people who depend upon their commission as a reward for their efforts may promise their customers certain quantity of the product, quality and delivery dates which the production department may find impossible to meet, thus causing conflict between the two units.

## INTER ORGANIZATIONAL CONFLICT

Conflict also occurs between organizations, which are dependent upon each other in some way. This conflict may be between buyer organizations and supplier organizations about quantity, quality and delivery times of raw materials and other policy issues. Such conflict could also be between union and management, between government agencies that regulate certain organizations and the organizations that are affected by them.

## THE CAUSES OF CONFLICT

Basically the causes of conflict fall into three different categories.

## COMMUNICATIONAL ASPECT

Poor communication can have a powerful effect in causing conflict. Misunderstood or partial information during the process of communication can make the differences between the success and the failure of a task. And any such failure for which the responsibility becomes difficult to trace can cause conflict between the sender of the communication and the receiver. Thus the problems in communication process like filtering of communication, semantic problems due to differences in background etc can animation to stimulate problems.

## BEHAVIOURAL ASPECT

These conflicts arise out of human thoughts and feelings, emotions and attitudes, values and perceptions and reflect some basic traits of a personality. Thus some people's values and their perceptions of situations are likely to generate conflict with others who have different values an perceptions. Behavioural conflict may also be based on personal biases regarding such factors a religion, race, sex, and so on. Behavioural conflicts can also arise when beliefs and values held by person are challenged. These are often culturally based.

## Structural Aspect

These conflicts arise due to issues related to the structural design of the organizations as whole as well as the design of its sub units.

*Some factors are*:

- *Size of the organization*: The larger the size of the organization, the more the chance for existence of conflict. Conflict is more likely because as the organization becomes larger, there is greater impersonal formality, less goal clarity, more supervisory level and supervision and greater chance of information being diluted and distorted as it is passed along.
- *Line- staff distinction*: This is one of the major causes of conflict. Line units are involved in operations that

are directly related to the core activities of the organization. Staff units are generally in an advisory capacity and support the line function. The conflicts between these two units arise because of different perceptions about their roles and responsibilities. Since staffs generally advise and the line decides and acts, the staffs often feel powerless.

- *Participation*: It is assumed that if the subordinates are not allowed to participate in the decision making process, then they will show resentment which will induce conflict.
- *Role ambiguity*: A role reflects a set of activities associated with a certain position in the organization. If these work activities are ill defined then the person who is carrying out these activities will not be able to perform as others expect him to, because his role is not clearly defined.
- *Design of work flow*: Poorly designed work flow structure and poorly planned coordination requirements lead to inter group problems and conflicts, specially when tasks are interdependent. For example, in a hospital, the doctors and nurses must work together since their tasks are highly interdependent. If they do not coordinate the activities well then there will be confusion and conflict.
- *Scarcity of resources*: When individuals and units must share such resources; capital, facilities, staff assistance and so on, and these resources are scarce and there severe competition to obtain these resources, then conflicts can become quite intensive. This is especially true in declining organizations where resources become even more scarce due to cut back in personal and services so that the concerned units become highly competitive for the available resources.

## CONFLICT MANAGEMENT

Various researches have identified various techniques in dealing with conflict between two or more individuals. Some of the primary strategies for dealing with and reducing the impact of behaviour conflicts are,

- *Avoidance*: In certain situations, it may be advisable to take a passive role and ignore the conflict altogether. From the managers point of view it may be specially necessary, when getting involved in a situation involving conflict would provoke further controversy or when the conflict is so silly in nature that it would not be worth the managers time to get involved and try to solve it. It is also possible that it may be best either to leave it to the concerned parties to solve it.
- *Smoothing*: This simply means covering up the conflict by appealing for the need for unit; rather than addressing the issues of conflict itself. If the parties within an organization have conflict, the supervisor may try to calm things down by being understanding and support to both parties and appealing them for co-operation by presenting an image of "one big family'.
- *Compromising*: A compromise in the conflict is reached by balancing the demands of the conflicting parties, and bargaining in a give and take position, to reach a solution. Each part gives up something and also gains something. This technique is very common in negotiation between the labour unions and management.
- *Forcing*: This is a technique of domination where the dominator has the power and authority to enforce his own views over the opposing conflicting party. This technique is potentially effective in situations such as president of a company firing a manager because he is considered as a trouble maker.
- *Problem solving*: This approach assumes that in all organizations, there will be differences in opinions, which must be, resolved through discussions and respect for differing viewpoints. In general, this technique is very useful in resolving conflicts arising

out of misunderstandings. A discussion of issues in a trusting environment can clear such misunderstandings.

## ELTON MAYO'S HAWTHORNE STUDIES

The Hawthorne Studies (or experiments) were conducted from 1927 to 1932 at the Western Electric Hawthorne Works in Chicago, where Harvard Business School professor Elton Mayo examined productivity and work conditions. The studies grew out of preliminary experiments at the plant from 1924 to 1927 on the effect of light on productivity.

Those experiments showed no clear connection between productivity- and the amount of illumination but researchers began to wonder what kind of changes would influence output.

## VARIABLES AFFECTING PRODUCTIVITY

Specifically, Mayo wanted to find out what effect fatigue and monotony had on job productivity and how to control them through such variables as rest breaks, work hours, temperature and humidity. In the process, he stumbled upon a principle of human motivation that would help to revolutionize the theory and practice of management. Mayo took six women from the assembly line, segregated them from the rest of the factory and put them under the eye of a supervisor who was more a friendly observer than disciplinarian.

Mayo made frequent changes in their working conditions, always discussing and explaining the changes in advance. He changed the hours in the working week, the hours in the workday the number of rest breaks and the time of the lunch hour. Occasionally, he would return the women to their original, harder working conditions.

### Relay Assembly

The investigators selected two girls for their second series of experiments and asked them to choose another, four girls, thus making a small group of six. The group was employed in assembling telephone relays - a relay being a small but intricate mechanism composed of about forty separate parts, which had to be assembled by the girls seated at a lone bench and dropped into a basket when completed. The relays were mechanically counted as they slipped down the chute. It was intended that the basic rate of production should be noted at the start, and that subsequently changes would be introduced, the effectiveness of which would be measured by increased or decreased production of the relays.

**Feedback Mechanism**

Through out the series of experiments, an observer sat with the girls in the workshop noting all that went on, keeping the girls informed about the experiment, asking for advice or information and listening to their complaints. The experiment began by introducing various changes, each of which was continued for a test period of four to twelve weeks. The results of these changes are as follows:

**Conditions and Results**

- Under normal conditions with a forty eight hour week, including Saturdays, and no rest pauses. - The girls produced 2,400 relays a week each.
- They were then put on piece-work for eight weeks.- Output went up.
- Two five minute rest pauses, morning and afternoon, were introduced for a period of five weeks.- Output went up once more.
- The rest pauses were lengthened to ten minutes each.-Output went up sharply.
- Six five minute pauses were introduced, and the girls complained that their work rhythm was broken by the frequent pauses- Output fell slightly
- Return to the two rest pauses, the first with a hot meal supplied by the Company free of charge - Output went up.
- The girls were dismissed at 4.30 p.m. instead of 5.00 p.m-Output went up

- They were dismissed at 4.00 p.m.- Output remained the same.

Finally, all the improvements were taken away, and the girls went back to the physical conditions of the beginning of the experiment: work on Saturday, 48 hour week, no rest pauses, no piece work and no free meal. This state of affairs lasted for a period of 12 weeks - *Output was the highest ever recorded averaging 3000 relays a week.*

## WHAT HAPPENED DURING THE EXPERIMENTS?

What happened was that six individuals became a team and the team gave itself wholeheartedly and spontaneously to co-operation in the experiment. The consequence was that they felt themselves to be participating freely and without afterthought and were happy in the knowledge that they went working without coercion from above or limitation. They were themselves satisfied at the consequence for they felt that they were working under less pressure than ever before. In fact regular medical checks showed no signs of cumulative fatigue and absence from work declined by 80 per cent.

It was noted too, that each girl had her own technique of putting the component parts of the relay together - sometimes she varied this technique in order to avoid monotony and it was found that the more intelligent the girl, the greater was the number of variations. The experimental group had considerable freedom of movement. They were not pushed around or bossed by anyone. Under these conditions they developed an increased sense of responsibility and instead of discipline from higher authority being imposed, it came from within the group itself.

## GROUP DYNAMICS.

The study of groups in work situation has been an important activity of behavioural scientist ever since the pioneering work of the Hawthorne Researchers over seventy years ago. The outcome of numerous studies into different aspects of the behaviour of groups is a considerable store of useful and practicable knowledge about the working of groups. Typical areas of research have included the study of group effectiveness, inter-groups competition, and group cohesiveness. Groups at work are formed as a direct consequence of an organization's need to differential itself. A group is basically a collection of individuals, contributing to some common aim under the direction of a leader, and who share a sense of common identity. Thus, a group is more than an aimless crowd of people waiting in an airport lounge or at a bus stop. A group has some central purpose, temporary or permanent, and a degree of self awareness as a group, and in the work situation most tasks are in fact undertaken by groups and teams, rather than by individuals. Groups are also widely used for solving problems, creating new ideas, making decisions and coordinating tasks.

These group functions are what the organization itself needs to fulfill its purpose. However individuals themselves need groups. Groups provide stimulus, protection, assistance and other social and psychological requirements. Groups therefore can work in the interest of organizations as a whole as well as in the interests of individual members. One of the earliest distinctions to be made between groups (arising from the Hawthorne investigations) was between formal and informal groups. Formal groups were those set up by the management of an organization to undertake duties in the pursuit of organization goals.

Some writers have described formal groups as official groups, to avoid the confusion that can arise when describing groups operating in an informally structured organization. Such groups may be informal in the sense that they have few rules, enjoy participative leadership and have flexible roles. Nevertheless they are completely official.

What is meant by informal organizations are those groupings which the employees themselves have developed in accordance with their own needs. These, of course, are unofficial. Every organization has these unofficial groups and research has shown how important they are for organizational effectiveness.

## CLASSIFICATION/TYPES OF GROUPS

There can be different types of groups that might exist in an organization. The most common way of distinguishing between groups is to categorizing the groups into formal or informal groups.

Formal groups are deliberately created by the organization in order to help the organizational members achieve some of the important the organizational goals. The informal groups, in contrast, develop rather spontaneously among an organization's members without a direction from the organizational authorities.

There are various types of formal groups that are found in an organization.

*These are*:

- Command group which is determined by the organizational chart depicting the approved formal connections between individuals in an organization. Examples of command group are Director and the faculty members in a business school, school principal and teachers, production manager and supervisors, etc.
- Task groups comprising some individuals with special interest or expertise, are created by the organizational authorities to work together in order to complete a specific task. Task groups are often lot restricted to the organizational hierarchy and can be cross-functional in nature. Examples of task group might be people working on a particular project. Standing committee is a permanent committee in an organization to deal with some specific type's f problems that may arise more or less on a regular basis. Examples of standing committees include the standing committee in a university to discuss various academic and administrative issues.
- Task force/ad hoc committee, in contrast, is a temporary committee formed by organizational members from across various functional areas for a special purpose. Meetings can also come under this category.

*Various types of informal groups are*:

- Interest groups are formed when a group of employees band together to seek some common objectives, like protesting some organizational policy or joining the union to achieve a higher amount of bonus.
- Friendship groups develop among the organizational members when they share some common interest like participating in some sports activities or staging the office drama, etc..
- Reference groups are the groups, with which individuals identify and compare themselves. These could be within the organization when a middle level executive compares himself with the higher level executive and longs for the perks and benefits enjoyed by the latter. The reference group might exist outside the organization as well when an individual compares himself with his batch mate working in other organizations or an ideal group of people he likes to have friendship.

## GROUPS NORMS AND GROUP COHESIVENESS

*Group development process*: A useful way of looking at the development of group was devised by B. Tuckman (1965) who saw groups as moving through four key stages of development. Later (1977) he added a fifth stage.

*The final model can be summarized as follows*:

- Forming is the initial stage of group development when the group members first come in contact with others and get acquainted with each other. This stage is characterized predominantly by a feeling of uncertainty among the group members as they now try to establish ground rules and pattern of relationship among themselves.
- Storming is the next stage that is characterized by a high degree of conflict among the members. Members often show hostility towards each other and resist

the leader's control. If these conflicts are not adequately resolved, the group may even be disbanded. But, usually the group eventually come in terms with each other and accepts the leadership role at the end of this stage.

- Norming is the third stage of the group development process during which the group members become closer to each other and the group starts functioning as a cohesive unit. The group members now identify themselves with the group and share responsibility for achieving the desired level of performance of the group. Norming stage is complete when the group members can set a common target and agree on the way of achieving this.
- Performing is the fourth stage when the group is finally ready to start working. As the group is not fully formed after resolving their internal conflicts of acceptance and sharing responsibility, they can now devote energy to achieve its objectives.
- Adjourning is the final stage when the group, after achieving the objectives for which it was created, starts to gradually dissolve itself.

Group norms can be seen to develop at Stage 3 in the analysis. Norms, in this context are common standards of social and work behaviour, which are expected of individuals in the group. Norms are rules of behaviour or proper ways of action which are accepted as legitimate by group members. Once such norms are influenced by organizational factors; such as policies, management style of superiors, and rules and procedures.

They are also influenced by individual employees, whose standards may or not be in line with those of the official organization. For Example, a group norm for the young men in an engineering workshop could be to follow a fashion of wearing long hair. This would conflict with organizational norms concerning the safety of employees in the workplace. Another example of a conflict between official and unofficial group norms can be drawn from situation where a group itself decides to operate a certain level of output over a given time, regardless of targets set by the management in their search for increased efficiency and productivity. The ideal situation, from an organization's point of view, is attained when the *unofficial* norms of the group are in harmony with the *official* norms of the organization. There is no doubt that part of the leadership role of a manager is to secure this harmony in his or her own part.

## GROUP COHESIVENESS

Group cohesiveness means the degree of attachment of the members to their group. This refers to the ability of the group members to stick together. It also implies to the ability of a group to attract new members. If group cohesion is high, the interaction between members of the group is high and the degree of agreement in group opinion is high.

A very cohesive group will demonstrate strong loyalty to its individual members and strong adherence to its established norms. Individual who cannot accept these norms are cast out from the protection of the group. As Tuckman's analysis shows, cohesiveness develops over time and a newly-formed group has little cohesiveness.

There are several factors which can help cohesiveness to develop in a group.

*These include the following*:

- Similarity of work
- Physical proximity in the workplace.
- The work-flow system
- Structure of tasks
- Group size (smaller rather than larger)
- Threats from outside
- The prospect of rewards
- Leadership style of the manager
- Common social factors (age, race, social status etc.).

In general the reason why people do develop into closely knit groups are threefold: because of those things they have in common, because of pressures from outside the group, and because of their need to fulfill their social and affiliation needs.

## STATUS

The existence of status is a common feature of every organized group whether it is society, organization, or work group. Status is the relative ranking that a person holds in a group, organization or society. A status is a position that has been determined as being important in the relationships of the group. It typically refers to a specific hierarchical position within a particular organization. There are four scales by which one can describe various types of status.

### ASCRIBED-ACHIEVED

This dimension of status measures the extent to which prestige or value is earned or is a matter of birth right. In the society, a certain amount of prestige is derived merely from being born into a prominent family. On the other hand a person may earn it through his own work and admiration of others.

### FUNCTIONAL-SCALAR

This is related with the vertical and horizontal positions. In an organization, the position of a person may be evaluated on the basis of its rank in the hierarchy.

### PERSONAL-POSITIONAL

This scale relates status to the extent to which prestige or value is based on characteristics of the individual himself or based on the position he holds without regard to the person who occupies it.

### ACTIVE-LATENT

This dimension arises because a person performing various roles may have different status with each role. For example a person may be lowly placed in an organization; consequently his status is very low in the organization. But if he is holding a high position in the trade union, this status may affect his working in the organization.

**Status and Group Norms**

Status has significant effect on the power of group norms.

High status members of groups often are given more power to deviate from norms than other group members. They are better able to resist pressure for conformity to group norms than low status members. This happens because high status members are highly valued by group members and there fore the latter's accept the behaviours of the formers.

## ROLES

A role is the pattern of behaviours expected of a person occupying a particular position in a social unit. Since a person may be part of several social units like family, friendship group, organization etc. he may occupy several positions at the same time. Even in an organization working as an employee, a person may hold a position; say chief accountant but the same person may be a superior, a subordinate, a member of finance committee and so on. In every such form of position, behaviours expected from him may be different. Thus there are certain actual behaviours and they create role identity. There are two elements that define this role identity; role perception and role expectations.

### ROLE PERCEPTION

An individual is expected to behave just as to his own perception in the group or organization. The person forms this perception on the basis of certain stimuli like job description, clues provided in training programmes, role narration by peers and so on. However this perception may or may not be correct. In order to correct this perception analysis of role expectations is required.

### ROLE EXPECTATIONS

Role expectations are defined as how others believe one should behave in a given situation. Combining both role perception and role expectations, actual role prescription for an individual may be developed.

## ORGANIZATIONAL CLIMATE

Every individual is different from others in his attitude,

behaviour and culture and so he requires a different kind of social and organizational environment. When a person joins an organization, he brings to it his individuality that affects the other members of the organization and is also affected by their behaviour and culture.

So each organization has its separate or individual climate in which its members develop. People who are fit in that climate or who make themselves fit in that climate continues with the organization and the rest who are quite unfit or fail to adjust themselves are forced to quit.

A sound climate is an asset for the organization and good management must protect it because it takes a long period to create a sound climate and people recognize the organization with its climate past. It can improve the climate by making sincere efforts.

*The study of the organizational climate has the following impacts on the organizational behaviour*:

- *It affects motivation, productivity and job satisfaction*: organizational climate can have major influence on motivation, productivity and job satisfaction. Climate determines the action and it creates few expectancies as to consequences. Employees can expect certain rewards; penalties and satisfaction or frustrations based on the organizational climate and the expectations tend to lead to motivation as shown by expectancy theory.
- *Contingency relationship*: There is a contingency relationship between the climate and the organization. It means climate of the organization is contingent upon the type of employees it has, the type of technology, workers education and the other like variables. For example research institute or department would certainly want a climate different from that of, workshop or an office.
- *It represents the entire social system*: Organizational climate represents the entire social system of a work group. *There are two aspects of a climate*:

(i) Work place itself

(2) Treatment to personnel from the management.

If employees feel satisfied while at work and if climate provides a sense of personal worth, it can be assumed that climate in that organization is favourable. As far as treatment from management is concerned, they will likely to be listened to and treated, as they are someone of value. They want that management should really feel and care about their needs and problems.

If these two are favourable, there prevails a good climate in that organization. Thus a good organizational climate is necessary' for the development of the organization. Good climate attracts good and efficient people to the organization, who, if satisfied, may contribute to the productivity of the organization.

## TECHNIQUES FOR MEASURING ORGANIZATIONAL CLIMATE

A number of instruments have been developed to measure the organizational behavioural climate. Generally these instruments try to measure the totality of the psychological environment in which people work.

*In order to measure the organizational climate, Litwin and Stringer have developed a nine point questionnaire covering*:

(1) Structure,
(2) Responsibility,
(3) Reward,
(4) Risk,
(5) Warmth,
(6) Support,
(7) Standards,
(8) Conflict,
(9) Identity.

By the use of this questionnaire, they concluded that different management approaches do create different organizational climate that affect the motivation, performance and job satisfaction to a great extent.

Likert, another authority developed an instrument known as Likert scale that focuses mainly on behavioural conditions and the management styles used. Likert scale covered seven characteristics.

*That is*:

(1) Leadership process used,

(2) Motivational forces,

(3) Communication,

(4) Interaction - influence process,

(5) Decision making

(6) Goal setting, and

(7) Control.

## ORGANIZATIONAL EFFECTIVENESS.

Organizational effectiveness, also called as organizational success or growth may be defined as the degree to which an organization realises its goals. An organization remains effective as long as it uses its own resources in an efficient manner and continues to contribute to the large systems.

The effectiveness of the organization should be measured because of two reasons. First those who are responsible for the management of an organization should know whether their organization is doing things rightly. If not what additional efforts are required.

Second an organization is a means for satisfying the needs of people in the society and the satisfaction of such needs is directly linked to organizational effectiveness. Because of these reasons, certain approaches have been developed for measuring effectiveness.

*Most important among them are*:

- *Goal Approach*: The most widely used approach for measuring organizational effectiveness is the goal approach and it attempts at measuring organizational effectiveness in terms of goal achievement by an organization. An organization being a deliberative and purposive creation, has some specific goal or set of goals. The effectiveness of the organization can be measured in terms of the degree to which these goals are achieved. This approach the effectiveness may be measured on the basis of profit, providing efficient service, high productivity, good employee morale, stability, motivation or satisfaction.

- *Behavioural Approach*:This approach takes in to account the behaviour of people in the organization; which ultimately determines the degree of goal achievement by an organization. This is because organizations as collectivity of people have one set of goals and individuals have another set of goals. The integration of individual and organizational goals affects the organizational effectiveness because each individual tries to satisfy his needs by working in the organization. If there is a high degree of integration between organizational and individual goals, a high degree of organizational effectiveness can be achieved.
- *Strategic constituencies Approach*: Under this approach, the organizational effectiveness depends on the degree to which an organization is able to satisfy different strategic constituencies (or interest groups). These strategic constituencies and their expectations may differ for different types of organizations based on the functions performed by them. They may be owners, management, employees, customers, suppliers, government and community. As these factors have their impact on the operation of the organization, satisfaction of their expectations is important for making an organization effective. In order to apply this approach, an organization has to
  - Identify the relevant strategic constituencies and their impact on the organization; and
  - Identify the expectations of these constituencies and the way for meeting these expectations.

# 12

# Stress Management

In the workplace, stress can affect performance. Individuals under too little stress may not make enough effort to perform at their best levels, while those under too much stress often are unable to concentrate or perform effectively and efficiently.

The relationship between stress and performance is complex. Employers, however, have primarily been concerned about the rising costs of overstressed employees. The Occupational Safety and Health animation of 1970 and many state laws hold employers liable for "all diseases arising out of and in the course of employment". This means that employers are often held liable for stress-related illnesses of their employees.

Most estimates place stress-related costs to companies between $100 and $300 billion per year. These costs include absenteeism, accidents, health care expenses, and lower productivity. For example, it has been estimated that approximately 75% to 90% of all visits to primary care physicians are job related along with more than half of the 555 million work days lost annually to absenteeism.

One study reported that typically 16 days per year are lost due to emotionally exhausted or depressed employees. Also, 60% to 80% of accidents are estimated to be due to employee stress. In addition, there are the costs of poor decisions made under excess stress, of fewer innovative ideas, and of replacing debilitated employees. Stress can result in physical, psychological, and behavioural responses. Stress has been implicated as contributing to a variety of physical disorders that include heart disease, high blood pressure, strokes, migraine headaches, cancer, gastrointestinal disorders. (e.g., heartburn, ulcers) along with asthma, diabetes, and multiple sclerosis. One study reported that a company spent $3,400 annually for one employee with anxiety headaches, which included the loss of productivity, doctor visits, and negative effects on coworkers.

Psychological disorders are not always readily identifiable, but symptoms include anxiety, depression, job dissatisfaction, maladaptive behavioural patterns, chemical dependencies, and alcohol abuse. Psychological disorders have been recognized as one of the 10 leading work-related diseases in the country today by The National Institute for Occupational Safety and Health (NIOSH). Finally, behavioural responses include the coping behaviours exhibited in dealing with stressful events.

Employers cannot ignore the stress of their employees, and it is in management's own self-interest to find ways to reduce it. However, stress is subjective, and people react to it in different ways. Some adapt while others tolerate it or try always to avoid it. Some go to pieces at the first sign of stress while others seem to thrive on it. Much of a person's reaction depends on the situation and their skills in prevention and reduction. Clarke, middle managers have the highest stress level simply because they are in the middle, which can cause a great deal of conflict. A survey conducted by the American Management Association indicated that 41% of middle management has more work than time.

Hall and Savery add that middle managers must respond to sometimes conflicting demands from governmental agencies, union representatives, and the community, in addition to their supervisors and subordinates. They further found that middle managers under 30 years of age felt more stress than older managers because of confusion over lines of authority. In addition, younger middle managers are often more stressed because they have less autonomy and closer supervision. In recent years, middle managers were subjected to stress from the recession of the eighties and subsequently from the increased use of participatory management and computer systems leading to many lay-offs. Lay-offs cause stress not only for those losing their jobs but also for those remaining. Ethnic minority workers, such as Black Americans and Hispanics, have also been identified as being more subjected to stress strictly because of their background. Research has also been conducted on the stress levels of women. It is widely believed that women as a group are more stressed and feel different stress than men. Jick and Mitz suggested that women experience psychological stress (e.g., depression, emotional discomfort) more frequently than men, who tend to experience more physiological stress than women (e.g., coronary heart disease, cirrhosis of the liver). Some of these differences in stress levels can be attributed to the socialization process of men and women, which brings about different perceptions of the workplace. Women are also expected to carry the burden of raising the children and performing household chores while holding a job, which increases stress levels. Levi has indicated that two to three times as many women as men are chronic worriers. In addition, women often suffer from stress due to work underload where under-promotion leads to women being clustered at the lower levels of many organizations.

Stress can have either a positive or negative source. However, the body cannot distinguish between them. Whether stress is primarily positive or negative depends on how individuals perceive and respond to it. For example, success on the job can carry a great deal of stress. Braham calls this the "success syndrome" and states that it affects one of five managers. He says possible symptoms include apathy, irritability, uninvolvement in projects, decline in productivity, marital problems, and excessive drinking or smoking. Other causes of workplace stress include: schedules and deadlines, fear of failure, inadequate support, problems with the boss, job ambiguity, role conflict, change, new technology, work overload or underload, repetitive work, excess rules and regulations, lack of participation in decisions, poor interpersonal relationships, career development factors (obsolescence, under/over promotion, organizational structure, organizational leadership, culture, and poor working conditions) that include the climate, overcrowding, politics, and communication problems. In addition, employees often have difficulty balancing work and family life and taking on more responsibility with less support. There are many stress effects. For example, overload has been found to result in increases in blood pressure, peptic ulcers, anxiety, insomnia, loss of appetite, irritability and depression. Role conflict and role ambiguity have been linked with lower job satisfaction and higher job-related tension. Perrewe and Vickory categorize stress effects into five areas: subjective (anxiety, fatigue), behavioural (alcoholism, restlessness), cognitive (forgetfulness, inability to make decisions), physiological (high blood pressure, breathing problems), and organizational (job dissatisfaction, absenteeism).

An extreme case of stress is known as burnout, a condition that occurs over time and it is characterized by emotional exhaustion and negative attitudes that include boredom, discontent, cynicism, inadequacy, and failure. Burnout usually occurs when a person experiences physical, psychological, or spiritual fatigue and can no longer cope. The literature identifies a variety of organization-based methods available to combat job stress. Task redesign, flexible work schedules, participative management, increased employee autonomy, employee fitness programmes, and assigning work within employees' capabilities are work-related techniques.

In addition, training that helps managers become better bosses (e.g., those who take time to help employees, show appreciation for employees' work, provide feedback) can also alleviate stress. Companies have even been using humour seminars to help relieve job stress. If stress training programmes are designed and implemented properly, they can reduce illness and absenteeism and improve productivity. In addition, Quick et al. identify other reasons for organizational stress-reduction programmes: to improve human relations and morale, lower health care costs, and improve the company's image with the community. However, some experts point out that a lot of money may also be wasted on stress-reducing programmes that don't work. For example, some organizations have been lured into phony stress management programmes such as trampoline therapy and accupressure. Often, the solution to combatting stress is personal - in other words, individuals learn to manage their own stress. Individual techniques include establishing goals and priorities, managing time efficiently, delegating, learning to communicate with others, changing behaviours, exercising, relaxing, and developing a social support network of friends, family, and colleagues. The purpose of our research was to examine the attitudes and perceptions of managers regarding stress and stress management. We attempted to ascertain how managers defined stress, the impact of stress on employees, and what they feel can be done to reduce stress levels or improve one's tolerance to stress.

A 60-question survey was addressed to the vice president of Human Resources and mailed to a random sample of 400 public and private organizations with 50 or more employees throughout a six county area of Western Michigan. These organizations represented a wide diversification of economic activities and industrial sectors. We received a total of 164 completed surveys for an overall response rate of 41% (or 45% excluding 35 questionnaires returned marked "no forwarding address"). Respondents were asked to identify their perception of stress. While the typical definitions, as noted, specify stress as "a nonspecific response of the body to any demand," the majority of our respondents (88%) perceived it as a condition of physical or mental strain.

This was consistent across organization type and size, organization level, position of respondent within the company, age, and sex of the respondent. A majority (88%) believed that some levels of stress can increase the productivity of the average person. The highest percentage of respondents who tended to agree with this statement were in the prime of their career between the ages of 30 and 39 (89%) and 40 to 49 (85%). Compared with other ages groups, those under the age of 30 agreed least with this statement (55%). It appears that more experienced respondents recognized that stress isn't all bad and that many can perform well under stress. We often assume that the higher an individual rises in management, the more stress is experienced. However, the survey indicated that the middle management level is perceived to be the most stressed (88% agreed), then line management (84%), top management (72%), staff (57%) and blue-collar employees (47%). In view of the large reductions in middle management jobs during the past decade, it could be that middle managers are feeling more stress, both from job loss and additional work loads.

Contrary to literature indicating that women tend to experience more stress than men in management, our respondents did not strongly agree with this statement (58% agreed). Respondents in the 30 to 49 age groups, however, were more likely to believe that as females move into top level management positions, they exhibit more signs of stress (59% agreed between the ages of 30-39 and 72% between 40-49). In addition, more female than male respondents indicated that females exhibited more signs of stress than men (62% and 54%, respectively).

It might be that females feel they are less accepted as they move into top level management and thus have more frustration and stress to deal with than their male counterparts. Alternatively, they have additional responsibilities placed on them not only at work but at home and, consequently, feel more stressed compared to males. As the size of the organization increased, fewer respondents believed that females in management exhibited more signs of stress (39% in organizations with more than 500 employees compared with 77% in organizations with fewer than 100 employees).

## SIGNS OF STRESS

Signs of stress were categorized according to whether they were overt (easily recognized) or covert (not easily recognized). Respondents endorsed all the signs of stress (73 to 84% agreement) except for vandalism/theft, with which a majority strongly disagreed (52%). The various signs of stress and the degree of agreement were as follows:

| Signs of Stress | % Agreement |
|---|---|
| *Overt*: | |
| Physical Illness | 82% |
| Attitude/appearance changes, aggression | 80 |
| Declining performance, poor attendance | 74 |
| Vandalism/theft | 17 |
| *Covert:* | |
| Insomnia, change in appearance | 84 |
| Depression, social withdrawal | 84 |
| Drug/alcohol abuse | 77 |
| Psychosomatic illness | 73 |

There were no highly discemible trends by demographics. However, those age 50 and older showed slightly less agreement regarding drug/alcohol abuse and physical illness as signs of stress.

## CAUSES OF STRESS

Stressors are stimuli that elicit a stress response. However, not all provoke a stress response in all individuals, nor do all individuals respond in the same way to the same stressor. Two categories were developed which identified a number of causes of stress: personal and work related. Items in the list of personal stressors were developed using the Holmes and Rare Schedule of Recent Experiences Survey, while items in the list of work-related stressors were based on the organizational Readjustment Rating Scale developed by Kuzmits. Items identified with the highest values in the two developed scales were used in our questionnaire.

Personal causes of stress included: death of spouse or close family member, divorce/separation, jail term, personal injury/ illness, marriage, change in health, and money problems. There was high agreement that each of the personal items were causes of stress (agreement ranged from 76 to 97%). Work-related causes of stress included: fired/laid off, demoted, poor performance appraisal, job overload, problems with boss, changes in conditions (no promotion likely, valued employee quit, long hours), job design/high job demands, boring/routine job, and positive situations (voluntarily have new job, promotion/success). Levels of agreement regarding these items as causes of stress ranged from 76 to 93%. The 30 to 49 age groups appeared to view positive situations as more stressful than did younger and older groups. Perhaps these middle-aged groups see career development as stressful. In addition, female respondents (85%) tended to perceive positive events as more stressful than did male respondents (57%). It might be that as females gain more success, they experience more stress because they feel less accepted by upper management.

## COPING WITH STRESS

Responses were demographically consistent regarding coping mechanisms. The majority agreed that while stress is induced by unique feelings and emotions (76%), most (74%) believe that individuals typically respond by working through a three-phase process consisting of alarm, resistance, and exhaustion. This response, developed by Hans Selye and called the "general adaptation syndrome" theory, has been used to explain the relationship between stress and the physical-physiological or psychosomatic symptoms.

While people may be similar in the general stages they go through, they vary in the actual methods used to increase their ability to cope with stress. We asked respondents which factors helped people increase their tolerance to stress.

*The techniques receiving the most agreement were as follows:*

| Technique | % Agreement |
|---|---|
| Healthy attitudes | 94% |
| Proper nutrition | 92 |
| Exercise | 90 |
| *Relaxation/sleeping/taking*: a break | 90 |
| Building a strong family life | 86 |
| Meet it head on | 85 |
| *Set limits/goals/priorities*: | 84 |
| Increase personal qualifications/skills | 70 |

Increasing qualifications and skill levels were perceived by individuals in the 20-29 and the 40-49 age groups as a better coping mechanism than by other age groups. Women also tended to indicate that increasing one's skill level was a positive way to manage stress (78%) compared with men, who respond (54%). It may be that as women become more competent in their jobs, their increased confidence makes stress more manageable.

Only 17% of the respondents indicated that high intelligence increased tolerance to stress. There was a strong relationship between the size of the organization and the use of goal setting, prioritizing, and setting of limits to manage stress. Respondents from larger organizations tended to perceive this as a coping mechanism more than those from smaller organizations. As an organization increases, it generally becomes more formal in its structure and places more constraints/limits, goals, and deadlines on individuals. Also, larger organizations tend to be structured into departments, and employees are more specialized, which again places limits on individuals in larger organizations compared to those in smaller companies.

As individuals moved up in the organization, the ability of a strong family life to reduce stress was seen as less effective than for individuals with lower positions. It may be that those in higher management positions have better abilities to use work-related coping mechanisms than those in the lower levels. For example, higher-level managers may receive more support from their peers or from the culture of the organization; they many have the ability to delegate many tasks; or they may be in a better position to change the stressful situation compared with those lower in the organization.

When asked who should be responsible for stress management, the majority of respondents (74%) felt that the responsibility should lie with the individual rather than the organization, because stress is viewed as a personal problem and stress tolerance differs among individuals. However, when comparing responses by type of respondents, agreement varied. Those from manufacturing organizations felt less strongly that individuals should be primarily responsible for stress management (66%) compared with those from service or public firms (80% each). The reason may be due to unions, which are more prevalent in the manufacturing industry and tend to view most issues affecting employees as ones that organizations should be aware of and try to handle.

Respondents over 49 agreed considerably less (58%) than younger age groups (72-77%) with the statement that individuals should be primarily responsible for managing their stress. It may be that higher-level managers tend to be older and use coping mechanisms that are work-related. It could also be that older employees with more experience have learned to recognize work-related stressors and understand that employees often are incapable of removing or reducing them without help from their managers and organization.

While most respondents believed that individuals should manage their own stress, they also recognized that organizations can't ignore over-stressed employees, because of the potential effects on productivity and profits. In addition, over-stressed employees may not do anything to alleviate their stress, or the method they choose may be ineffective. Therefore, when respondents were asked what they perceived the best approach to be if an organization were to help to manage employee stress, the majority (70%) felt that wellness centres would be effective. Respondents from firms with less than 100 employees (81%) and firms with over 500 employees (76%) tended to perceive organization-wide coping mechanisms as beneficial, compared with those from medium-sized firms (53%). Medium-sized firms may be less employee-oriented than smaller firms and may lack the resources larger firms can devote to coping strategies.

In response to the question regarding present stress management practices of respondents' firms, over half (60%) indicated that their organization encouraged employees to receive professional help. However, smaller firms appeared to be less likely to do this (37%). It may be that in smaller firms there is less anonymity among employees than in larger firms and, therefore, receiving professional help may be viewed more negatively. Younger respondents were less supportive of professional help for employees than were older respondents. A company may be more likely to recommend professional help to individuals who have more responsibility and status (and thus tend to be older), because they may feel more responsible for and have a stronger desire to retain a valued employee. Other organizational techniques used included providing wellness or health programmes to employees (41%) and providing stress management training for interested employees (33%). While the majority of the respondents indicated their organizations provided some type of stress management help, almost one-third (32%) said otherwise.

Stress is inescapable and is induced by good and bad situations. Our respondents defined stress as a condition of physical or mental strain or physical/emotional wear that can be the result of a real or perceived threat. While many respondents indicated that some stress can increase productivity, many experts indicated that over-stressed individuals would be happier and would live longer if they could identify and handle their stress more effectively.

Contrary to popular opinion that it is more stressful at the top, our respondents perceived stress to be higher among middle-level mangers. This is probably a function of positions that put middle-level managers in situations where they may frequently be at odds with either those under or those over them and where they lack control and autonomy compared with top management.

We found much agreement among the respondents regarding signs of overt or covert stress along with the perceived causes of stress, which may be classified into personal and work-related stressors. Respondents also indicated that individuals need to take responsibility for managing their stress and noted that tolerance can be increased by using exercise and relaxation techniques, developing healthy attitudes, and building strong family support. However, recognizing that many stressors are work related, respondents also indicated that providing organization-wide techniques would help employees manage their stress and also help the organization avoid the negative effects of stress on productivity. However, only over one third indicated that their organizations actually do provide wellness centres.

Any form of stress management should contribute to the goals of both the organization and the individual. Employees should perceive they are going to benefit or they will not voluntarily participate. organizations must believe the benefits will outweigh the costs or they will not establish any stress management programme.

*A stress management programme should include the following*:

- Identifying the major stressors in the workplace and assessing which they can control.
- Helping employees identify their major personal sources of stress.
- Developing goals, or the programme may not be as effective as possible and the results will be difficult to measure. The goals should be clear, as specific as possible, and measurable. They should focus on attitudinal adjustments, modification of behaviours, and any skills to be acquired. In addition, individuals and organizations must perceive the goals as realistic and attainable.
- Support by top management.
- Communicating with employees about the benefits of stress management. Explain what stress is along with the health implications of excess or dysfunctional stress. Employees should be encouraged to lead healthier lives by lowering their stress on the job as well as at home.
- Assisting employees in identifying their own stressors and stress tolerance levels. Before learning how to deal with stress, employees first have to identify those stressors they react to because not everyone responds the same way to the same stressors. To aid this process, organizations might provide health risk appraisals which test for their employees' levels of stress.

- Making sure employees learn to recognize symptoms of excessive and dysfunctional stress. For example, symptoms often include intestinal distress, rapid pulse, frequent illness, insomnia, persistent fatigue, irritability, nail biting, lack of concentration, and increased use of alcohol/drugs. Common methods used to help identify stressors and symptoms include self-report measures, behavioural measures and physiological stress measures.
- Developing individualized programmes that meet the needs of their employees. Programmes should be topic-specific.
  - Strategies that employees can initiate include relaxation techniques, meditation, developing a good support system, undertaking outside hobbies, learning to set realistic goals, organizing their time, and learning when to say "no" before taking on more than they can handle.
  - Organizations should do more than simply provide stress management techniques. If the causes of stress can be reduced or eliminated, they should be. Organizational-level strategies might include redesigning employees' jobs, improving the selection, placement and orientation of new employees, providing employees with more participation and autonomy in decision making, disseminating information, providing needed education and training, reducing work loads or the work pace, modifying work schedules to be compatible with demands and responsibilities outside of work, conducting time management programmes, clearly defining work roles, providing opportunities for career development, and providing emotional and task support.
  - Exercise and maintaining a nutritious diet are two of the most agreed upon stress management techniques. Organizations can help employees by

providing information and access to physical recreation facilities or equipment by either establishing on-site facilities or provide memberships to local health clubs.

  - One type of organizational stress management programme available is to provide employees with access to an employee assistance programme, a corporate psychologist, a toll-free hotline, or some other form of counseling assistance. These programmes can deal with a variety of problems that range from learning to cope to dealing with substance abuse.

- Communicate with employees. Providing more information about their jobs and other factors that affect them will help employees feel more in control of their circumstances and can help build cohesion. Organizations must also communicate and describe the stress management strategies available to employees and help them develop personalized action plans.
- Programmes should be implemented in stages. If all aspects of a programme are implemented at one time and parts of the programme fail, employees will lose faith in the programme and in management. This will be another cause of anxiety and stress for the employee.
- Help employees keep a positive perspective on life and feel a sense of purpose. It is important for employees to feel they are making a valuable contribution to the organization.

Work typically encompasses more time than any other single activity. Employees are putting more and more emphasis on deriving satisfaction and quality in their life from their jobs. Unfortunately, for many people, work holds many sources of tension, anxiety, frustration, and conflict which have negative effects on them and their employers.

# 13

# Crisis Management

It was a classic case requiring crisis management. A group of union gold miners walked off the job. Another group of miners from the same union crossed the picket line. Then, on the morning of September 18, 1992, a mysterious explosion killed nine miners. Accident or homicide? Striking member of the Canadian Association of Smelter and Allied Workers claimed it was an accident caused by mine managers who had violated safety regulations. Police, on the other hand, investigated the case as a mass murder. Fortunately, most companies with labour unions will never deal with a crisis of this magnitude. However, crises do occur, and the way they are handled can be a key element in a firm's survival and financial health. Crisis management is the term generally used to describe the process of handling these troublesome events.

In labour relations, a crisis usually revolves around some type of contract dispute. A strike, for instance, has the potential to stir up labour unrest and simultaneously cripple operations. To deal effectively with such a crisis, organizations are encouraged to develop a crisis management plan. This associate examines crisis management in relation to organizations that must deal with labour unions and offers suggestions for dealing with labour-related crises.

## CRISIS EVENTS IN LABOUR RELATIONS

"A crisis is a major, unpredictable event that has potentially negative results. The event and its aftermath may significantly damage an organization and its employees, products, services, financial condition, and reputation". Labour relations have the potential to embody all of the above facets of a crisis. Crisis events that are specific to unionized organizations include picketing, strikes, violence, and negative public perceptions of management.

## PICKETING

While picketing can be fairly peaceful, it can also be troublesome, especially if it disrupts business activities. The Pittsburgh Press witnessed this in 1992 when strikers blocked replacement delivery drivers from entering the compound entrance.

Rather than go on strike, members of Hotel and Restaurant Employees Local 25 walked the picket line and sounded bullhorns to take their message directly to guests. Jefferson management tried unsuccessfully to get a restraining order on the bullhorn use, although the judge did set guidelines, designating only one bullhorn between 7:00 a.m. and 8:30 a.m. and two horns after that until 9:00 p.m. Thus, the picketing did include some degree of guest discomfort. Since some of the rooms command a hefty thousand dollars a night, any discomfort could be seen as a crisis event for management.

## STRIKES

The 1994 Teamster strike at UPS emphasized another form of business disruption that can approach crisis proportions. Although the strike lasted only 11 hours, major UPS clients such as Lands End and ATandT were severely affected by the lack of deliveries. In addition, a UPS spokesperson estimated the company would lose in excess of $5 million because of the strike.

### Violence

The Ravenswood Aluminum Corporation was the scene of a particularly nasty labour dispute from late 1990 to 1992. Preparations for the impending conflict began early as management installed new fences around company property, erected video surveillance cameras, hired a new security guard service, and brought in refrigerated boxcars of food. The situation became a crisis when a security guard was shot and seriously wounded while on duty. The town of Ravenswood became seriously split between loyalty to the strikers or the strikebreakers. The feud even spilled over to churches. In one example, a strikebreaker entered a church and approached the alter only to witness union workers and their families suddenly exiting the sanctuary. A crisis such as Ravenswood emphasizes the extent of the stakeholders involved - employees, town citizens, outside suppliers, and customers. While preparations for the crisis had been made by management, the "perception" of such preparations angered strikers and their supporters.

**Negative Public Perceptions**

Royal Oak Mines operates the gold mine described at the beginning of this associate where nine miners were killed by an explosion. The tension leading up to the explosion was fueled by the company's move to replace strikers with 150 replacement workers from Southern Canada - an expedient not widely practiced in Canada. After the explosion, management described the animation as terrorism and vowed to open the mine within a week. This stance, especially in view of the loss of life, did not soothe feelings among those loyal to the strikers. Indeed, strikers called the explosion an accident, not terrorism. Rick Cassidy, vice president of the union commented, "We were pissed off at them", "but nobody wished that fate on them". In reviewing the definition of a crisis event, one can see that public perception damage occurred to Royal Oaks. In addition, its reputation was affected as the town of Yellowknife split between those loyal to the strikers and those opposed. When picketing, strikes, violence, and negative public perceptions occur, the results can hurt the organization and its stakeholders.

Because of the unique risks in these labour situations, organizations are encouraged to adopt crisis management measures to soften potentially harmful effects of labour strife. In managing any crisis, management needs to consider what should be done before, during, and after the event.

## CRISIS MANAGEMENT: BEFORE THE CRISIS

No matter what industry or labour environment an organization operates in, the key to effective crisis management is advance planning. Labour problems usually give some signals before they actually occur: the strike that is threatened if a contract is not reached, the picketing that will develop as a result of the strike, the labour violence that may occur when workers cross the picket line, and the negative press that may result if "enthusiastic" security guards are employed. Such signals should not come as a surprise and management should be prepared for each step in the crisis process.

*Before the crisis, three steps should be taken*:

1. *Form the crisis management team*: The crisis management team should be in place before any crisis actually occurs. Prior to a crisis, the team's function is to develop and plan for worst case scenarios, described next. The size of the team will depend on the particular organization; however, smaller teams consisting of 10 or fewer members are recommended. Potential team members should include the plant manager, the industrial relations manager, the public relations manager or equivalent, the company CEO or representative, the company legal counsel, a financial officer, and a representative from supervisory management.
2. *Develop worst case scenarios*: A key step is to develop worst case scenarios that are applicable to an organization's particular environment. These prepare management to animation proactively in the best way possible to handle the crisis. For example, suppose the crisis management team at Company A anticipates that negotiations are not going to produce a contract and that a strike is inevitable. The worst case scenarios are now drawn and attention is focused on how to operate the plant while the strike is going on. In some cases, management may decide it is best to discontinue operations during the strike. Even the time of year is important in drawing worst

case scenarios, as strikes are generally shorter and less violent during cold weather months.

3. *Define standard operating procedures that should be taken prior to the crisis event*: The next step is defining procedures that should be standard prior to the crisis. Since most labour unrest stems initially from a strike, the team should first define what areas are most relevant to strike preparation. For example, will replacement workers be used and, if so, what should be their access to and from the plant? Should security guards be used, and if so, how? How will supplies and products be moved to and from the plant. Should surveillance equipment be used?

## THE USE OF MANAGERS AND NONUNION PERSONNEL DURING A STRIKE

Some companies can continue to operate without replacement workers. Instead, management, supervisors, and clerical employees can be called on to fill in during the duration of a strike. In planning for such an event, pre-training should be provided for all personnel who may be called upon to keep the facility operating.

## THE USE OF REPLACEMENT WORKERS

The use of replacement workers is an extremely sensitive issue for union members. Such workers represent a potential loss of jobs for union members, and thus, will understandably illicit strong protests from the union. The advantages and disadvantages of using replacements should be weighed carefully. Management must consider the emotional, post-strike climate of the organization and determine if using replacements is absolutely necessary. If replacements are used, they should be told exactly where to park their vehicles and how to enter and exit the plant. In some cases, it is advisable to house management and workers within the facility during the strike.

### The Use of Security Guards

Management should always be aware that the use of

security guards represents an especially obnoxious affront to strikers. This aversion goes back to the days when security guards purposely harassed, beat, and even killed coal miners. Therefore, the decision regarding security guards should be carefully evaluated. This decision will be determined, in part, by management's prior decisions on maintaining operations and using replacement workers.

If guards are used, key decisions must be made. For instance, where will security guards be stationed? Their placement could make the difference between peaceful picketing and a violent confrontation. In addition, the proper training of security guards should be addressed. For example, they should have training in crowd and strike control tactics. Guards who are sent to intimidate strikers will only diminish the chances of a smooth labour settlement. Also, it is recommended that an outside agency supply security guards rather than using in-house personnel. Once the strike is over, the outside guards leave and take any community ill with them.

### Movement of Supplies and Products

Plans should be drawn for the routing of incoming supply trucks and outgoing deliveries. Access routes should be safe, since most violence occurs at these critical points. In addition, all suppliers should be notified within 45 days of an anticipated strike.

### Use of Surveillance Equipment

If surveillance equipment is used, care should be taken that surveillance activities are legal and are not conducted in a manner that may intimidate strikers. Surveillance activities cannot occur before a strike is actually called.

### Protection of Plant and Equipment

In some cases, additional protection of plant and equipment may be necessary. Acts of sabotage and vandalism occasionally occur during a labour dispute. Phone lines may be severed, transformers destroyed, and key equipment damaged by disgruntled workers. Increased lighting in strategic areas and the posting of security guards are prudent steps in protecting these important assets.

## Protecting Company Personnel at Home

Although occurrences are rare, company personnel have been harassed, threatened, and even shot at while at home. Management should decide whether to take steps to increase the security of these individuals.

## *Crisis Management: During the Crisis*

A major theme throughout the crisis management literature is the need for the organization to communicate effectively with the public.

*Brewton outlines the following three steps*:

1. *Focus on the public's desire for information*: Strikes, picketing, and labour violence crave public attention. The manner in which management addresses the media indicates to the public how the crisis is being handled. If management appears defensive or unwilling to comment, the public will perceive this response negatively. For example, public opinion of Royal Oaks, the scene of the gold mining explosion described earlier, reached a low when management refused to respond to faxed requests for interviews.
2. *Appoint an official spokesperson*: Ideally, only one person should talk with the media. This insures that conflicting accounts do not surface from within the same organization; otherwise, management may appear confused and disjointed. While the company CEO or president could be a good choice as spokesperson, the public relations officer may also be appropriate.
3. *Professionalize the presentation*: The message to the public via the media should be communicated in a professional manner. Rushed interviews of management should be avoided. Instead, a planned encounter with the press is encouraged. Formal press releases, press kits, and news conferences are desirable, since they give management the resources

and time to put their most positive image forward. Such messages should present management's side of the situation without focusing undue criticism on the union.

## CRISIS MANAGEMENT: AFTER THE CRISIS

- *Open channels of communications*: The period following the resolution of a labour dispute should focus on recovery and restoring normal day-to-day operations. Relationships between supervisors and employees may have been strained. Indeed, supervisors and employees who usually speak daily with each other may not speak during a strike. Open communications between management and labour should be encouraged by both sides.

While a variety of interventions are available to enhance communications, creating labour-management committees may offer some promise in improving hostile relationships between the two parties. Labour-management committees consist of representatives who work together to discuss short- and long-term objectives of the organization. Practical outcomes of these discussions that can aid in the aftermath of a labour crisis include the use of newsletters, attitude surveys, employee recognition programmes, and information on the organization's revenues, employment trends, and technology advances.

- *Ask the right questions*: The major issue in crisis management of labour disputes is not so much how to avoid strikes; indeed, that is more of a function of the negotiating parties. Instead, crisis management deals with mitigating the impact of labour unrest to minimize the dysfunctional outcomes that may result. In other words, crisis management attempts to reduce the damage to both sides.

*Questions that need to be addressed during this stage include*:

- Was the media handled wisely?
- Were security personnel properly used to minimize confrontations and prevent unnecessary violence?

- Should strike insurance be acquired?
- Were entrance and exit points properly manned and secured?
- Should the plant continue to operate in the event of a future strike?
- Do current provisions of the contract require modification in the future?

Since each labour crisis is different, the assessment stage will vary according to the particular organization, its industry, and the labour union involved. Labour unrest represents a unique form of crisis many organizations should prepare for. While the results of such unrest are almost always negative, a crisis management plan can help soften the impact.

# 14

# Organizational Change and Development

Most kinds of social science somehow have to cope with a challenge which is conceptualized in many ways: System vs. actors, structure vs. event, structure vs. process, etc. All these concepts, not to say dichotomies, aim at designating the static and respectively the dynamic aspects of social phenomena.

The need to apply/make use of these kinds of concepts may, in a simplified way, be explained by the fact that when we write about some social phenomenon in order to understand it, it will not suffice just to 'say what happens/has happened'. Everything that happens to people, everything people do, does not simply happen or is simply done. All events take place within frames, whether these are acknowledged or not by the actors.

This is common wisdom for social scientists, but perhaps not for common people, at least not to the same extent, or in the same way. However this may be, social scientists usually consider their awareness of the social structures within which people animation as being among the strengths of social science as such. Thus, the focus on structural features of social phenomena, structural explanations etc, is quite strong in many of the disciplines in the social science.

In the field of organizational studies this kind of structural bias has been noticed for a long time, and it has been criticized from a number of different angles. At the most general level, the point is made that the social structures within which humans animation are themselves created by human actions.

Another kind of critique, addressing the conceptual practice of social scientists, rather than the practice of people who make society, questions the kinds of theorems, dogma or phrases which say that people animation within frames. How can we decide, who is to decide, or from what position to decide, what is inside and outside the frames? But there are also other kinds of frames at work, which are not always noticed by the social scientists: the theoretical framework of social science itself. And perhaps it may also happen, that this framework works to put social science 'outside' the real dynamic, and thus the structure of the social phenomena under study?

The theoretical framework is made up of concepts, models and perspectives that in turn are made up by words. They have come into public existence by means of the words written in publications. And, as we know, words may refer to things, but words are not identical with the things they refer to. That is what Hegel wanted to remind us of, when he once wrote: "The word 'dog' cannot bark". Of course, we know this very well. That is why it seems to be necessary to be reminded of it again - and again: The fact that we use words when we talk and write about any social phenomenon is so obvious that usually we do not pay any attention to it. The consequence is that all the time we run the risk of mistaking a word for a phenomenon.

*You may think*: no researcher is that stupid. But this is not a question of being intelligent. Let me present an example of this kind of mistake: our use of the word organization'. About this, Karl Weick once wrote: "The word organization is a noun and therefore a myth. If you look for an organization, you will never find it. What you will find is events that are linked to each other, events that transpire through walls, corridors, time schedules etc.. It is these events which we wrongly turn into a concrete substance, when we talk about an organization. Instead of talking about organizations, we should talk about organizing".

Weick's point is that we may, without really noticing it, turn what takes place as events into what seems to be a structure. In most approaches to organization theory the word organization' is so common in use that it has become an almost self-evident term, and in turn this use works as evidence for the existence of the phenomenon. In organizational studies, a number of approaches have been developed during recent decades to cope with challenges like this. Among these are different ways to apply some kind of narrative approach: various strategies of 'telling the story'. Also action research approaches often represent, explicitly or implicitly, a kind of critique of overly structural approaches in organizational studies.

However, the structural bias of organizational studies is not criticized by action researchers just for theoretical reasons, but also for practical ones. Structural analyses of organizational phenomena may very well present the main reasons why things work the way they do, why the situation is as it is, but such analyses do not necessarily present much knowledge on how to change the situation, how to improve it, how to make things work differently. To come to knowledge of some structural aspects which condition the way people animation in particular organizations, does not automatically lead to a way, or a possibility, to animation to change these general conditions.

organizational studies often seem to be performed as if their addressee is a very determined collective actor, who is capable of acting in order to change general structures as soon as knowledge of what changes ought to be made is provided. But even though it is usually possible to create some general knowledge, there are usually no corresponding possibilities of some 'general action'. Organizational change usually takes place by means of very differentiated forms of actions, as a practical process performed by a great number of actors coping with a multitude of details. In short, changing organizational structures takes place by a multitude of organizational events.

As we have seen, Weick poses the problem strikingly. But what about his suggestion for a solution? If he is right that organizations in practice are made up by events, will it help to talk about it in terms of verbs rather than nouns? Will it help to condemn the word organization and use the word organizing instead? I do not think so. Instead of talking about organizing, we have to do some organizing. Because, as we know, the word organize' cannot organize. Weick's theoretical point is quite right, but to make his point have some practical impact, we have to make some practical steps. This is exactly the point where action research differs most radically from descriptive research. To clarify this point, I will start by making a simple, pragmatically conceived distinction between practical discourse and theoretical discourse.

To have theoretical knowledge of something means to understand it. To make practical changes in something means to do something with it. This simple fact may help us to make a quite useful distinction between what as suggested, call respectively theoretical discourse and practical discourse: a theoretical discourse is undertaken in order to understand something, while a practical discourse is undertaken in order to do something.1 By differentiating between theoretical discourse and practical discourse, the main difference between action research and descriptive research comes to the fore: The arena of descriptive research is almost exclusively the theoretical discourse, while action research also enters the arenas of practical discourse, that is, we engage in some kind of dialogue and cooperation with the actors in the field.

The participation of researchers in practical discourses may take place in many ways. There are many approaches, many positions. But, across the different positions that action researchers take in this question, there is a challenge common to all: how can we get into a position to actually carry out action research in order to promote democratic development in practice? Again, the conditions around the globe are quite different. Within working life, the quality of the relations between the social partners is quite important. In Scandinavia these relations are generally known to be relatively good.

In Norway the labour market parties have, for 40 years, given their policy support to action research projects within working life. Part of the aim of this action research has been to contribute to the democratization of working life. However, policy support is not equal to financial support. And even though there is a general agreement at the top level between the labour market parties, the decision to involve themselves in action research projects is made at the enterprise level, by local management. Among the actors of working life, not least among the most powerful ones, that is, the owners and the management, the interest in contributing to the democratization of working life may be rather modest. In the West, capitalism and democracy may be regarded as true-born twins, but they are not identical twins.

The relationship between political democracy and economic democracy is one of tensions. The interest for these questions seems to be far greater among social scientists and social researchers than among the actors of working life. Against this background: does the knowledge we have as action researchers constitute a kind of power of knowledge, strong enough to not only match the power of the actors of the basic units of capitalism, the enterprises, but to contribute to practical change?

## THE POWER OF KNOWLEDGE AND THE POWER OF JUDGMENT

*Lets examine this question by means of an example*: Norske Skog Folium is a paper mill with about 400 employees; this associate mill is part of an international corporation with about 9.400 employees. The union leader at this associate mill knew our approach from a presentation we had given at a conference. Our approach, emphasizing broad participation in development processes as a strategy of democratization, appealed to him. He persuaded the top manager at this associate mill to have a meeting with us.

The development process we were invited to advise them on was one of organization development. In order to survive as a paper mill producing paper of special qualities, the performance of the production had to be improved. On this the top management and the union leaders were in agreement. However, not surprisingly, they had different views on how to reach this goal. Both views concerned the organizational structure. To simplify a bit, the union was concerned mainly with making the organizational structure less hierarchical, and to increase the involvement of the employees in questions pertaining to their own workplace and questions of improvement and development. One condition for obtaining this they considered to be removing the foremen. The management was concerned mainly with creating teams among the workers on the shop floor, in order to improve the performance of the employees.

The union leader was not really negative to team-organization; his view was that removing the foremen was also a necessary condition in order to make team-organization work in practice. Neither was the management totally negative to removing the foremen. In addition, both the union leader and the management were aware that among the rank and file at the shop floor, there were lots of negative attitudes towards the concept of team-organization.

Now, such was the different views of these powerful actors at this enterprise. What, then, about the power of knowledge? How could scientific knowledge help to mediate between these two views? As you have noticed, the local parties were not in diametrical opposition to each other, but their opinions were different enough to block any practical progress: they were not able to agree on what to do or how to proceed. Their expectation of us was that we should advise them as to what kind of new organizational structure would be the smart one, and advise them on how to get there.

In fact, our judgment was that the best solution would be to both remove the foremen and to create a team-based work organization; in addition we thought they should also create a more team-based management. However, to present our thoughts in the form of a general model of a new organizational form, would not have been a very smart thing to do. The result might very well have been that the union leaders and the management had come to an agreement about our suggestion as a model for a new organizational structure. Nevertheless, the problem of how to proceed, in order to make the new structure also really lead to a better performance, would have remained - as the main problem. This is because, to our knowledge, a new, less hierarchical and more democratic structure, does not automatically lead to a better organizational performance. Of crucial importance is the very process by which the organizational changes are made.

This was our judgment, based on our - let us call it scientific - knowledge. But, we also knew that simply to present this knowledge to them (union/management), would not work. The power of knowledge does not work that way. Since theories are made up by words, any knowledge of any phenomenon is a certain kind of interpretation of this phenomenon. And, even though the local actors may lack knowledge of the kind of organizational theory that we have as researchers, they do not lack theories. They simply have other theories, in the form of their own interpretations. In other words: Solid knowledge is not a solid. Thus, there is no open space in the heads of the local actors into which our knowledge simply may be 'poured in'. In order to make our knowledge, our theories or interpretations, relevant to the local actors, we have to relate to their interpretations.

Therefore we have to get knowledge of their interpretations. These interpretations usually are manifold, rich in content and not to be found in a database from where they may be printed out and read. For us to "read" their interpretations, and for them to "read" ours, we have to enter into some kind of dialogue with each other. This means that the way we contribute with our theoretical knowledge cannot simply take the form of a theoretical discourse, in which we try to make the local actors come to an agreement with us on a common understanding of what is the situation. Rather, our contributions have to be presented within a practical discourse, where we try to find answers to the question about what they can do (in this situation).

In this sense we may say that the power of knowledge is dependent on our ability to enter into a practical discourse, in the form of a dialogue whose outcome to a large extent is dependent of the 'power of the better arguments'. We make this allusion to Habermas' well-known phrase deliberately. As researchers, we are not in the position to make decisions (on what to do). The management has the exclusive right of making decisions, eventually in some kind of cooperation with the union. Our chance to influence these decisions is given by the quality of the arguments we are able to provide during the dialogue. Our status as researchers, as representatives of a scientific community, does not make our arguments any stronger. Confronted with the actors that hold the powerful positions in capitalist enterprises, we do not occupy a strong position. We are not stronger than the strength of our arguments. Thus, what is decisive is the content of our arguments.

The content of our arguments, then, is not to be simply derived from our theoretical knowledge of organizational structures, processes of organizational change etc. One important reason is that the dialogue between the parties at the enterprise and us often takes on a course that is not possible to foresee.

Suddenly we find ourselves discussing issues that, to be dealt with properly, require life experience quite as much as theoretical knowledge. Another reason is that sometimes we have to really create arguments, invent new arguments, on location, so to speak. That is, we have to create new arguments on the basis of the understanding that we develop in the course of the dialogue with the local actors.

This means that in order to try to create practical results that are in accordance with our theoretical knowledge, we have to admit that the power of knowledge is not powerful enough, if left to itself. The power of knowledge has to be supplemented by the power of judgment. It is necessary to have a sensible power of judgment, in order to understand what takes place in the particular dialogue we participate in, and on that basis to create those particular arguments that are apt in this dialogue.

To put it into a formula: the power of knowledge is dependent on the researchers' ability to participate in practical discourses based on of the power of the better arguments, and this ability is in turn dependent on a sensible power of judgment. For these reasons, what will be the content of the better argument will differ from case to case.

*In the case of Norske Skog, the kinds of arguments that turned out to be most powerful were these:*

- Instead of recommending any particular theoretical model of the future organizational structure, we recommended them to agree upon what kind of development process to organize.
- Among the rank and file there were lots of sceptical attitudes towards teams. A suitable way to cope with this would be to invite all employees to participate in well organized dialogues to give their answers to three questions: a) What do they consider to be the main problems of the factory? b) In what way might team-organization be helpful in solving these problems? c) If a team-based work organization should be developed and implemented, how then is it best to proceed?
- On the basis of these dialogues, in which practically all employees (plus management) should participate, the question of how to organize the process of organizational development could then be decided upon.

Last, but not least, we also gave them ¢ promise'. We offered to take care of organizing the dialogues based on broad participation. As a part of accepting our arguments, they also accepted this offer. Thus, in order to create a process of democratic development, not only theoretical resources were required, like the power of knowledge, the power of the better arguments and the power of judgment.

Also our practical skill in the organizing of development processes, based on broad participation, was required. In other words, for action researchers it is not sufficient to have theoretical knowledge of the concept of practical discourse. It is necessary also to have the skill to participate both in the organizing of and in the performance of practical discourses.

Now, to make a long story short: the management made their decision on a process based on broad participation, and we kept our promise to participate in organizing it. This process included three dialogue conferences, comprising 200 participants; a subsequent decision on developing models of team organization in a number of project groups; establishing a steering committee; working in project groups; new dialogue seminars on theoretical models of teams; creation of teams; selecting team leaders and, in the end, to use the ordinary management vocabulary, the 'implementation' of teams.

We organized the dialogue conferences and participated in various kinds of critical events along the process, like meetings in the steering group, in some of the project groups, etc. In short, we participated both in the organizing of and in the performance of the practical discourse that was undertaken at Norske Skog. Some of this kind of project work is well known to everybody who has experience of this kind of processes; it is rather trivial and relatively easy to perform. Therefore, we would like to highlight a less well known, or perhaps less acknowledged, aspect of this kind of processes. This aspect concerns the relation between dialogue and action. From words to deeds: that is the logic of this relation.

But very often this logic is conceived in a too linear way. One thinks that in order to be able to take the step from dialogue to action, the dialogues have to generate a common understanding. Such a common understanding, a kind of consensus, is considered necessary as a common ground for action. But this conception may very well be a misconception, or a misunderstanding. As a matter of fact, a very common misunderstanding, common both to practitioners and to theorists who are experts in organization theory, is the following: They think that if the future solution on organizational problems becomes sufficiently detailed and then agreed upon, the practical steps to create this solution will follow almost automatically.

But, what is called a "solution" is, however detailed, still a solution on paper, that is, a theoretical solution. Both theorists and practitioners happen to make mistakes here: The words by which the solution is conceptualized are treated as if they were identical with the practical solution. But the real phenomena are different from the words by which they are conceptualized. Thus, regardless of the degree of details agreed upon in the theoretical draft of a solution, the practical steps to be taken do not follow automatically, as if the real action is simply a practical consequence of the theoretical cease. This kind of mistake as regards the real status of a solution on paper is more likely to happen within a theoretical discourse than within the practical discourse. But also practitioners may easily be victims of the temptation to enter into theoretical discourse. And this may very well happen while they are in the midst of performing a practical discourse.

Therefore, to those we collaborate with. Not as a theoretical point, presented as a piece of knowledge; literally we have to find practical answers to theoretical disagreements among the practitioners. That is, at certain phases in the process of organizational development, we have to point out that what will make progress is not to agree upon some particular solution. What will make progress is to agree on what practical steps to be taken next, in order to organize, or to continue, the process by which the practical solution is to be generated.

For these reasons the point is not to create a common understanding by means of dialogues. Rather the point is to create common dialogues, a common practical discourse within the organization(s). What is needed in order to develop more democratic work organizations is not a common theoretical understanding of what a democratic organization might look like. What is required is a common practical discourse, which allows for everybody to participate, and which allows for different understandings and interpretations to come to the fore. Thus, the really big challenge in this kind of democratic organization development is to organize those who perform the action, the local actors, in practical discourses.

To obtain this, researchers cannot animation as if we are some kind of distant observers of theoretical knowledge. We have to animation as one among other kinds of social actors that are engaged in the practical change of working life. What kind of practical discourses may be organized on this mutual basis will depend on a lot of specific circumstances, from the institutional character of working life and work life research, to the personal idiosyncrasies of the participating researchers. It goes without saying that the relationship between theoretical and practical discourse is not to be organized in a strict instrumental way. In the Scandinavian action research tradition we have, together with the parties of working life and cooperating enterprises, made lots of theoretical and practical efforts to organize practical discourses of a kind that allows for broad participation; in principle everybody (all) concerned shall be invited to participate.

Since most people are at job to perform their work, not to perform dialogues, you can imagine that to create a practical discourse that allows for everybody to participate requires quite carefully organized devices. The totality of events, arenas and forums that together form a practical discourse that allow for everybody to have a saying in an OD process, may be compared to the forums of public debate at the societal level, the public sphere. In this sense, the practical discourse is organized as a kind of internal public sphere within the enterprise.

Notwithstanding all the differences between the public sphere of society and the internal public sphere within enterprises, there are some important similarities. The public sphere is a medium for reasoning, and thereby it is a source of legitimacy. Whatever one says, whatever one claims to be true, somebody else can contest it. The decisive factor is not who makes the claim, but the reasons put forth to support it, respectively contest it. And questions of what to do with some phenomenon or problem may turn out to be also a matter of how to understand the problem, what would be a legitimate interpretation of the matter. For these reasons, the public sphere is obviously a 'medium' where theoretical and practical discourses may be linked.

This is also the case with the internal public sphere in enterprises. What to do with some issue is indeed dependent on how to understand it. This implies that also the so-called practitioners from time to time have to undertake some kind of theoretical discourses, in order to come to a better understanding of the issues at stake in their process of practical development. Or, to phrase it otherwise: the practical discourse also has its 'moments' of theoretical discourse. These moments, and these issues, obviously may be linked to the theoretical discourse of researchers. But what kind of 'input' is required from the theoretical discourses of the research community is not that obvious.

Sometimes, some 'piece of knowledge' that is common place within the research community is needed. But, it may also be a need for knowledge of a kind that has quite other sources than the field of management and organization studies: the social sciences in general, as well as the humanities. Art and literature are also sources of knowledge, especially the kind of knowledge that is required to provide new interpretations of seemingly well-known phenomena.

This kind of knowledge may turn out to be quite as actionable as the huge amount of knowledge that is produced by the standard procedures of management and organization studies. Because, the crucial point about creating actionable knowledge is not at all to avoid the creation of general knowledge, neither to dismiss theoretical discourses. The crucial task is to organize 'local orders of discourse' in ways that make it possible for any relevant, whatever general, knowledge to come to work in local settings.

To organize public spheres within private enterprises is just one way to cope with this task. As we have tried to demonstrate by the example from Norske Skog and the perspectives presented thereby, this approach indeed makes the researchers involved come closer to the events than is the case by most other research methods. As action researchers we are not just close to the events; we are literally part of the events, we even participate in creating the events.

Knowledge of organizational structures normally is required as an integral part of action research methods as methods for generating both new ways of working and new kinds of knowledge. However, the kind of knowledge of organizational structures and dynamics required, in order to support/promote organizational change in processes that are based on extended participation from both management and employees, also comprises a kind of theoretical/practical competence, concerning challenges/questions like:

- Which kind of knowledge to apply in the particular situation/context,
- How to apply this knowledge in a way that makes it work in the particular context,
- What kind of new theoretical points or practical devices have to be created in order to make progress in each particular context?

From the experience of coping very specifically in different kinds of action research projects with these kinds of challenges, action researchers contributing to organizational change will gain a lot of knowledge that may also contribute to the discourse on organizations, by writing publications that address this discourse. But still the question is: does this closeness to the events produce a better ability to present a new and better understanding of organizational structures and organizational events?

There are action researchers who argue that the closeness to the events, in particular by means of the common responsibility for organizational change between action researchers and practitioners, represents a kind of privileged methodological position compared to other research methods. From this kind of perspective, narratives from action research projects may appear an adequate mode of writing publications. However, also within the community of action researchers a broad spectre of arguments has been presented against this perspective.

## THE GENESIS OF GENERAL WRITINGS ON ORGANIZATIONS

During the last century, in particular after WW2, theories of organization have been proliferating. The more or less explicit rationale of all this theorizing may be stated in rather simple terms: the better we understand organizations, the better organizations as suggested, be able to create. However, after more than half a century of experience with organization theory as a kind of 'cross-disciplinary discipline', the interrelationship between the features of organization theory and the organizations of our society is not easy to state in simple terms. In fact, the multitude of experiences of the troublesome relation between organization theory and what is supposed to be its object of study, organizations, have given rise to an increased interest in making organization theory (OT) an object of study in itself.

The question of 'to whom do we write', or 'whom do we address', is a constituent part of the texts that we write on organization theory and organization studies. Not in the sense that there is a limited number of singular addressees to which each specific text is directed. Rather, the point is that there are just not any particular, empirical addressee(s), but some imagined addressees (or group/community of addresses) we have in mind when writing. We write publications to make them public, and what we write and how we write is affected by how we imagine our readers and their reading.

Since the question of whom we write for has been shifting throughout the times, we should begin at the beginning, that is, the beginning of organization theory as it is presented in this book by W. Starbuck, *'The Origins of Organization Theory'*. He has studied texts on management and organization from remote times and civilisations and has made an interesting observation: The history of organization theory contrasts with the history of managerial thought. When people began to compose texts about organized activities, between 2,000 and 3,000 years before the Christian era (BCE), they focused on managerial practices rather than on organizations as such. Several writers proposed general principles for managerial practices before 1000 BCE, so one can say that theories about managing have existed for at least 3,000 years.

These writings often said nothing about the organizational contexts in which managing was to occur. When the writers did make statements about organization, they did not generalize. They wrote about specific organizations... This bifurcated pattern persisted over the next 3,000 years.... we have been able to find only a few authors who proposed generalizations about organizations as distinctive social systems before the late nineteenth century. The reason for this persistent, bifurcated pattern Starbuck finds by applying a simple perspective of sociology of knowledge: "Evidently, people saw the results of organized activities as being products of actions taken by individuals, so they formulated prescriptions about actions individuals should take".

But there is more to be said about this 'persistent pattern' of writing than to say it depends on 'a way of seeing'. It depends more literally on a way of talking. As we remember, Starbuck does not make the claim that organizational matters were not written about at all. What he tells us is that these texts describe only one specific organization and do not make any generalization. Even when such a text states principles, it does not make any suggestion that these principles "also apply to other organizations". This is obviously not just because the writer does not regard the object of his description as an organization, it is also due to who is regarded the addressee of the text.

In the case of a Chinese text known as The Officials of Chou, which was written around 1100 BCE and among others contains "job descriptions for the many officials in the king's service, ranging from the prime minister to household servants", the addressees are obviously not other (royal) leaders, but the leaders in this singular 'organization'. The text is probably written in order to maintain its procedures, rules and structure, in short, its way of working. Both the leaders and the officials may change, but the organization is to be maintained, thus the specific descriptions are made to serve as specific prescriptions.

This sheds some light on the relationship between the use of generalizations in writing and the users of the writing, the addressees. The context of The Officials of Chou is singular, known both to the writer and the reader, and therefore the descriptions (of jobs, procedures) can work as prescriptions, or even instructions, on how to act. The conditions for making use of the text as work instructions, is mainly knowledge of the specific organization for which the text is written. For such a text to be of any use in another organization, this organization would have to be not just a similar one, but an identical one. Therefore, even when the text states principles of how to act, the question of application of these principles outside the context of which it is written is not addressed.

This kind of writing is, as demonstrated by Starbuck, in great contrast to the writing on principles of leadership. The addressees of these texts are not a limited number of individuals within one singular context, known to both the writer and the reader. The written text addresses readers across specific contexts of action. Thus, the context of use of any of these texts is not identical to all readers; it is a number of different contexts with certain similarities that form the background of both the writing and the reading of texts on leadership. And what is regarded similar across various contexts which are not identical and thus different, is exactly such common aspects which come to be considered general features, of which generalizations can be made in writing.

The question then, is: how is it possible to compare different realities and find out about differences and similarities? By what means, or by what medium, are such different contexts brought in contact with each other? Such questions may give raise to enormous problems of both philosophical and empirical kinds, and we do not pretend to be able to give a full answer. But an unavoidable part of the answer on what made it possible to bring different contexts together and make comparisons, is that ancient leaders had experiences from different contexts, and that the medium to compare these was by means of linguistic communication, mainly oral discussions, gradually supplemented by written texts. Thus, the medium for comparison was, and still is, language.

With this simple fact in mind we may realise more of what is at stake in the 'persistent, bifurcated pattern' which Starbuck discovered. In the ancient times Starbuck has focussed on, writing general statements on leadership obviously made sense, while writing general statements on organizations obviously did not. Why? The answer to this question may make us become more aware of the conditions for writing organization theory today. Therefore, even though the answer is rather obvious, as suggested, present it some more in detail than otherwise would have been necessary. The main preconditions for writing on leadership in ancient times, we have to assume, were two: Firstly, that there existed a kind of oral discourse on leadership, which provided the vocabulary required for writing texts. Secondly, that this discourse was a kind of practical discourse, in the sense that the participants who made up this discourse mainly were leaders practicing some kind of leadership, discussing how to perform leadership, on the basis of their personal experience.

In such a discourse, to be of common interest for the participants, important common features of performing leadership will have been among the crucial issues. Thereby linguistic expressions that refer to common aspects of leadership are generated, be it in the form of phrases, maxims, concepts or lines of reasoning. In short, a vocabulary for conversations on common aspects of leadership is created. This makes clear that the existence of a common discourse among people experienced in leadership is the precondition for these texts to be read in a way that makes the reader get a specific understanding of the general terms, which in turn is the condition for the texts to be useful, i.e. applicable in practice. In this sense, this ancient discourse on leadership is indeed a practical discourse: The discussions, writing and reading are undertaken in order to figure out how to perform leadership, not in order to come to a general understanding of what kind of phenomenon leadership is. The texts are written within a practical discourse. It is worth noting that their character of being general does not by itself make these texts constitute any theoretical discourse.

Obviously, there were no people who gathered to form a corresponding discourse on organizational matters or issues at that time and place in history. Thus there was no common vocabulary, no possibilities of communicating on similar experiences across different organizational contexts. Such a discourse did not really take shape until from the late nineteenth century on. The kind of people who formed this emerging discourse were not just leaders and managers, but also engineers, middle management and others who experienced working life from within private firms, public administration etc.. These different kinds of people made various kinds of experiences from different kinds of organizations. Among others a common element was the experience that the way the work was organised affected the performance of those who worked in the organization.

By discussing these kinds of experiences a certain vocabulary, or rather certain vocabularies, for addressing organizational issues was gradually developed. In these early phases persons with practical experience from organizations, be it private or public ones, were among the main contributors. Y. Shenhav has been doing extensive research on this period in USA, and he argues that around the turn of the former century there existed a systematic discourse about organizations in the United States. This discourse, that was already categorized in 1912 as 'a smaller sister of sociology, as a science of human nature'6... was infused into American sociology 'from below' during the first half of the twentieth century. This engineering/managerial discourse invented the 'organization' as a reified epistemological concept and celebrated the idea that it is worthy of intellectual and academic attention. One implication of the emergence of this discourse of organization was that managers became increasingly aware that the performance of leadership was just one of the main 'parameters' or conditions that influenced the performance of the employees.

The other main parameter was the organization, organizational forms and procedures. Hence the need to understand the matters of organization in order to form the best kind of organizations and organizational performance. It is well known that among the prominent contributors to organization theory in this early period, before WW2, we find people highly experienced in management like F. W. Taylor, H. Fayol, C. Bernard and others. But it is also worthwhile noting that a large part of the writings on organizations in this early period was by authors who were less prominent, but who nevertheless to a large extent were people with their main professional experience from work organizations, both in industry and other sectors, even public administration. Based on their various experiences, these authors did look for properties common to organizations of all kind.... they used the plain language of managers, they rarely attempted to compare organizations from different eras, and they focused their thinking on how to make organizations more effective: How should organizations be organized? Their prescriptions resemble 'The Officials of Chou', but unlike the authors of 'The Officials of Chou' they sought to generalize7 across many organizations....

We may now see one important reason why it lasted about 3 millennia from the general writings on management to the occurrence of texts making generalizations on organizations. Not until the turn of the former century there had been established something like a discourse on organization, which provided the vocabulary necessary for writing texts on this issue. And this vocabulary was, just analogous to the ancient vocabulary on leadership, generated within a mainly practical discourse: people who were rich in experience from lots of different organizations performed a discourse on what were the important common features of organizations, in order to make them better. Thereby it became possible to write in general terms on organizations, and to have these writings make sense to the audience of readers.

Until WW2, the discourse on organization, by which indeed general perspectives and theories of organization were developed, by and large remained a practical discourse. This is not just because such a large part of the authors was experienced with organizational life, it was also because the large part of this literature was written in order to answer questions of what to do about organizations. Like in the United States, the authors were "searching for general properties of organizations that could lead to prescriptions". By these efforts those authors created lots of theories, perspectives, and concepts that enriched the vocabulary of organizational discourse. Many general aspects were discussed: the need of functional differentiation, coordination and hierarchy, procedures, relations between line and staff, spans of control, etc. The texts were written to help create organizations with better, that is, more effective performance.

The focus on structure, on organizational forms, became gradually more important: "...a gradual change took place, and documents written during the 1920s began to view organizations as integrated systems and to discuss the structures of this system", not just because the structure appeared to be the most important single feature/property of organizations. The focus on organizational forms was due to the fact that the addressees of these texts were those who were in charge of forming organizations, of influencing the decisions on what structural form organizations should have: managers, engineers, consultants. The discourse on organizations was indeed a practical discourse.

Thus, during the first half of the twentieth century, it would not make sense to claim that the discourse on organizations was divided into a practical discourse and a theoretical discourse. This divide did not happen until after WW2. Before WW2 it was usually simply assumed that the writers were experienced in the topics they wrote about. The quality of its reasoning and suggestions. Nobody considered it necessary to give an account for the empirical foundations of the text. But after the WW2, this situation changed: The late 1940s and early 1950s saw two changes in the character of writings about organization theory... For one thing, the two streams of thought abut organization - sociological writings about bureaucracy and managerial writings about organizational effectiveness - discovered each other.

For another thing, authors began to speak about the empirical bases for their theories. With the entry of writings based on research projects in the discourse on organizations, two kinds of changes occurred that created new kinds of relations between the discourse of organizations and the phenomena that this discourse is about. Firstly, the base of direct experiences from organizations as a foundation for writing was narrowed down. This is because the experience from managing organizations and working in organizations was gradually substituted by 'second hand' experiences in the form of empirical data, provided by the expanding number of methods for undertaking empirical studies. These methods, as we know, by and large consist of various techniques for either looking at/listening to people or communicating with them (orally or in writing), in order to construct written fragments labelled and stored as 'data'. Thereby direct, personal experience from organizations as real phenomena is in effect downgraded, and the virtual reality of written fragments claming to represent experience (hence the label 'empirical data') is upgraded, notably, within the emerging research-based discourse on organizations.

Secondly, this narrowing down of experience is 'compensated' by widening considerably the vocabulary of discourse on organizations; not just sociological but also anthropological and psychological concepts, terms and perspectives entered the discourse on organizations. In the wake of these two kinds of changes the discourse on organizations underwent significant transformations, and its divide into one theoretical and one practical discourse took place. The theoretical discourse took on the shape of what we today. The practical discourse per definition remained mainly within working life, but was by no means unaffected by the growth of the theoretical discourse, that is, the establishment of OT as an academic enterprise in universities, business schools and research institutes. Neither were these two discourses totally separated; an increasingly complex pattern of interfaces was an integral part of this development.

The actual complexity of this interface seems to be not fully recognized by organizational theorists. In accordance with a very persistent figure of thought, or manner of thinking, within the communities of social science and research, organizational research included, the relation between the theoretical and practical discourse is considered a hierarchical relation. The theoretical discourse resides over the practical discourse. Against this background it seems that organizational theorists hope that the knowledge of OT sooner or later will move down the hierarchy until it reaches the actors within organizations, as if knowledge might be transferred by some irrigating system. Nevertheless, this kind of notion may be some of the reason why there is one significant transformation which seems to have avoided any attention in the writings on the development of organization theory. What we have in mind is that as the theoretical discourse on organizations, organization theory, gradually developed after WW2, research based writings on organization theory increasingly show signs that there are simultaneously two addressees of these texts: The main addressee continue to be the actors in charge of forming organizations within working life, management, engineers, personnel management etc., but in addition also other organization theorists (or organization theories) become important addressees.

The reason is, a bit simplified, that with the growth of organization theories based on empirical research any author also enters into a competition with other, different research approaches. Of course, there had been competing theories also earlier, but with the introduction of research methods and scientific norms of presentation, it became commonly assumed among the competitors that the best scientifically based theory would be the legitimate 'winner'. It was commonly assumed that any winning price for any such theory was just a 'travelling trophy' - the logic of research and science deem this activity to be work in progress.

Thus, to undertake research projects on the basis of empirical methods in order to create a comprehensive, general theory of organizations became regarded the best way to create actionable knowledge of management and organizations. This general perspective became rather soon commonly accepted among the performers of organization studies. However, there was no corresponding common acceptance of neither methods nor theories to be used. Thus the competition between different approaches and 'schools' of organization theory and organization studies about which of them provided the best general theory of organizations was established as the one main horizon of almost all the various research approaches.

This competition between theories became not only the main horizon, but also the main driving force. Since it turned out in practice that any research programme, approach or 'school' in organization theory was able to cover only certain aspects of the phenomenon of study, each new approach would rather soon be contested by another new approach, which claimed to cover those aspects neglected or let out or undiscovered by the former approach.

However, common for each new approach was the ambition of creating a general, comprehensive theory of organizations, being able to cover all main aspects of organizations, ambitions that were not fulfilled, but which paved the way for new, not less ambitious approaches. In the 50s and 60s, this was the logic of the 'rise and fall' of a number of theoretical approaches of organization studies and organization theory.

During the 70s and 80s it was gradually acknowledged that the new approaches not necessarily had to replace the prevalent one(s); the concept of scientific progress was supplemented by the concept of pluralism: Different approaches or schools might coexist in a (not too) friendly competition. This 'competition' between research approaches has deeply affected the construction of and the content of organization theory from the second half of the former century until now.

Since long the primary addressee of the writings on organization theory have become other theorists, other writers, in short, researchers and academicians. At the same time the style of writing has continued to be one which presumes that the real, final addressee are the practitioners 'in charge' in organizations, those who are in a position to form and change organizations. The upholding of this 'double addressee' is, though largely unnoticed, conditioning the kind of writing that still dominates organization theory.

The rationale of writing organization theory, 'to create a better understanding of organizations in order to create better organizations' is thus maintained, in spite of the fact that 'a better understanding' no longer refers to the understanding of the practitioners performing their work within organizations, but rather to the understanding of those who are performing the theoretical discourse on organizations, the theorists. In practice, writing in order to improve the 'understanding of organizations' has become writing scientific publications which try to improve the kind of theoretical understanding of organizations that the author regards as the more or less prevalent, and, not a bene: more or less unsatisfying dealt with, within the theoretical discourse on organizations.

Thus, this unacknowledged 'double addressee' has led to a style of writing which is based on the (tacit) assumption that a comprehensive, general theory of organizations and organizational phenomena is inherently actionable. This situation in the coexistence of organization theory as a "Positive Science", as an "Interpretive Science", as a "Critical Science" and as a "Post-modern Science". organizational theorists no longer believe that there will be 'one best theory', nor do they believe in just one direction of theoretical progress. Pluralism has become part of the contemporary 'normal science' in organization theory.

But this pluralism is not very plural as regards theoretical perspectives on the question of practical application of organization theory. This problem is 'solved' by a certain style of writing, which is based on the unnoticed confusion of the addressees of the writing. The main problem with this style of writing is not that the aim is to create general theories. The problem is the very content of the theories, or rather the lack of content; they tend to be too abstract, too poor in content. The assumption that knowledge based on scientific methods and scientific concepts is inherently actionable has made the writing of organization theory being imprinted by a peculiar mixture of constraints and freedom: on the one hand the repertoire of research methods is limited by what counts as methods for generating empirical data. This limitation also limits the multitude of kinds of real organizational experience that should have been at work in the process of creating organization theory. On the other hand, there is in principle no limitation of the new theories and concepts that can be applied as frameworks and perspectives by which the sparse data may be interpreted. By this particular mixture of constraints in methods and freedom of theories that govern the 'normal science' in organization theory, we today witness an ever growing proliferation of theoretical perspectives being applied to rather tiny empirical data.

## CONTRIBUTION FROM ACTION RESEARCH ANDTHEORETICAL DISCOURSE

On the basis of my critical diagnosis of the development of contemporary organization theory, it should now be possible to develop an answer to the question whether, and how, action research may contribute to make it better in the future. It is obvious that the contribution from action research cannot be to write just narratives from the field. Such narratives would easily be read as just another empirical study of organizations. In this way, narratives from action research may as well work to sustain the common style of writing organization theory.

However, it is the very style of writing, the conceptual schemata and the general form of the theoretical frameworks that flourish within organization theory, which has to be challenged. Thus, the most important kind of contribution from action research to the improvement of organization theory seems to be to present the kind of general criticism that on the basis of the experience and knowledge from action research appears to be most pertinent.

To begin with, we have to emphasize one thing: the 'moral' of my description of the split of the discourse on organizations into a practical and a theoretical discourse was not intended to be that the problems of today might be solved by returning to the good, old days when most writings on organizations were based on the personal experience of professional managers etc. In fact, one of the reasons why professional academics and researchers entered into the discourse on organization after WW2 was that they were quite dissatisfied with the content of the discourse dominated by 'amateurs' who wrote texts in which they tried to formulate general principles of organizations, based on their experience as managers etc. This discontent was very clearly expressed by one of the founding fathers of OT as a multidisciplinary discipline, Herbert Simon: "In particular, Simon attacked the idea that principles of organization and management are useful, and he pointed out that every principle seemed to contradict an equally plausible principle. He asserted that a more 'scientific' approach to the study of organizations would eliminate the contradictions".

The title of the substance in which he first expressed these ideas is "The Proverbs of Administration". His analogy with the theoretical generalizations of the 'amateurs' of organization theory and proverbs is quite illuminating; not just for how Simon conceived these generalizations, but also for his conception of organization theory as scientific. As we know proverbs may be regarded as condensed, general expressions of a multitude of life experience, but as we also know, there are numerous examples of proverbs contradicting each other. The project of erasing contradictions between different general statements, theorems and principles and to create a comprehensive, general theory which consists of empirically based generalizations that do not contradict each other, is based on the assumption that in order to guide action, a theory cannot consist of statements that contradict each other.

If a theory contains contradictory statements, how can we know which is true, and which one to animation in accordance with? A general theory free of contradiction will solve this problem, and thus work better to guide action. This conception of the usefulness of a general theory was approved not only by organization theorists, but by many social scientists and social researchers as well, and to a great extent it still is. What is neglected in this conception is that for any general statement, principle or theoretical knowledge to guide specific action, the person(s) who want(s) to apply it cannot rely on a general theory/knowledge of what situations it applies to. The relation between general knowledge and specific situations goes the other way round: the actor (each person) has to judge in what situation it may be applied. The ability to make such judgments is equal to the power of judgment one has. Proverbs are created on the base of life experience, and they are created in the confidence that most people are sufficiently experienced to have developed a power of judgment strong enough to apply the right kind of proverb to the right kind of situation. The existence of proverbs that, if compared as general statements regardless of any specific, practical context contradict each other, is literally a theoretical problem; it represents no problem for actors who are able to judge what proverb to apply to what situation/context. That is, people with a sensible power of judgment.

Exactly the same goes for the ability to apply the kind of knowledge that is required in the kind of situation or kind of event one is into (at the moment). No theory, however comprehensive, coherent and rich in content can contain a kind of 'complete map' of the situations of its possible relevance for action. Theoretical knowledge has to be put into use, no knowledge is inherently actionable. That is, knowledge has to be put into use within some particular event by somebody partaking in this event. In order to judge what knowledge is suitable to apply in each particular situation it will be necessary to make use of one's power of judgement. That is an effort which requires more than invoking one's repertoire of theoretical knowledge of organizations.

The power of judgment is dependent on many kinds of experience and many kinds of knowledge, which cannot be organized within one theoretical perspective where the relations between the various kinds of knowledge and experience are structured in one strict logical order. Making use of the power of judgment goes beyond the realm of logic. Making use of the power of judgment is literally a making: it means to perform an act: the judgement is to be made, and it is always a risky business in the sense that no criteria, no logic or no theory can in beforehand tell what will be the right judgement. A sensible power of judgment is shown by the quality of the judgments made. This little exercise perhaps reveals the hidden assumption that seems to have motivated the project of creating comprehensive, general organization theory free of contradictions in order to guide action: Such general theories will/may reduce the dependence on peoples' power of judgment; the theory itself would, if worked out sufficiently comprehensive, logically coherent and empirically validated, contain in itself its own criteria for practical application.

Even though the theoretical approaches of today are not as rigidly conceived in this respect as was H. Simon's initial project, we may recognize a very closely related kind of disbelief in, or dissatisfaction with, making the question of practical application of organization theory being dependent on the power of judgment. This disbelief is of course not articulated explicitly, but we may recognize this belief the practice of writing: organization theories that claim to satisfy the criteria of a good, reliable and valid scientific text are presented as if they were inherently actionable.

The most common way of imagining this presumed actionability of theories goes like this: The main building blocks of theories are concepts. As we know concepts refer to only general aspects of any phenomenon, and so do also the concepts used in organization theory. It is usually imagined that for a general theory to be practically applicable in some local context, the more concrete elements of the specific context/situation have to be put into the general theoretical framework in accordance with the conceptual order of the general theory.

Thereby the relationship between the general concepts and the specific context is imagined established, and thereby the scientifically based knowledge is considered specific enough to be actionable. When the local actors know what the theory means in their case, they can animation upon it. However, this kind of relationship between the general concepts and the specific context is established only in theory, that is, in the imagination of the authors of these kinds of theories. In the real world it is not possible to put the concrete elements of the local context and the local events into the conceptual framework of the theory; that is possible only in the virtual world of theory, or imagination. In practice it goes the other way round: For a theory to become actionable knowledge, the elements of the theoretical framework, the concepts, have to be put into the local context, by means of some kind of communication, some kind of conversation/discourse.

As the meaning of words and concepts is no inherent feature of the term but dependent on the way words are used, and the context within which they are used, no conceptual meaning can simply be transferred into a new discourse, as if it was a fixed entity. The meaning will somehow be reconstructed; it takes on a particular meaning in the particular discourse where the concepts are in use8. Thus, the concepts put into use in a practical discourse may very well turn out to be actionable, but which one and in which way is never to be predicted.

What can be predicted, on the basis of experience and knowledge from action research projects, is that only some concepts and certain parts of the theoretical framework will show up as relevant in the practical discourse. Also knowledge and concepts that are not all part of one particular theory, will have to be applied. This means that the conceptual framework as a whole, as a general theory, no longer really works as a framework. The local reconstruction of a specific understanding of specific organizational phenomena in this sense works as a deconstruction of the general understanding that is represented by organization theory.

Thus, experience and knowledge from action research does not only subvert the common belief in most organization theory, that general knowledge, if it is systematically developed and presented in a conceptual order free of inner contradictions, in principle is actionable knowledge. Also the common belief in the need for a theoretical framework in order to undertake organization studies may be subverted. The need for a conceptual framework is commonly considered necessary because the most important general concepts are regarded as representing the most important general aspects of the phenomena in question, the organization(s). The conceptual model, the theoretical framework, is regarded nothing less than a general model of the most important features or aspects of the phenomenon of study. The common belief is that without any such conceptual framework, in which the logical order of the relations between the concepts in the framework represents the real order of the relations between the general aspects of the phenomenon, the researcher will be not able to grasp the essential general aspects of the phenomenon of study.

On the basis of my knowledge from the practical discourses of organizational life that we are confronted with in action research projects, we look upon this belief in disbelief. By our participation in practical discourses in numerous action research projects, we regularly experience how little of the vast literature on organization theory is relevant in efforts of organizational change, of creating better organizations and better organizational performance. This is not only due to the fact that lots of other kinds of knowledge and experience are relevant than knowledge of the main subjects of organization theory. Quite as much it is due to fact that the quality of the concepts of organization theory is insufficient. The main problem is not that the concepts are of a general nature; the main problem is simply that they are too poor in content, too abstract.

The concepts that are circulating within the theoretical discourse of organization theory suffer from the lack of being enriched and developed by direct, personal experience from the practical discourse and the real events that take place within organizations. The theoretical discourse of organization theory considers itself as self-sufficient with knowledge of organizational phenomena developed by means of the methods of constructing empirical data. In this way the theoretical discourse on organizations literally abstracts bits and pieces from the practical discourse and the organizational events, it is no surprise that the knowledge generated appears to be rather abstract. In this way empirical studies mainly have the function of giving sense to the general concepts within the theoretical discourse, rather than having the function of giving a richer understanding of the real events that take place in organizations. With the proliferation of new theoretical approaches and concepts, organization theory has in the last decades developed many different ways to express more or less similar and rather well known aspects of organizational phenomena. To put it bluntly, both to experienced organizational theorists and to practitioners, many attempts to make renewals in organization theory appear as an exercise in expressing common insights by uncommon terms. organization theory thus runs the risk of trivializing itself, like a funny dressed person who appears boring as soon as s/he starts speaking.

What is worse is that organization theory by this research practice continues to run the risk of mistaking a word for a phenomenon. Since organizational structure is no longer the main issue in organization theory, Weick's warning about the risk of making "events into structure" is perhaps no longer the most important warning to make. However, the same risk pertains to other features of organizations. There are lots of other aspects than the organizational structure that has become subject of conceptualization, and the awareness of the importance of organizational processes and events has been increasing.

But also the concepts developed to cover other general aspects of organizational events nevertheless tend to take a structural turn, in the sense that they together make up the structure of the theoretical framework that is the main feature of any theoretical approach of organization studies. Since any theoretical framework tries to cover the main features and events of organizations, the creation of such frameworks always implies transforming abstracted aspects of events into concepts. Therefore we are permanently confronted with the risk Weick warned us against: to make events into a concrete substance by means of the concepts we use.

Thus, it is an open question whether such writing will be an example of taking a word for a phenomenon. It will depend partly on the quality of the text, partly on the quality of the reading. In any case, any concept is so to say referring only to the surface of the real events, or rather: part of the surface. In order to judge whether this is the essential part, as is presumed by the construction of theories, concepts and theoretical frameworks, some kind of confrontation with 'the real thing' is required.

However, as long as the concepts and methods of descriptive organization studies work to keep organization theory producing a theoretical discourse that preserves itself from getting comprehensive experience from the practical discourse within organizations, from within the events, such kinds of confrontations are rare, to say the least. The need for comprehensive experience from within the events is substituted by the quest for a comprehensive theoretical framework as a necessary precondition for performing organization studies and generates organization theory.

But since this framework works to keep the researchers away from any criteria for validation beyond those that are to be found only within the theoretical discourse, any theoretical framework may as well work as a shelter that makes researches partially blind or deaf to grasp the essential aspects of the organizational phenomena they are confronted with, as it may help to grasp them. For this reason, the most apt contribution from action research to the theoretical discourse on organizations seems to be to repeat the question presented at the beginning of this associate: Maybe the theoretical framework of organization theory works to put organizational research 'outside' the real dynamic of organizations?

To those who like myself fear that the right answer to this question would too often be 'yes', it may be of some help to remind that the theoretical framework we find within organization theory is not upheld by strong theoretical arguments and unquestionable scientific standards. Rather, it is upheld by a practice, that is the practice of writing and the practice of performing organization studies. This practice has, as we have seen, changed considerably throughout history, and we have implicitly argued that considerable changes are still needed. Neither the earlier practice nor the contemporary practice is governed by any kind of collective or common reason. Like any scientific community, we have no ultimate principle to rely on except for the principle that the scientific discourse is a public discourse. The necessity of writing publications and the freedom of advancing public criticism are the main principles, or mechanisms, by which improvements in the process of knowledge generation may occur. In other words: there is no other principle that warrants the quality (and the truth) of scientific knowledge other than the principle of the scientific discourse being public.

The main reasons for the need of advancing critical perspectives in the contemporary discourse on organizations we have presented throughout this associate, by diagnosing some of the main general characteristics of the development of organization theory. To recapitulate: Firstly, the split of the discourse on organizations in a practical and a theoretical discourse. Secondly, the style of writing that thereby emerged, where organization theory is written both as if the addressee is some general actor and with other organization theories as the real addressee.

Thirdly, the predominant belief that a comprehensive theory of organization is inherently actionable, and, last but not least, the thereby connected belief that working out comprehensive theoretical frameworks is a necessary condition for undertaking organization studies. All these features have to a large extent worked to prevent researchers from using research methods which may give them rich experiences from within the practical discourse of organizations. The result of all this is a discourse on organizations which is rich in theoretical frameworks but rather poor in content.

On the basis of experiences and knowledge from action research where direct involvement in the practical discourse within organizations is an integral part of the research projects, action researchers have a unique potential for working out a deeply needed criticism of the above sketched predominant features of organization theory. However, this potential is of little value if such criticism remains just part of an oral culture within the community of action researchers. In that case the value of this potential for critique may even be negative in the sense that it works to support prejudices against general theories as such, among action researchers. Thus, in order to take advantage of this potential for critique, the criticism has to be worked out and presented publicly. Only when presented as a publication within the discourse on organization theory, the value of this potential can be tested, and contested. A criticism which does not make itself publicly available for criticism is no critical theory.

Thus, against the background of the lines of reasoning presented in this associate, as suggested, conclude by suggesting in general terms what might be a strategy for action research to contribute to the improvement of organization theory: a combination of advancing methods for constructive practice within the practical discourse of organizations, and advancing critical theory within the theoretical discourse on organization theory. The aim of this associate has been to present one example of this strategy.

# 15

# Organizational Culture

The concept of organizational culture (OC) has been widely adopted in both professional and academic literature. OC is commonly related to the shared value system of an organization, and provides the basis for managerial judgement about what is the right and wrong way of doing things. Writers such as Connor and Becker and Dose argue that managers' perceptions of the OC existing in their workplace are key determinants of their work attitudes, and thus provide an important framework for understanding managers' decisions and behaviour at work.

In particular, the study of the relationship between management accounting systems and managers' OC perceptions has attracted continuing research interest. Goddard and O'Connor have shown, for example, that the link between managerial BP and managers' OC perceptions has significant implications for managerial job-related outcomes. In this associate, we aim to extend the literature on the relationship between managerial BP and job-related outcomes by testing empirically a model that includes the effect of two dimensions of managers' OC perceptions.

Budgetary participation (BP) relates to the involvement of managers in the budgetary process and their influence over the setting of budgetary targets. The argument that managers' participation in budget setting affects job-related outcomes such as performance is premised on two explanations. First, models based on psychological theories suggest that participation is related to performance through identification and ego-involvement with the budget goals. This, in turn, leads to enhanced motivation and commitment to the budget. Second, from a cognitive perspective, participation is seen to improve the flow of information between superiors and subordinates, leading to higher quality decisions. Similarly, participation may promote better performance through facilitation of learning and knowledge acquisition.

There is evidence, however, that BP is not always beneficial. Studies have found that a variety of factors, including perceived environmental uncertainty, job difficulty, organizational structure, and budget emphasis in performance evaluation may moderate the relationship between BP and managerial job-related outcomes. For instance, Gul et al. found BP to be negatively related to managerial performance in less decentralised (i.e. more hierarchical) situations.

The role of OC perceptions, however, has attracted only limited research attention. The importance of these perceptions was underlined in a three-case analysis undertaken by Flamholtz. Flamholtz concluded that 'if a firm's culture and its core control system are not synchronised, it is not likely that even a well integrated core control system will actually influence behaviour in its intended ways'. More specifically, managers in one of Flamholtz's cases described their OC as being highly rules-oriented and tradition-bound, and therefore felt that BP was only 'pseudo'. Thus, when a zero-based budgetary system was introduced, these managers failed to make any significant budget cuts.

A more recent survey-based study by O'Connor utilised Hofstede's measure of power distance, and found that this variable moderated the relationship between managerial BP and role ambiguity. O'Connor's results indicated that BP has a stronger negative effect on role ambiguity for managers perceiving low power distance than for those perceiving high power distance. In a later survey of managers in a large public sector organization, Goddard reported a positive association between participative budgeting and managers' perceptions of a more managerialist, efficiency-oriented culture.

In summary, prior research provides evidence that the relationship between BP and managers' job-related outcomes is affected by perceptions of particular OC dimensions. The problem with these studies, however, is that they have treated different value dimensions of OC as independent entities, and therefore failed to deal with the complexity inherent in the multi-dimensional nature of OC. Marcoulides and Heck have drawn particular attention to this issue, and have noted that combinations of value or perceived OC dimensions may have interactive effects. Marcoulides and Heck have called for researchers to adopt more rigorously defined models that take into account the interactive contribution of the different value dimensions that determine the link between management accounting system and organizational outcomes.

The present study recognises this gap in the literature and presents an empirical examination of the moderating role of managers' OC perceptions on the relationship between BP and two managerial job-related outcomes: job-related tension and managerial performance. The profile of OC dimensions developed by O'Reilly, Chatman and Caldwell provides the basis for understanding managers' OC perceptions. For this study, innovation and attention to detail are the two focal OC dimensions because they represent critical components of modern managerial strategies and practice, including continuous improvement, flexible budgeting, and total quality management.

In particular, innovative OC has attracted research attention because it is an important factor in creating a firm's competitive advantage. While organizations tend to cultivate differing levels of innovation based upon their business strategy, research findings suggest that organizational structure and processes need to be aligned with the level of innovative OC. Russell and Russell argue that, as organizations adopt a more innovative OC, employees prefer more organic structures and participative management processes. We thus expect that, as managers' perceptions of innovation increase, increasing BP by these managers will lead to more favourable job-related outcomes. We also propose that managers' perception of attention to detail is an important moderating factor in determining the relationship between their participation in budgeting and job-related outcomes. The OC dimension of attention to detail relates to the level of importance placed by organizational members on precision and accuracy in completing tasks. In the manufacturing industry examined in our study, attention to detail may vary depending upon factors such as manufacturing strategy and the level of technology of the organization.

Chatman and Jehn argue further that, as attention to detail decreases, decision-making processes become less reliant on analytical models and depend more on subjective judgement. Dependence on more subjective decision-making processes, however, tends to increase the risk of errors and misjudgement. As such, participative budgeting is expected to become more useful in a low attention to detail OC because it provides managers with an opportunity to review and to exchange job-relevant information in a more systematic manner, resulting in improved decision quality.

We thus expect that, when managers' perceptions of both innovation and attention to detail are low, BP will lead to more favourable job-related outcomes. When managers' perceptions of innovation are high, on the other hand, we expect BP to lead to more favourable job-related outcomes, regardless of the level of attention to detail. In summary, we propose a three-way interaction between managers' perceptions of innovation, their perceptions of attention to detail, and their participation in budget setting affecting their job-related outcomes. The resulting model includes managers' perceptions for innovation and attention to detail as moderators of the relationship between BP and managerial job-related outcomes (job-related tension, managerial performance). We discuss in more detail the two focal managerial job-related outcomes for this study and develop our specific hypotheses.

## HYPOTHESIS DEVELOPMENT

### JOB-RELATED OUTCOMES

In the present study, we focus on two job-related outcome variables: job related tension (JRT) and managerial performance. Job-Related Tension Hopwood has noted that JRT reflects those aspects of a job that give rise to individual frustration and anxiety. Such aspects include situations where individuals are subject to excessive demands, or where they are not appropriately equipped to handle particular work situations. The consequences of JRT are generally adverse for the individual, producing anxiety, depression, and physical illness, and leading ultimately to dysfunctional behaviour at work. Managerial Performance Mintzberg has noted that managerial performance encompasses a variety of tasks such as planning, investigating, and coordinating activities; and selecting, evaluating and supervising staff. Notwithstanding this, prior studies have successfully assessed managerial performance using an omnibus index based on the instrument developed by Mahoney, Jerdee, and Carroll.

The Relationship Between JRT and Managerial Performance Dunk and Jamal report the relationship between managerial performance and JRT to be negative. We expected this to be the case in the present study, although there is also evidence that the relationship can be relatively weak, or even non-existent. Separate analyses were therefore undertaken in the present instance for each of the two dependent variables.

## THE RELATIONSHIP BETWEEN

### Budgetary Participation

The present study is based on the underlying proposition that a manager's OC perceptions serve as an important cognitive filter through which he or she comes to understand what constitutes desirable attitudes and acceptable norms of behaviour at work. In turn, individual managers' perceptions of the different OC dimensions provide a basis for their judgement on the appropriateness of decision-making structures and processes when carrying out their tasks. We argue that, for managers perceiving an OC that is high in innovation, participation in budget setting is going to be seen to yield greater benefits in terms of information exchange, role clarity, and managerial motivation, regardless of the perceived level of attention to detail. In the following paragraphs, we expand on this point, dealing first with the effect of innovation, and then with attention to detail. Innovation Consistent with O'Reilly et al., we define the OC dimension of innovation in terms of the following values: being innovative and willing to experiment with new ideas, being opportunistic, not constrained by many rules, and willing to take risks.

Thus, managers who perceive their organization's OC to be highly innovative are likely to pursue projects that are novel, untested and risky. Given that innovation often involves trial and error, with little certainty of outcomes and of the means for achieving outcomes, managers in a highly innovative OC are likely to face high uncertainty in their work-related roles as well. With increasing uncertainty, BP is expected to improve managerial performance as well as to reduce managerial JRT. This is because participation provides the opportunity to share job-relevant information that can improve managers' decisions and, ultimately, their performance.

At the same time, managers' JRT is likely to be reduced because participation provides the opportunity to cope with the increasing ambiguities and stress (related to developing new and untested projects) by sharing relevant information. Further, participation can also provide opportunities for managers to gain access to resources that can be used to buffer task performance from the unanticipated effects of other factors. This tends to lower JRT, since managers are likely to feel less threatened with work demands that they are unsure of meeting, given the uncertainties inherent in new and creative projects.

Attention to Detail Again consistent with O'Reilly et al., we define the OC dimension of attention to detail in terms of values relating to being precise, analytical, careful, and detail-oriented. Our contention is that, for managers perceiving an innovative OC, differences in the managers' perceptions of the level of attention to detail do not affect the impact of BP on JRT and performance. For instance, in the case of managers perceiving high innovation but low attention to detail, taking on risky and innovative projects will be seen to be important while their decisions are likely to be based on more subjective judgements and less precise assumptions. Unfortunately, such decision processes increase the risk of adopting inaccurate assumptions when setting budget targets in a more uncertain environment. BP therefore would enhance decision making for these managers by improving the exchange of relevant information between them.

Further, managers perceiving high innovation and low attention to detail must also deal with the uncertainty and stress that result from a less stable environment and a more subjective decision-making system. Managerial role expectations are likely to be less clear in a culture where creative, non-standard ventures are encouraged. Participation in budgeting would thus help to communicate these role expectations, thereby lowering role ambiguity and JRT. Similarly, in the case of managers perceiving high innovation as well as high attention to detail, BP will continue to be beneficial. In this situation, managers not only face a highly uncertain work environment, but the added pressure of adopting more accurate estimates in decision-making. Thus, because of their high attention to detail, these managers are likely to make use of all possible sources of information in order to improve the accuracy of their decisions. Since information availability is improved through participation, participative budgeting will lead to more analytical and accurate decision-making. It follows therefore that managerial performance should be enhanced in this context.

Further, participation in budget-setting provides the opportunity to buffer managers' estimates against unanticipated factors, and possibly to share the risks involved in making budgetary decisions in dynamic situations. As such, managers' JRT ought to decrease as BP increases for managers who believe that they are operating in an OC that is high on both attention to detail and innovation. In summary, when members' perceptions of innovation are high, regardless of the level of attention to detail, we expect increased BP to be associated with decreased JRT and improved managerial performance.

## MANAGERIAL JOB-RELATED OUTCOMES FOR MANAGERS PERCEIVING LOW INNOVATION

In situations when managers' OC perceptions of innovation are low, BP may not be perceived to be as helpful or as necessary as when managers' perceptions of innovation are high. This is because, when low innovation is perceived, the values of conservatism and risk aversion are more dominant than creativity, and thus the environment and managerial tasks may be perceived to entail less uncertainty. In this respect, Judge, Fryxell and Dooley found that 'less innovative units behaved more like traditional bureaucratic departments'.

The role of BP as a vehicle of information exchange becomes less important for managers perceiving low innovation. We argue, however, that BP will have value for managers perceiving low innovation only if attention to detail is low. We elaborate on this in the following paragraph. In the case of managers perceiving low innovation but high attention to detail, managers are likely to contend that, while innovative ideas may be important, keeping within set rules, policies, and regulations should take priority. At the same time, planning and decision-making will be based on careful analyses and an emphasis on precision.

As a result, standardisation of managerial duties and roles can be expected to be high. Brownell and Merchant, when job standardisation is high, there is minimal improvement in the flow of information between managers. In fact, managers' personal input or ideas can become easily discouraged and/or rejected if it is not within the set guidelines. Thus, for managers perceiving low innovation but high attention to detail, encouraging participation in budget setting may be construed as pseudo-participation.

Consequently, increasing BP for such managers could become more threatening and less motivating leading to increasing frustration and higher JRT. Further, managers perceiving pseudo-participation may be prone to adopt inefficient usage of time in preparing paperwork. For example, as we noted earlier, Flamholtz found in one of his cases that managers in a large banking institution viewed their participation in a zero-based budgeting system to be only pseudo. Consequently, their reaction was not to make any real budget cuts as required by senior management. Instead, they carried on to report budget estimates based on the traditional guidelines. Such dysfunctional behaviour is clearly detrimental to managerial performance.

In summary, for managers perceiving low innovation but high attention to detail, we expected to find that BP would be associated with increased JRT and reduced managerial performance. By contrast, in the case of managers perceiving both innovation and attention to detail as being low, increased participation in budget setting is going to be associated with reduced JRT and increased managerial performance. This is because managers who view their OC as being low in both innovation and attention to detail are prone to perceive a more conservative environment that is less detail-oriented.

The primary threat is for such managers to become complacent and to be reactive (rather than proactive) to changes. Miles and Snow, for example, identified organizations they termed 'reactors'. Such organizations tend to be locked into an inefficient, complacent managerial style where managers lack planning and coordination structures. Thus, compared to an OC that is low in innovation but high in attention to detail, an OC that is low on both innovation and attention to detail is likely to entail a lack in proper managerial decision support systems. BP therefore may provide both the opportunity and the incentive for managers to aim for higher performance levels.

Further, managers who perceive low innovation and attention to detail OC tend to have a greater tendency to base their decisions on their own personal judgements. With budgetary targets being more predictable (since innovative OC is seen to be low), the opportunity for greater subjective decision making promotes true, rather than pseudo-participation. Managers, in turn, have an opportunity to become more involved, confident, and committed towards their budgetary targets, since they are able to exercise their own discretion. Consequently, managers' JRT will decrease because managers are able to target and to plan performance schedules based on their own volition. Further support for such an argument may be derived from Gul et al., who found that BP in situations of high managerial autonomy was associated with better managerial performance.

In summary, for managers perceiving low innovation and low attention to detail, BP is expected to be associated with decreased JRT and increased managerial performance.

## HYPOTHESES

- *H*1: There is a significant three-way interaction between innovation, attention to detail, and BP affecting managers' JRT.
  - *H*1(a): For managers perceiving high innovation, increasing levels of BP are associated with lower levels of JRT, regardless of their perceptions of attention to detail.
  - 1(b):For managers perceiving low innovation, increasing levels of BP are associated with lower levels of JRT when their perceptions of attention to detail are low, and higher levels of JRT when their perceptions of attention to detail are high.
- *H*2: There is a significant three-way interaction between innovation, attention to detail, and BP affecting managerial performance.
  - *H*2(a): For managers perceiving high innovation, increasing levels of BP are associated with higher levels of performance, regardless of their perceptions of attention to detail.
  - *H*2(b):For managers perceiving low innovation, increasing levels of BP are associated with higher levels of JRT when their perceptions of attention to detail are low, and lower levels of performance when their perceptions of attention to detail are high.

A random sample of 62 companies was selected for this study from the 623 food manufacturing organizations listed in the Kompass Australia business directory, and employing more than one hundred people. Manufacturing companies were chosen for consistency with research into BP and job-related outcomes. Food manufacturers were selected because this industry provides a variety of strategic and management approaches, while controlling for extraneous industry variables. Companies with less than a hundred employees were not expected to have clearly defined areas of responsibility to which managers are appointed. The human resource manager of each company was initially contacted to identify those managers in each firm with a distinct area of responsibility.

Subsequently, 263 managers were contacted and requested to take part in the research. No restriction was placed on the areas of responsibility from which managers could be selected. A questionnaire with a cover letter, together with a reply-paid self-addressed envelope, was mailed to each manager. A follow-up telephone call was made in order to check on receipt of the questionnaire, and to promote a higher response rate One hundred and twenty-four responses from 37 companies were returned.(3) Five, however, were excluded from the study because of incomplete responses, and four more were excluded because respondents were from an inappropriate level (e.g. managing director or line-supervisor). A further response was deleted because acquiescent response (all items responded to in the same direction). This left 114 useable responses. The respondents' ages ranged from 25 to 50 years. They had held their current positions for an average of 3.8 years (range: 1.7 to 9.7 years) and had been employed by their respective companies for an average of 12.8 years (range: 2.5 to 34.5 years). The average number of employees in their area of responsibility was 81 (range: 24 to 230 employees). Ninety-five per cent of the respondents were male.

## INSTRUMENTS

### Managers' OC Perceptions

This instrument was developed by Windsor and Ashkanasy, and based on the O'Reilly et al. (1991) OC questionnaire. It consists of an introduction paragraph and 26 response items. The introduction states: 'Every organization has its own culture which is a set of values that might be expected or implicitly required of members of that organization.' Respondents were asked to write a number in the box adjacent to each of the 26 °C values to indicate the extent to which they perceived that value to be important in their organization. Response options varied from 1 (not at all) to 5 (to a very great extent). The 26 items cover the seven °C dimensions identified by O'Reilly et al. The present study focuses on two of these dimensions: innovation and attention to detail.

Managers' perception of innovation was measured using the five items identified by O'Reilly et al. These value items are: 'being innovative', 'being quick to take advantage of opportunities', 'having a willingness to experiment', 'risk-taking', 'having no rules—not being constrained by many rules'. Cronbach alpha reliability for the scale in the present study was acceptable (0.71). Managers' perception of attention to detail was measured based on the four items identified by O'Reilly et al. Items are: 'paying attention to detail', 'being precise', 'being analytical' and 'being careful'. Cronbach alpha reliability of the scale was good (0.78).

**Budgetary Participation**

The Milani six-item, seven-point Likert type instrument was used to measure BP. As an example, one of the items required respondents to indicate extent of their involvement in setting the budget on a 7- point scale, where 1 represented 'none at all' and 7 represented 'all of the budget'. This instrument has been used and tested extensively in many other studies, and has provided high internal reliability. Cronbach alpha obtained in the present study was very good (0.83).

**Job-Related Tension**

The 15-item scale developed by Kahn, Wolfe, Snoek and Rosenthal was used to assess managerial job-related tension. It measures four dimensions of job stress: role ambiguity, role conflict, role overload and resource inadequacy. Respondents were asked to use 7-point Likert-type scales to rate the frequency with which they are bothered by potentially stressful events, such as being unclear on the scope and responsibilities of the job, feeling one has insufficient authority or qualifications to carry out assignments, and feeling that one must do things against one's better judgement. Cronbach alpha for this scale was also very good (0.84).

## Managerial Performance

A self-evaluation instrument developed by Mahoney et al. was used to measure managerial performance. Respondents were asked to rate, on a 7-point scale, their own perceived performance on an overall rating, plus ratings on sub-dimensions of planning, investigating, coordinating, evaluating, supervising, staffing, negotiating, and representing.

Following the procedures adopted by Mahoney et al. and Brownell and Hirst, reliability of the overall rating was checked by regression against the eight sub-dimensions. The regression explained 50% of the variance of the overall rating score, which is acceptable given that studies have reported an R-squared of 0.47 to 0.79. On this basis, scores on the overall rating scale were adopted as the measure of managerial performance in the present study.

## Analysis Models

A significant value for the coefficient in both regressions was required to support the main hypotheses. Further, because interaction regression models were used in this study, the approach of centring the independent variables (by using deviation scores) was adopted to reduce the correlations between the product terms and the component parts of the independent variables.

Deviation scores for all the independent variables in the regression models were calculated by subtracting raw scores from the overall mean score. Tolerance of greater than 0.10 was achieved for all the independent variables in the regression models used, indicating that multicolinearity was not present in the centred data. To test sub-hypotheses (H1(a) and (b); H2(a) and (b)), the following regression models were used. For the sub-sample of managers perceiving high innovation, the value of the coefficient was expected to be non-significant, thus supporting sub-hypotheses H1(a) and H2 (a). By contrast, Hypotheses H1 (b) and H2(b) were supported if the coefficient was significant for the sub-sample comprising managers perceiving low innovation 6.

## DESCRIPTIVE STATISTICS

The correlations were all in the directions expected. In particular, there was a significant negative correlation between JRT and managerial performance although, as we anticipated, this was weak, with only 16% variance shared between the two variables.

## INTERACTION TESTS (H1 AND H2)

As the first step, we examined results of equation 1, which includes the three-way interaction between managers' perceptions of innovation, attention to detail, and BP. Statistical interpretation of the results followed the approach adopted by Lau, Low, and Eggleton and Jaccard et al. The analysis indicated that there was a significant three-way interaction affecting JRT, but not managerial performance. This provides support for H1 but not for H2. The JRT regression model explained 25% (adjusted) of the data variance, with the three-way interaction accounting for an additional 4% of variance above the two-way model.

## TESTS OF SUB-HYPOTHESES: 6.3.1 JRT

The three-way interaction in respect of JRT was significant (supporting H 1). Therefore, to determine if the effect of the interaction between BP and attention to detail on JRT differed between managers perceiving low innovation and those perceiving high innovation, the innovation perception scores were dichotomised at the mean.

As expected, the effect of the interaction between attention to detail and BP on JRT was not significant for managers perceiving high innovation. An examination of the main effects of BP based on the results of equation 2 (the additive model) indicates the coefficient for BP was significant. Thus, for managers' with high perceptions of innovation, BP was negatively associated with JRT for both high and low levels of of attention to detail, as predicted in hypothesis 1(a).

For managers whose perceptions of innovation were low, the interaction between attention to detail and BP on JRT was significant. JRT was negatively related to BP for low attention to detail, but that this effect was attenuated for high attention to detail. This supports H1(b) in respect of perceptions of low attention to detail, but not in respect of high attention detail. Nonetheless, the result does indicate that, for high BP, JRT was relatively higher for managers high in attention to detail in compared low attention to detail.

## MANAGERIAL PERFORMANCE

Results indicated that there was a significant and positive relationship between BP and managerial performance. There were no significant interactions between BP and either of the two OC dimensions, however. In particular, the anticipated three-way interaction for managerial performance failed to reach significance at p 0.05. Further analyses of the two-way interactions between attention to detail and BP, based on equation 3, for each of the low and high innovative sub-samples also indicated no significant results relating to BP. Consequently, H2(a) and (b) are not supported.

The results of the present study support the proposition that managers' OC perceptions affect the impact of BP on managerial job-related outcomes. More specifically, BP was shown to be associated with favourable managerial job-related outcomes for managers perceiving high innovation. It appears that, for managers perceiving high innovation, BP contributes to lower JRT and higher managerial performance, irrespective of their perceptions of attention to detail.

For managers whose OC perceptions are low in both innovation and attention to detail, BP plays an important role in the planning and coordination processes, as well as motivating managers who face a higher risk of becoming complacent and using sub-standard decisions tools. This then serves to reduce JRT because of greater role clarity. Managers therefore experience greater confidence in setting performance targets. In contrast, for managers perceiving a low innovation accompanied by high attention to detail, the effect of BP on JRT was attenuated.

While not fully supportive of H1(b), this result indicates that high BP is associated with relatively high JRT for managers perceiving high attention to detail. For these managers, their work roles are likely to be driven by highly procedural processes with an emphasis on precision and care. Budgetary target setting can become stressful in this circumstance, since managers feel their participation is pseudo. Thus, there is little opportunity for them to become committed. Such findings support arguments by Waterhouse and Tiessen and Gul et al. that, in situations where there are set rules and a lack in decision-making autonomy, BP may not be useful.

It appears from our results, however, that this interactional effect does not carry over to affect the positive association between BP and managerial performance. Instead, this result is consistent with the view that BP leads in general to higher performance outcomes. A corollary of this finding is that, while we found managerial performance to be negatively related to JRT, the two constructs can be impacted differentially by organizational variables such as OC perceptions, and should therefore be considered separately in future studies of determinants of managerial job-related outcomes.

The results of this study indicate that managers' perceptions of OC have a significant moderating effect on the relationship between BP and managers' job-related outcomes. The implication of this finding for practice is that designers of organizational control systems need to consider the impact of managers' perceptions of their OC. In particular, changes to the emphasis placed on managerial participation in the budgetary process need to consider managers' perceptions of innovation and attention to detail. In this respect, there are some interesting parallels between these findings and those reported in the general job design literature. For example, Wall, Jackson, Mullarkey and Parker found that task uncertainty moderates the link between job control and performance.

These results should, however, be interpreted in light of six potential limitations. In the first instance, only two OC dimensions were studied. We argue that the two dimensions included in the present study are those most relevant to modern organizational control systems and practices. OC is a multidimensional concept, however, so that the influence of the two value dimensions studied may be subject to an interaction with other value dimensions. The present study was limited to consideration of two OC dimensions because of sample size limitations, and the difficulty of interpreting high order interactions. It is also arguable that the particular operational definitions of OC employed in the present study may not be optimal. Literature in the OC area provides different definitions and typologies of culture. Future studies could attempt to identify an appropriate control design for culture-types defined under these alternative perspectives.

The second limitation concerns the use of individual-level data. We argue that this is justified in the current study because the focus is on individuals, whose job-related outcomes are affected by personal perceptions of culture. Nevertheless, there clearly is scope for future studies to examine the effect of the interaction between OC and BP and its effect on organizational-level outcomes.

A third limitation is that the present study was based on data collected at a single point in time. Although OC is a relatively stable construct, environmental changes can cause perceptions of OC to change. Ashkanasy and Holmes, for example, tracked perceived culture changes in public accounting firms during a period of merger activity, and found that perceptions changed not only in the merging forms, but also in the firm not involved in mergers. In this case, changing perceptions of OC can result in mismatch between control systems in use and the extant OC. A longitudinal study may aid in understanding how budgetary and other accounting control systems are implicated in the changeover and how this may affect managers' JRT and performance. The fourth limitation concerns the nature of self-report questionnaire data. Self-report measures of performance can be affected by leniency bias, although Heneman reported that self-report measures may be subject to less leniency and range restriction than other measures. Our results also may be subject to common method bias. Again, this issue may not be so important in this study because of the variety of different measurement scales we have used. Further, since we do not focus on simple relationships between variables, there is less likelihood of this problem emerging.

Fifthly, our results involve interpretation of high-order interactions that may be difficult to replicate successfully. We acknowledge this limitation, and suggest that further research using larger samples be undertaken to verify our findings. The sixth and final limitation of our research is that we did not address fully the precise mechanisms proposed in the development of the various hypotheses.

For example, further research can be undertaken to test the existence of pseudo-participation in situations when managers perceive low innovation and high attention to detail. Notwithstanding these limitations, the present study has emphasized that organizational governance procedures need to match managers' OC perceptions if the benefits of these procedures are to be realised. As such, this study contributes a further nomothetic validation of the influence of managers' OC perceptions on the effectiveness of BP on managerial job-related outcomes.

# Organizational Effectiveness

Increasingly, organizations are integrating data from employee opinion surveys with other organizational data systems. For example, strategic planning can be enhanced by linking survey data and systems such as sales data, absenteeism data, or client service ratings. The purpose of linking survey data with other measures of organizational effectiveness is to determine which of the work environment factors assessed by an employee survey are actually related to organizational outcomes. This information is used by organizations to determine how to select organizational development activities that achieve the greatest improvement in organizational effectiveness. Ittner and Larcker reported that up to 23% of US companies used modelling procedures to link different types of performance data.

Research based on the integration of data systems is increasing. We refer to this type of analysis as 'linkage research'. Unfortunately, linkage research is not feasible for all organizations. For example, specific measures of effectiveness may not be available at a particular point in time. In this associate, we present an alternative approach, termed the 'quasi-linkage approach' that uses only employee survey data. A key advantage of this approach is that organizations need invest fewer resources to conduct analyses. We first describe the benchmarking approach that is typically adopted in organizations, and discuss the advantages of linkage research compared to benchmarking. We then introduce 'quasi-linkage analysis' and discuss its benefits and limitations. The quasi-linkage approach uses only a single source of data:

employees of the organization. One of the main concerns when analysing data from a single sources is that relationships between the work environment factors and effectiveness outcomes might be inflated. That is, common method variance might spuriously increase the link among key measures and bias organizational decision making. We examine ways to reduce common method variance and, therefore, enhance the utility of analyses.

We then discuss other considerations when conducting quasi-linkage analysis. First, it is important to show that the criteria measure has external validity and is related to measures that might be used in a more fully developed linkage analysis. Second, the level of analysis should be considered when determining what kind of processes and outcomes should be linked.

One of the most common uses of employee survey data is benchmarking: the comparison of survey results within and between organizations. Benchmarking provides comparative data, from which it is possible to determine whether a given mean score or percentage of agreement represents a good, average or bad result. The key strength of benchmark comparisons is that they provide a standard from which to evaluate the organization's performance, and identify critical issues, sources of concern and areas of success in the workplace.

Although benchmarking is useful for identifying strengths and weaknesses, it is limited to providing static or structural information about the state of an organization. It does not provide dynamic information about how the organization functions. However, when the benchmark process is conducted in isolation, managers might easily assume that organizational resources should be directed towards improving those measures with the lowest scores were obtained. This approach assumes that each organizational attribute measured in the survey is equally important for organizational effectiveness, an assumption that needs to be tested. Benchmarking is particularly useful for comparing effectiveness outcomes rather than determining what are the factors that underpin effectiveness. Linkage research supplements the benchmarking process. Ideally, if strengths and weaknesses in organizational performance have been identified from the benchmarking process, linkage research can guide strategies for improvement. Specifically, survey data is matched to other organizational databases, such as the Human Resources information system, finance records, and sales data.

Then, analyses are conducted to determine which of the work environment factors measured in the survey are statistically related to the effectiveness measures that the organization wishes to target. By identifying which work environment factors are related to organizational effectiveness, these analyses indicate where organizational resources should be directed in order to bring about improvement. Because these analyses are based on actual data collected from the organization, rather than a theoretical model of how things ought to be, they provide a more meaningful and accurate model of organizational effectiveness.

However, there are several barriers to the linkage research process. First, due to the need to protect confidentiality, it is usually not possible to link individual responses to the survey with organizational records for individuals. At best, the data linkage process can only be carried out at the work group level, which significantly reduces the number of observations, and thus, the power of the analyses to detect relationships. This issue is most relevant for small organizations.

Second, linkage research requires that there is a common field that can be used to match survey data with data from other organizational measurement systems. Unfortunately, this kind of common field does not always exist. For example, survey responses tend to be identified according to work group membership, or respondents' location in the organization, whereas financial data (including measures of absenteeism and turnover) tend to be grouped according to cost centres.

In our experience, it is unusual for cost centres to map consistently to the work group structure in the organization. Some work groups will be associated with multiple cost centres, whereas in other instances there will only be one cost centre associated with an entire division of the organization. If financial data only exists at the divisional level, it will be necessary to also aggregate survey data to the divisional level, which again results in a loss of power for the analyses. The alternative is to manually create a new common field, determining on a case-by-case basis, how work group data and cost centre data should be aggregated in order to link the two databases. This process is time consuming and demands a high level of expertise in both statistical methods and organizational structure. Consequently, this process may be beyond the reach of some organizations.

Third, it may not be possible to find non-survey measures for each of the relevant dimensions of organizational effectiveness. For example, some organizations do not have systems in place to record when employees have been absent from work. Other organizations do not have measures of client satisfaction. Nevertheless, these organizations might still want to know how to reduce absenteeism or improve client satisfaction. Even when the organization does have these data, it might be difficult to access it, either because the data holder is protective of his or her turf, or because of concerns about breaching confidentiality.

## QUASI-LINKAGE – THE ALTERNATIVE

The quasi-linkage approach provides the same strategic information as that provided through linkage research, namely, which work environment factors are most closely related to organizational effectiveness. It does so by building self-report measures of organizational effectiveness into the employee opinion survey.

It is then possible to analyse the relationship between the work environment factors assessed in the survey, and self-report measures of organizational outcomes, to identify which work environment factors are most closely related to the self-reported organizational outcomes. The issue of common method variance is a major concern for the quasi-linkage approach. Common method variance is a summary term that refers to biases in relationships that are due to the variables being measured with the same method. When both work environment factors and effectiveness measures are measured from employee ratings, the relationship between these measures will be inflated if raters tend to respond to survey items in a consistent way. For example, some respondents exhibit an acquiescence bias, which is a tendency to agree with items, regardless of content. The effect of such a bias is to inflate the relationship between survey measures.

There are a number of techniques that can be used to minimise common method variance. One of the simplest is to have two different versions of the survey, one measuring the work environment factors, and the other containing the effectiveness measures. Half of the employees in each work unit provide ratings on work environment factors, and the other employees in the work unit rate the effectiveness measures.

When this approach is adopted, the data have to be aggregated to the work unit level as it is not possible to link ratings at the individual level. Although this approach is feasible in larger organizations, the reduction in statistical power for smaller organizations with fewer than thirty or forty work units, means that relationships between work environment factors and effectiveness measures might not be detected. Under these circumstances it is necessary to employ some of the alternative procedures for dealing with common method variance.

## ILLUSTRATING THE QUASI-LINKAGE APPROACH

We describe a case study where we used the quasi-linkage approach to increase the value of information derived from a staff survey. We conceptualise the quasi-linkage approach in terms of three stages.

Stage one is concerned with survey content. Stage two involves comparing organizational scores on the effectiveness measures to benchmark data, with the goal of identifying areas for improvement. Stage three involves analysing the data to determine the relationship between work environment factors and effectiveness measures. We describe how each of these stages were carried out, after first providing some background on the organizational context. The organization was a government agency, consisting of approximately 1,300 staff, working across ten business units. The organization is responsible for policy development and service delivery to the public.

The organization conducted an employee opinion survey annually, with the dual goals of developing and monitoring their people management strategies, and investigating workplace issues impacting on employees, such as leadership, communication, and performance management.

Since the survey was intended to develop and monitor people management strategies, senior management were keen to obtain strategic information from the survey that could be used to guide organizational improvement efforts. The quasi-linkage approach was therefore relevant to their needs, and they were enthusiastic about adopting it.

# Index

## E



## F



## G



## H



## I



## L



## M



## N



## O



## P

## Q



## S



## T



## W